Linguistic Approaches to Literature (LAL)

Linguistic Approaches to Literature (LAL) provides an international forum for researchers who believe that the application of linguistic methods leads to a deeper and more far-reaching understanding of many aspects of literature. The emphasis will be on pragmatic approaches intersecting with areas such as experimental psychology, psycholinguistics, computational linguistics, cognitive linguistics, stylistics, discourse analysis, sociolinguistics, rhetoric, and philosophy.

For an overview of all books published in this series, please see
http://benjamins.com/catalog/lal

Editors

Volume 17

Cognitive Grammar in Literature
Edited by Chloe Harrison, Louise Nuttall, Peter Stockwell and Wenjuan Yuan

Cognitive Grammar in Literature

Edited by

Chloe Harrison
Louise Nuttall
Peter Stockwell
Wenjuan Yuan

John Benjamins Publishing Company

Amsterdam / Philadelphia

The paper used in this publication meets the minimum requirements of the American National Standard for Information Sciences – Permanence of Paper for Printed Library Materials, ANSI z39.48-1984.

Library of Congress Cataloging-in-Publication Data

Cognitive Grammar in Literature / Edited by Chloe Harrison, Louise Nuttall, Peter
       Stockwell and Wenjuan Yuan.
    p. cm. (Linguistic Approaches to Literature, ISSN 1569-3112 ; v. 17)
    Includes bibliographical references and index.
    1. Cognitive grammar. 2. Discourse analysis, Literary. 3. Creativity (Linguistics)
       4. Literature--History and criticism. I. Harrison, Chloe, editor.
P165.C638   2014
415--dc23   2013049282
ISBN 978 90 272 3404 9 (Hb ; alk. paper)
ISBN 978 90 272 3406 3 (Pb ; alk. paper)
ISBN 978 90 272 7056 6 (Eb)

John Benjamins Publishing Co. · P.O. Box 36224 · 1020 ME Amsterdam · The Netherlands
John Benjamins North America · P.O. Box 27519 · Philadelphia PA 19118-0519 · USA

Table of contents

List of contributors

Sam Browse is a researcher in the School of English at the University of Sheffield. His work focuses on developing a text-driven approach to metaphor in discourse, and his interests encompass literary, political, economic and journalistic forms of public discourse. He teaches stylistics, discourse analysis and critical theory.

Marcello Giovanelli is a Lecturer in English in Education at the University of Nottingham. He has teaching and research interests in educational linguistics, pedagogical stylistics and cognitive poetics. He has written two English language textbooks and has recently published a monograph on *Text World Theory and Keats' Poetry* (Bloomsbury 2013).

Craig Hamilton is Associate Professor of English Cognitive Linguistics at the Université de Haute Alsace. He has held previous positions at the University of California-Irvine, the University of Nottingham, and the University of Paris. He published the first major article applying Cognitive Grammar to a literary work in 2003, and has since published widely on cognitive linguistic approaches to modern literature.

Chloe Harrison is Lecturer in Stylistics in the Department of English and Languages at Coventry University, where she teaches applied linguistics, literary stylistics and cognitive poetics. Her research work develops a Cognitive Discourse Grammar of contemporary literature, drawing primarily on Cognitive Grammar and cognitive linguistics in general.

Alina Kwiatowska is Professor of Linguistics at the University of Łódź. Her research focuses on aspects of cognitive linguistics, stylistics, and visual semiotics. During her term as President of the Polish Cognitive Linguistics Association, she organized a conference on cognitive poetics (2010), and edited the volume *Texts and Minds. Papers in Cognitive Poetics and Rhetoric* (Peter Lang 2012). Her most recent publications explore the interfaces of the visual and the verbal.

Ronald W. Langacker is Professor Emeritus at the University of California, San Diego. He devised and developed Cognitive Grammar, and has published over 20 books and around 200 articles, including the seminal and definitive volumes in CG. He has also worked on and published extensively on the linguistics of Uto-Aztecan languages. His work has been translated into several languages and he has served as President of the International Cognitive Linguistics Association.

Clara Neary is Lecturer in English Language and Linguistics at the University of Chester, where she teaches both literary and non-literary stylistics, cognitive poetics, media discourse and the linguistics of creativity. Her research publications include articles on Indian literature in English, life writing, and the stylistics of global literatures.

Louise Nuttall is a researcher in the School of English at the University of Nottingham, where she holds an Arts and Humanities Research Council award. Her work investigates the presentation and effects of mind-style and characterisation in 20th century literary prose fiction, drawing on a set of related approaches within cognitive linguistics and cognitive psychology.

Todd Oakley is Professor and Chair of Cognitive Science at Case Western Reserve University in Cleveland, Ohio, where he is also a Fellow of the Institute of Origins and Professor of English. He is the author of *From Attention to Meaning: Explorations in Semiotics, Linguistics and Rhetoric* (Peter Lang 2009) and co-editor (with Anders Hougaard) of *Mental Spaces in Discourse and Interaction* (John Benjamins 2008), as well as 30 research papers and chapters.

Anne Päivärinta is a researcher in the School of Language, Translation and Literary Studies at the University of Tampere, Finland. Her work focuses on embodiment in Dylan Thomas's writing, with particular interest in bringing together Conceptual Metaphor Theory and literary stylistics.

Mike Pincombe is Professor of Tudor and Elizabethan Literature at Newcastle University. He teaches the literature and critical theory in this period, and also supervises doctoral work in creative writing. In his research he brings structural and semiotic analyses to bear on the literary texts and systems of Renaissance literature. He has published over 60 papers and 9 books and editions, including *The Oxford Handbook of Tudor Literature* (with Cathy Shrank, Oxford University Press 2009) and *Elizabethan Humanism* (Longman-Pearson 2001).

Michael Pleyer is a researcher in the Anglistisches Seminar at the Ruprecht-Karls-Universität in Heidelberg. His work centres on evolutionary linguistics, developmental psychology and cognitive science, with an interest also in multimodal and popular literary works. He has presented his research in over 20 talks and has published 11 research papers.

Christian W. Schneider is a researcher in the Anglistisches Seminar at the Ruprecht-Karls-Universität in Heidelberg. He works in Gothic literature, particularly in an American context, and with a specific focus on popular culture, comic book studies and the cognitive literary theory of multimodal and graphic texts.

Peter Stockwell is Professor of Literary Linguistics at the University of Nottingham. He is the author and editor of over 70 research papers and more than 20 books, including *Cognitive Poetics* (Routledge 2002), *The Language and Literature Reader* (with Ron Carter, Routledge 2008), *Texture: A Cognitive Aesthetics of Reading* (Edinburgh University Press 2009) and *The Handbook of Stylistics* (with Sara Whiteley, Cambridge University Press 2014).

Elżbieta Tabakowska is UNESCO Professor of Translation Studies and Intercultural Communication at the Jagiellonian University, Kraków. She is the author of over 100 scholarly articles and her books include *Cognitive Linguistics and Poetics of Translation* (Gunter Narr 1993) and *Language and Imagery: An Introduction to Cognitive Linguistics* (Kraków 1995). A collection of papers, *Cognition in Language*, was published in her honour (Tertium 2007).

Wenjuan Yuan is Lecturer in English Language and Literature at Hunan University, China, where she teaches literary linguistics and cognitive poetics. She took her doctorate from the School of English at the University of Nottingham, with research in the exploration of cognition and kinetics in the poetry of William Wordsworth. Her current work develops this cognitive poetic reading of Romantic poetry and her wider research interests include a cognitive approach to comparative literature.

Acknowledgements

Craig Hamilton would like to thank colleagues at the Jagiellonian University Kraków, Freiburg University, and Nottingham University for feedback on earlier versions of his chapter. Michael Pleyer and Christian Schneider are very grateful for the financial support of the Soheyl Ghaemian Travel Fund for Scholars, courtesy of the Heidelberg Centre of American Studies; the contributors and editors are also pleased to acknowledge the permission of the author/illustrator Alison Bechdel and Houghton Mifflin Harcourt publishers for permission to reproduce copyright material from *Fun Home* in Chapter 3. Research appearing in Chapter 6 was funded by the Arts and Humanities Research Council. The poem in Chapter 10 is copyright Siegfried Sassoon and is reproduced by kind permission of the Estate of George Sassoon. Mike Pincombe would like to acknowledge and thank Zsolt Almási, Agnes Ecsedy, and especially Kinga Földváry for their help with his translation and on points of Hungarian grammar in Chapter 11. Vincent van Gogh's (1888) *De Slaapkamer* ('The Bedroom at Arles'), which appears in Chapter 14, is held by the van Gogh Museum, Amsterdam. The 'Cognitive Grammar in Literature' project was supported financially by the Poetics and Linguistics Association (PALA), to whom we are very grateful.

Foreword

Ronald W. Langacker

A not uncommon criticism of Cognitive Grammar (CG) is that it lacks empirical support. It is an assessment that I strongly disagree with. Highly constrained in the kinds of structures it permits, CG has nonetheless been applied successfully to a wide array of phenomena in diverse languages, straightforwardly handling classic descriptive problems in a unified manner with reasonable claims to cognitive plausibility. It deploys a broad yet limited set of descriptive notions, each supported on a number of independent grounds. In being developed and justified primarily based on considerations of this kind, CG is like most any linguistic theory.

It goes without saying that other, more external sources of empirical validation are both welcome and (at least in the long term) necessary. There are numerous possibilities: psycholinguistic experiment, corpus investigation, neural imaging, computer modeling, acquisition studies, and practical applications (like language teaching). These are important and revealing, but while they all have their place, they also have their limitations. Certainly there is room in this arsenal for the application of CG notions to the study of literature. Does this enterprise count as 'empirical'? Perhaps not in the narrowest sense, but I believe it qualifies in a broader sense appropriate for language. Success in generating useful insights on the part of literary analysts can be taken as a significant source of validation.

The enterprise is daunting, for both me and those engaged in it. In my case it reflects the absence of any real expertise, with the consequence that applying CG to literature has never been central to my thought or method. However, I have always recognized its potential and applauded the fact that, in the broader movement of cognitive linguistics, literature has been a major concern for many scholars. To non-linguists, the enterprise is daunting for several reasons: the multiplicity of approaches even in cognitive linguistics, the complexity of their technical formulations, the often confusing and inconsistent terminology, and the sheer difficulty of applying even clearly formulated ideas to specific cases. The results are bound to be imperfect; but even imperfect efforts advance our understanding.

Especially compared to formalist approaches, cognitive linguistics has definite advantages for analyzing literature. Most obviously, it accords a central role to meaning, offering a well-developed conceptual semantics that bears directly on phenomena crucial for analyzing literary texts. The speaker (or writer) is seen as actively engaging in an elaborate process of meaning construction. An inherent aspect of this process is construal, our multifaceted capacity for conceiving and portraying the same situation in alternate ways. Even for prosaic language, the meanings constructed are richly imaginative, with metaphor, metonymy, fictivity, and mental space configurations being both pervasive and fundamental. A key point (often missed) is that conception, instead of being insular, is a primary means of interacting with the world, including other minds. Based on our ability to simulate the experience of other conceptualizers, each with their own perspective, speaking (or writing) is an intersubjective process aimed at negotiating a shared contextual awareness.

The cognitive linguistic view of meaning implies that ordinary and literary language forms are continuous rather than dichotomous. Other notions, more specific to CG, are also relevant for literary scholars. At least in principle (practice, of course, is another matter) the framework is fully comprehensive, dealing in a unified manner with any aspect of language structure. In particular, it provides a unified account of lexicon and grammar, which form a gradation consisting solely in assemblies of symbolic structures (form-meaning pairings). Hence the central claim that grammar is inherently meaningful: by using a certain grammatical element one is always imposing a certain construal. Also, since conception is taken as encompassing anything we experience, and sounds are apprehended and mentally represented, phonological structure is included in conceptual structure. An expression's phonological shape is therefore a facet of its overall meaning. One consequence is that there are no true synonyms. Another is that CG-based analyses extend in seamless fashion even to the phonological aspects of poetry.

While I do not feel qualified to judge them from the purely literary standpoint, I have enjoyed and profited from the papers in this volume. I have been particularly impressed by how inventive the authors have been in finding ways of applying cognitive linguistic notions, some of which I would never have thought of myself. Despite their number and variety, I have been convinced that these applications are only scratching the surface of what is possible.

I can only agree with the comment by Pincombe that there are limits to what CG can offer literature. And he is certainly correct that typical CG diagrams, when worked out in careful detail, are too complex and cumbersome for large-scale practical use. I might note that such diagrams are merely heuristic, not formal representations, and not the only way CG descriptions might be presented. In any case they reflect (and even vastly underestimate) the actual complexity of the phenomena; as in any field, methods will have to be found for analysis on a larger scale. But in the foreseeable future, any description based on CG notions will have to be highly selective, like those in this volume. I also agree with Stockwell that the extensive CG application to literature will require and inspire significant elaboration of the framework. It is something I look forward to.

CHAPTER 1

Introduction

Cognitive Grammar in literature

Chloe Harrison, Louise Nuttall, Peter Stockwell &
Wenjuan Yuan

1.   The practice of literary linguistics

The modern discipline of *literary linguistics* – also called *stylistics* – has a long
history stretching back into antiquity and the classical study of *rhetoric*. Across
all that time, it has been taken as axiomatic that we should apply our current best
knowledge of how language and mind works whenever we study the patterns
and effects of literature, the most prestigious form of language in use. All literate
human cultures and communities in all periods of past time have engaged in creating and sharing literary works, as far as we are able to determine, and wherever
we find evidence of literature, we also usually find evidence of literary analysis.
This takes a range of forms, from interested chat and comment right through to
complex theoretical and political statements. All such commentary is literary criticism, and its practice indicates both the universal, common concerns of humans
and our condition as well as the particularities of individuals and literary texts.

   In our own and in the last centuries, literary criticism has become institution-
alised on a wider scale than ever before. A great deal of journalistic and university
activity in the field of literature falls into the bracket of *cultural studies*, with an
emphasis on historical context, authorial biography, and ideological analysis. The
fundamental truism that literature is written in language, and the study of language should thus be central to the training of any literary critic, is often neglected.
Where a literary critic pays proper attention to linguistic matters, the analysis
is very often either at a rather amateurish level or is informed by an extremely
outdated view of modern linguistics. Even stylisticians with a range of contemporary models from current linguistic theory at their disposal have sometimes
fallen comfortably into the application of an established standard framework for
literary analysis. These approaches have typically relied on functional linguistics,

pragmatics, critical discourse analysis, and the corpus techniques associated with applied linguistic description.

We believe literary critics (especially stylisticians) should always be ready to explore our best current thinking about language in literary analysis. There is of course in general an intellectual agility in this constant refreshment of perspective. However, in the context of this book we also believe there is a particular value in thinking about the ways in which literary creativity, patterning and readerly effects can be illuminated by Cognitive Grammar. It is our belief that the many contributions contained in this volume set out at least an initially persuasive case for the usefulness of Cognitive Grammar in literary criticism.

2.   Cognitive Grammar: an overview

Cognitive Grammar represents a specific practical and theoretical approach to language within the broader discipline of cognitive linguistics. Cognitive linguists view all forms of language as rooted in the same basic cognitive mechanisms involved in other areas of experience in our wider encounters with the world. Viewed this way, language in all its discursive manifestations can (and in fact should) be analysed in terms of our understanding of cognition developed across the cognitive sciences. Furthermore, the organisation of language in *grammar* suggests a means of accessing this cognitive structure, providing an insight into our minds and mental experiences:

> Not only is it meaningful, it also reflects our basic experience of moving, perceiving and acting on the world. At the core of grammatical meanings are mental operations inherent in these elemental components of moment-to-moment living. When properly analysed, therefore, grammar has much to tell us about both meaning and cognition.   (Langacker 2008a: 4–5)

For cognitive linguists, language (and the conceptual structure it reflects) is *embodied*; it is grounded in our physical, bodily experiences as human beings. Furthermore, this embodied experience has an important social and cultural dimension. Cognitive linguists recognise the specific uses to which language is put within a sociological context, and their role in shaping the linguistic system. In this sense, cognitive linguistics shares a functional approach to language allied in many respects with that of systemic-functional linguistics (see Nuyts 2007). An underlying presumption of this volume is that a cognitive grammatical approach to contextualised linguistic choices, and particularly the 'goal of psychological reality' towards which it strives (Langacker 1987: 56), has distinct advantages for the stylistic analysis of literature.

Within cognitive linguistics, a range of cognitive approaches to grammar has been developed in parallel. Of these, *Cognitive Grammar* as devised by Ronald Langacker (1987, 1991a, 1991b, 2002, 2007a, 2008a, 2009) is the most well-established and richly developed, and the framework to which most attention is devoted within this volume. Also significant, however, are construction grammars such as those of Adele Goldberg (1995) and Bill Croft (2001), and related grammatical work by Leonard Talmy (2000). Though sharing many of the same principles and assumptions, these approaches draw together key concepts in slightly different ways. In the context of a multifaceted and evolving cognitive linguistics, the literary application of a cognitive approach to grammar may engage with, and indeed benefit from, this scope and flexibility.

The cognitive analysis of grammar is also closely related to the study of *cognitive semantics*. This area of research focuses specifically upon conceptual structures and the processes involved in their construction, which together make up a model of meaning in terms of *conceptualisation*. Though sometimes distinguished in terms of focus, the two disciplines are mutually supportive (see Evans & Green 2006: 48). In order to talk about the mental experiences corresponding to and manipulated by linguistic forms, we must draw upon concepts and theories within cognitive semantics. These include, but are by no means restricted to: the organisation of our encyclopaedic knowledge of the world through *categorization* and *prototypicality* (e.g. Lakoff 1987), the role of embodied experiences in terms of *image schemas* (Johnson 1987), *force dynamics* (Talmy 1988) and *conceptual metaphors* (Lakoff & Johnson 1980, 1999), and the construction of meaning through the blending of *mental spaces* (Fauconnier 1997; Fauconnier & Turner 2002). All of these concepts are relevant to the application of Cognitive Grammar, and will emerge at different points during the analyses found in this volume.

2.1 Constructions

In Langacker's Cognitive Grammar (referred to as CG in this and subsequent chapters) grammar is viewed not as a self-contained formal system but one in which all items are 'meaningful' in their own right. These are modelled as *linguistic units* and consist of a 'phonological' and a 'semantic' structure, connected by a symbolic relationship or a form-meaning pairing. Grammar consists of the patterns through which such units are combined to form *constructions* or *symbolic assemblies* of increasing size and complexity. Rather than viewing lexicon and syntax as separate concerns, CG views the two as a continuum of symbolic structures of varying complexity (Langacker 2008a: 15–20).

CG is a 'usage-based' model (see Langacker 2000) and views linguistic units as derived from a number of *usage events*, or instances of language use within a particular context. If repeatedly constructed in this manner, a complex structure will undergo progressive *entrenchment,* gaining centrality within cognitive organisation, until it achieves 'unit status'. The set of units shared by a group of individuals within a speech community is termed *conventional linguistic units.* A language, in CG, consists of 'a structured inventory of conventional linguistic units' which provides the resources for expression (Langacker 2008a: 222). Conventionalised patterns of language use (or assemblies of units) result in generalised *constructional schemas.* Once formed in this way, schematic units act as templates for the construction and interpretation of new linguistic expressions and provide a measure of 'well-formedness' against which such novel instantiations may be judged. The extent to which a unit is activated as an appropriate resource for *coding* a conceptualisation, and the extent to which an expression appears 'well-formed' or natural for this purpose is thus relative to the linguistic community in which the interlocutor is situated (Langacker 2008a: 220–27).

This framework is comparable with the approach taken by the group of models collectively termed *Construction Grammars* (Fillmore et al. 1988; Goldberg 1995; Croft 2001). These models share with Langacker's a view of lexicon and grammar as an inventory of symbolic units, and privilege the description of such constructions as opposed to a 'rule' based account of sentence composition. However the two types of framework, formulated independently, differ significantly in their theoretical approach and the nature of their specific interests. Langacker's detailed account of the cognitive processes involved in the formation and use of such symbolic units, in particular the factors involved in *construal,* lends this account an extra dimension, and one which is particularly useful for the discussion of literature.

2.2   Construal

The semantic structures activated by an expression through a combination of units represent just one aspect of its meaning. Of equal importance is the way in which this content is *construed.* Construal describes our 'ability to conceive and portray the same situation in alternate ways' (Langacker 2008a: 43). This applies to all encounters with language, including that of a producer (e.g. a writer) who makes choices in coding his or her conceptualisation, and the receiver (e.g. a reader) who conceives meaning based upon these linguistic cues or instructions. While the possibility of variable construals is far from new, what is most interesting perhaps is the systematic breakdown of the different *ways* in which they may vary, provided within various cognitive grammatical accounts (Langacker 2008a; Talmy 2000; Croft & Cruse 2004). In Langacker's model, the way in which a situation is construed may differ in terms of multiple interrelated dimensions, roughly categorisable as *specificity, prominence, perspective* and *dynamicity* (Langacker 2007: 435).

Generally speaking, a construal involves the relationship between an individual conceptualiser and a conceived situation, or the conceptualisation (meaning) evoked by a linguistic expression. As already indicated, in a discourse situation there are usually two conceptualisers involved; in reading this is most simply the writer and reader. A good way to represent this general construal configuration is seen in *Figure 1.1* below.

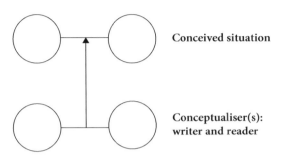

Figure 1.1. The construal configuration (adapted from Verhagen 2007:60)

Following Verhagen (2007), the different dimensions of construal can be identified with different aspects of this configuration. *Specificity, prominence, dynamicity* (and other related notions such as *action chains*) involve the structuring of the conceived situation and its component elements, or the uppermost 'horizontal level' of *Figure 1.1* (Verhagen 2007:59). *Perspective*, on the other hand, pertains to the structuring of the 'vertical relation' between this content and its conceptualisers. Significantly, this 'vertical' dimension includes various aspects of the communicative context and discursive background within which the construal takes place.

2.3   Specificity

Taking the horizontal dimension first, we may construe a situation with as much precision or specificity as is appropriate for our communicative needs and aims (Langacker 2008a:55–7). The linguistic choices available to us can often be arranged in taxonomic hierarchies reflecting a degree of increasing specificity:

> *living thing > person > adult > cognitive linguist > the coffee-drinking cognitive linguist*

As a dimension of construal, a highly specific expression such as 'a bright cold day in April' will evoke a more finely-grained conceptualisation of the situation to which we are introduced than 'one day'. The inverse of specificity is *schematicity*. Schematic characterisations such as *living thing* or *day* capture the basic commonalities of their more specific *instantiations,* related in terms of categorisation.

Our ability to form schemas through the *abstraction* of such instantiations, and recognise the relationships between them, is viewed as an important way in which our inventories of units are structured. Indeed, all expressions that are categorisable into grammatical classes within CG, such as verbs or nouns, are viewed as instantiations of an underlying schema.

2.4   Prominence

Prominence refers to the directing of attention within the conceived situation. The concept draws upon the notion of 'figure and ground', originating within gestalt psychology and which has exerted an extensive influence within cognitive linguistics (see Ungerer & Schmidt 2006: 163–206). This refers to the observation that, in visual perception, certain elements tend to 'stand out' as a salient 'figure' against the background of the visual field. The notion has been previously applied to literature, predominantly as a study in *foregrounding* (see Culler 2002; Hakemulder 2004; Kuiken & Miall 1994; van Peer 1986; van Peer, Hakemulder & Zyngier 2007). With its roots in Russian Formalism, the analysis of foregrounding is defined as 'giving unusual prominence to one element or property of a text, relative to other, less noticeable aspects' (Baldick 2004: 100). Foregrounding functions through the relationship between *deviation* and *parallelism*, which can occur at any level of language: from clausal to discourse-level (see Culler 2002 for a summary). Sometimes the foregrounded textual element crosses these categories, but this merely helps the poetic cohesion – an equilibrium between the foreground and background that forms a 'powerful aesthetic structure' (van Peer 1986:7).

In CG, this perceptual distinction is also significant in our conceptualisation and is identified at multiple levels of linguistic structure. One kind of prominence is the *profiling* of an expression's content against its conceptual 'base', or the interrelated knowledge domains activated for its interpretation (Langacker 2008a: 66–70). Consider the words *eye, nose, cheek* and *chin*. Each designates a different 'profile', though presupposing the same conceptual base of *face* against which this entity makes sense. In each case the profile singled out for focused consideration acts as the 'figure' in the resulting conceptualisation. This conceptual base is further subject to a figure/ground distinction in terms of its *scope*. While *face* in this example can be seen as the 'immediate scope' of these focused entities, this aspect of the ground is itself relatively prominent in relation to a wider knowledge domain or 'maximal scope' of *human body*.

Linguistic expressions may profile either a 'thing' or 'relationship' in CG. When a relationship is profiled, a second type of prominence – a *trajector/landmark alignment* – is observed amongst its participants (Langacker 2008a: 70–73). Differences in this kind of prominence account for a semantic distinction between sentences such as (1) and (2) below, which profile the same relationship against the same conceptual base, but differ through their contrasting choice of trajector (tr), or the focal participant being assessed in relation to the landmark (lm) (or ground). Relational profiles may be further subdivided into static or *atemporal relationships*, as in those coded by prepositions such as 'above' or 'below' (along with adjectives and adverbs) and those that evolve through time, as in the *process* coded by verbs such as 'moved'. In (3) the profiled process includes the *path*, or trajectory along which the cloud moves in relation to the city.

1. The cloud (tr) is above the city (lm).
2. The city (tr) is below the clouds (lm).
3. The cloud (tr) moved over the city (lm).

Our construal of such relationships within trajector/landmark alignments is based on our embodied experiences, or more specifically, the basic mental representations or *image schemas* built up through our bodily experiences of the world. In CG, image-schemas (such as those for ABOVE, BELOW and OVER) provide templates for the conceptualisation of situations and the psychological sense of 'well-formedness' in their expression.

2.5   Action chains

In CG, the embodied basis for our construal of processes and events within clause structure is extended beyond this basic distinction between trajector and landmark. The grammatical roles of entities participating in a process profiled by a clause are related to a number of *archetypal roles*, based once again on our embodied experiences (Langacker 2008a: 355). Crucially, a distinction is made between an *agent* (an active participant who wilfully carries out an action) and a *patient* (a passive participant that is affected or changed in some way by this action). Interacting with these entities are other participants which fulfil roles of *instrument*, *experiencer, mover* and *zero* (Langacker 2008a: 356).

   The interactions between these participants derive from another image-schematic model, named the 'billiard ball model' (2008a: 355). This represents 'our conception of objects moving through space and impacting one another through forceful physical contact' and characterises our most basic and general experience of the world. This archetypal conception underpins the system of *force dynamics* described in detail within cognitive semantics (Talmy 1988, 2000). Based on this experiential reality, the corresponding conceptual structure for a clause is modelled in CG as an *action chain* (see *Figure 1.2*) or a 'series of forceful interactions, each involving the transmission of energy (double arrow) from one participant to the next' (Langacker 2008a: 355–6). The various participant roles are distinguished in terms of their transmission of energy along this chain, between an agent (the 'energy source') and a patient (the 'energy sink').

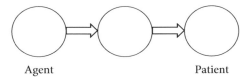

Agent   Patient

Figure 1.2. An action chain (based on Langacker 2008a: 356)

Though this conceptual structure is seen to underlie all clausal relationships, its linguistic presentation is once again subject to construal. Prototypically, in the *canonical event model* (Langacker 2008a: 357) the subject and trajector of a clause is the agent in this action chain, profiled in relation to a patient as object (as in [4] below). However, our attention may be directed to different portions of this action chain, and different participant roles attributed prominence within a trajector/ landmark alignment, as in (5) and (6):

4.   Darren smashed the vase with a football.
5.   A football smashed the vase.
6.   The vase smashed.

This event structure can be compared with different types of transitivity relations described in Systemic Functional Grammar (SFG) (Halliday & Matthiessen 2004: 168–78). Transitivity, in this account, is the grammatical system responsible for organising the 'flow of events' of which our experience is composed, into 'a manageable set of *process types*' (Halliday & Matthiessen 2004: 170). The detailed typology of processes provided by this account, and the analysis of their cumulative effect across the length of a text, has proved a highly effective tool for stylistic analysis. While CG does not set out a typology of this kind, clear overlaps can be identified with the types of participant roles engaged in the processes described in SFG. Indeed, the two accounts might be seen as complementary in terms of their different merits. The force dynamic foundations of CG allow us to begin to characterise an experiential basis for these distinctions in psychologically realistic terms. Furthermore, the direct connection CG makes between our grammatical choices and conceptual representations adds a cognitive specificity to the function of 'clause as representation' described in SFG which is particularly beneficial in accounting for the experience of reading literature.

2.6   Dynamicity

Dynamicity describes the way in which this conceptualisation develops through *processing time* (Langacker 2008a: 79). Langacker conceives of our cognitive processing in terms of mental scanning, or a basic movement between stimuli involving a process of *comparison*. A significant type of scanning described by Langacker is a *reference point relationship*, or our 'ability to invoke the conception of one entity in order to establish "mental contact" with another' (2008a: 83). In Langacker's account an initial 'reference point' affords access to a number of potential targets, or activated knowledge domains which collectively make up its *dominion*. As one of these possibilities is focused, the others fade into the background, and a fresh dominion is activated for the new target. Langacker's account of our tendency to 'scan along a chain of successive reference points' (2008a: 85), discussed mainly at the sentence level, is one which can be extended to the network of associations which operate across entire texts (Stockwell 2009a).

Different types of scanning are also available for the construal of a situation. *Summary scanning* examines multiple entities in a cumulative manner, building up a group or 'gestalt' which can then be apprehended 'all at once' as a unified whole (Langacker 2008a: 107). It is through this mechanism that we profile 'things' during the processing of nominals, for example *a cloud*. It is also the way in which we profile static relationships such as *the cloud above the city*. Sequential scanning on the other hand is the operation involved whenever we track a change or event through time. This mechanism views individual 'states' (or the relationship between entities at any moment) one by one, with each state decaying in turn as the subsequent one is accessed (Langacker 2008a: 111). This type of scanning takes place whenever we profile a process, such as that coded by a verb like 'moved'. However, the same profiled content may be construed in either fashion (dynamically or holistically) dependent on the kind of scanning adopted in its mental access. Compare the alternative construals:

7.   The rain fell heavily.
8.   There was a lot of rain.

While the rain in (7) is conceived dynamically, in (8) the various positions of this trajector along its path are added up into a single gestalt which can be conceived of holistically, like a multiple-exposure photograph. In its simplest terms, the dynamicity of a construal can be viewed once again as a matter of prominence, or the extent to which the temporality of a situation is made prominent as part of its resulting conceptualisation.

2.7 Perspective

Returning to the configuration in which such construals take place (see *Figure 1.1*), the final dimension of construal pertains to the 'vertical' relationship or *viewing arrangement* between this conceptualised content and the communicative context in which it is evoked (Langacker 2008a: 73). In CG, the interactive space from which this conceived situation is metaphorically 'viewed' by the conceptualiser(s) is termed the *ground*. One aspect of perspective construed within language is the *vantage point* assumed by a conceptualiser within this ground, comparable with the broad notion of point of view within stylistics. The particular spatial or temporal position from which a situation is conceptualised is made explicit through the use of deictic terms such as *here, now, tomorrow,* as well as verbs such as those which distinguish *come outside* from *go outside*. This vantage point need not be that of the actual discourse participant (e.g. the writer or reader) as we regularly adopt a fictive point of view, like that of a fictional character: *Simon knew that he would be in grave danger if he went outside.*

A second component is the extent to which entities at the two levels of this viewing arrangement are *subjectively* or *objectively construed*. Central to the linguistic interaction modelled in the viewing arrangement is the joint focusing of attention upon the 'object of conception' (Langacker 2008a: 77–8). When attention is focused in this way, the conceptualisers or 'subject of conception' are implicit or construed with *maximal subjectivity* in the ground. Consequently, as shown in *Figure 1.3(a)*, the object of conception, *the painting on the wall* is construed with *maximal objectivity*. However, our attention may also be directed to the conceptualisers and their vantage point e.g. through the use of pronouns 'I' and 'you': *I love that painting*. In such instances, represented in *Figure 1.3(b)*, our attention is redistributed: the conceptualiser is now more objectively construed, and the content presented more subjective. Being once again a matter of relative prominence, however, these alternative construals are best seen as opposite extremes of a continuum between which most linguistic expressions are situated.

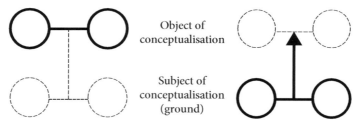

Figure 1.3. (a) Maximally objective construal   (b) Maximally subjective construal
(Verhagen 2007: 61)   (Verhagen 2007: 62)

In fact, a truly 'objective' construal in language is difficult to find, as in CG the *ground* features at least implicitly in the meaning of all linguistic expressions (Langacker 2008a: 259–62). Any indication of speaker attitude or evaluation connects the content with this context to some degree. More generally, a conceived situation is situated in relation to the ground by what Langacker terms *grounding elements*. Nominal grounding elements such as demonstratives and articles (e.g. *the* painting, *that* painting) specify a particular referent for focused conceptualisation in relation to the conceptualisers' shared knowledge. Clausal grounding, through tense and modality, specifies the status of such referents and the situations in which they interact, in relation to present moment of the communicative situation, and the *conceived reality* accepted as true (Langacker 2008a: 298–306).

2.8   Discourse

In CG, discourse is comprised of usage events (Langacker 2001, 2008a: 457). The construal relationship described here applies to every usage event in which linguistic expression takes place, and is thus central to the manner in which linguistic units are formed and applied in a process of progressive entrenchment. As previously suggested, this arrangement, and the conceptualisation achieved, is fundamentally social or interactive. Usage events include not only awareness of the ground or communicative situation, but also of the wider discourse context in which it takes place. The total body of knowledge shared by the interlocutors as the basis for communication at any given moment during discourse is modelled in CG as the *current discourse space* (*CDS*) (Langacker 2008a: 463–7). This space includes apprehension of the ongoing discourse including current, previous and anticipated usage events, and the full range of shared contextual knowledge required for comprehension. Based on this model (*Figure 1.4*), our conceptualisation or interpretation of discourse is a dynamic and incremental event, which draws upon a context that is evolving and continually updated.

The succession of usage events through which this conceptualisation unfolds may be of any size in CG, consisting of words, clauses, conversational turns etc. One form of organisation that seems particularly useful is that of *attentional frames* which, often coinciding with clauses, are characterised as 'successive windows of attention, each subsuming a manageable amount of conceptual content' (Langacker 2008a: 481–2). Though lacking detailed investigation, the conventional patterns involved in *structure building* at this discourse level are said to suggest a continuum with those identified in grammatical composition (2008a: 489). The argument that 'there is no definite boundary between grammar and discourse' (2008a: 499) is one which merits further investigation within cognitive linguistics. While the CG of clause and sentence level structures is well established, its

Current Discourse Space (CDS)

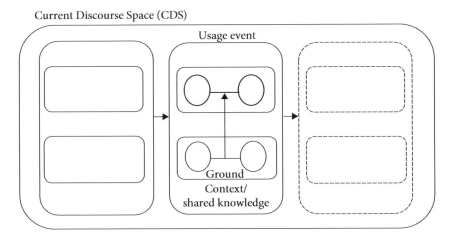

Figure 1.4. A Cognitive Grammatical discourse model (adapted from Langacker 2007:426 and 2008:466)

application to discourse has received less attention (see Langacker 2001, for its most detailed investigation). For the purposes of stylistic analysis, the extension of clause-level concepts across stretches of text, and the theoretical and practical considerations in doing so, are of primary significance. Several of the chapters in this volume consider the nature and consequences of such extrapolation in literary contexts.

3.   Literary adaptations from CG

Though grammatical models aim for universal and comprehensive applications, the exploration of different domains of language may often illuminate certain aspects of the grammar that remain particular to that language practice. Other concepts in the grammatical model might seem relatively minor in general but acquire special significance in the context of, for example, the literary domain. This is not because there is any particular systematic pattern that can definitively be called *literary language* (for formalist applications of this label, see Genette 1980; Greimas 1971; Propp 1968; Todorov 1977), nor because literature is special in some mystical, obscure way, but it is because the history and traditions of literary genres and the characteristic patterns of literary reading practices render the object of analysis complex. Literary reading – perhaps more than most other forms of engagement in language – is a form of consciousness. A Cognitive Grammar analysis of literature needs to pay special attention to the effects

PART I

Narrative fiction

CHAPTER 2

War, worlds and Cognitive Grammar

Peter Stockwell

1. The grammatical battleground

For much of its modern history, the field of literary linguistics has drawn predominantly on systemic-functional grammar for its analysis of clause relations in literature. This is perhaps not surprising, for reasons both of conceptual coherence and historical accident. Literary linguistics developed particularly in Europe from the work of the Moscow Linguistic Circle and the St Petersburg group in Russia in the 1920s, and from Prague School structuralism in 1930s Czechoslovakia – both had a strong influence on the British linguists J.R. Firth and his student M.A.K. Halliday. New Criticism in the US, *stylistique* in France and *Stilistik* in the German-speaking countries all drew on a range of approaches to language between the 1930s and the end of the 1950s, but one of the first and perhaps the most influential examples of modern stylistics is Halliday's analysis of William Golding's *The Inheritors*. Presented at a conference on linguistic style in August 1969 in Bellagio, Italy, and published in 1971, Halliday applied his own developing systemic-functional model as a sociologically grounded alternative to the psychological approach being developed by Chomsky and others in generative grammar.

Perhaps not only because of its European provenance but also because of this early explicit example of applied stylistics, the field in Europe expanded through departments of literature at just the same moment that literary studies and linguistics were becoming estranged from each other in the US. There were some brave attempts to apply transformational-generative notions for literary analysis (for example, Ohmann 1964, and Traugott & Pratt 1980, and see Caink 2013), but by the early 1980s most stylisticians had realised that the Chomskyan distinction between competence and performance left the analysis of the surface texture of literary works as a highly peripheral activity in modern linguistics. By contrast, systemic-functional grammar offered a model based on the familiar rank-structure approach to linguistic levels, with a seamless reach up from phrase and clause into text, discourse and register. For stylisticians needing to find a systematic connection between linguistic organisation and readerly interpretation, SFG quickly established itself as the paradigmatic grammar in the field. In particular, its capacity for the analysis of ideological and interpersonal dimensions of language in literary, institutional and political texts has broadened its use into media studies and critical discourse analysis.

However, the central status of SFG in literary linguistics is based on a coincidence of common concerns rather than any necessary and exclusive properties. There have been several approaches within stylistics that have drawn on pragmatics (Gricean language maxims, relevance theory), or sociolinguistics (particularly in narratology), or cognitive psychology (of worlds and schemas), or corpus linguistic techniques (for the exploration of text and textuality), but for the most part any close analysis of grammar at the clausal level has defaulted to SFG whenever stylisticians needed to explore transitivity relations, the assignment of participant roles, or the nature of lexical instances of these roles. Of course, all of these matters are also central to other grammars, and the general neglect of alternative grammatical models in literary linguistics needs some explanation. Perhaps there has been a sense that SFG works well enough for the job in hand; perhaps it is felt that its ideological reach gives it an advantage; perhaps there is a notion that a common currency of description has been established and so there is no need for radical innovation.

Each of these possibilities can be countered in general, and specifically in the context of this book with reference to Cognitive Grammar. Aside from the pure intellectual excitement in exploring new grammatical ways of accounting for literary organisation, there is a value in returning again to interrogate standard forms of description, in order to ensure that the results of an analysis have not simply by habitual practice become artefacts of the analytical system. In other words, the implicit comparison of a Cognitive Grammatical account alongside a SFG account can serve as a useful refreshment of the latter. Secondly, the impressive reach of SFG into interpersonal and ideological matters can be set also as a useful requirement of other grammatical approaches to stylistics. In this respect, we can treat SFG stylistics as a benchmark for any adequate model of analysis. The use of Cognitive Grammar in literary stylistics must be at least as good as previous practices, in order to justify overcoming the inertia of sticking with the same paradigmatic model.

Most important, however, is the first issue mentioned above – the assumption that SFG is perfectly adequate for the needs of stylisticians. It is true that there is an emphasis in SFG not so much on producing a well-formed parsed description as on matching the analytical account with the social reality that the linguistic utterance encodes. However, the historical divergence of SFG from broadly generativist approaches has also entailed a relative neglect of the psychological modalised in a variety of ways including modal verbs of various types ('would have believed', 'might scrutinise') or modal adverbs, particles, adverbial phrases and other forms ('perhaps', 'It is possible that', 'impossible or improbable', 'curious to recall', 'fancied there might be', 'perhaps' again, and 'ready to welcome'). The passage contains a very high density of examples of this projected unreality. As Langacker (2008a: 304) observes, 'Because they profile force tending toward an action, the source verbs [of English modals] are both *force-dynamic* and *future-oriented*'. Furthermore,

> their essential import is offstage and subjectively construed. This import reflects the original notion of potency directed towards an event's occurrence. Being subjectively construed, this potency no longer resides in the clausal trajector (by definition, the onstage focus of attention) but rather in the ground.
>
> (Langacker 2008a: 304)

The modals in the passage ('would have believed' and 'might scrutinise') belong to the class of nonimmediate modal forms. Even for an event located explicitly in the past (both in the verb form 'have believed' and in the grounding 'in the last years of the nineteenth century'), these forms nevertheless indicate an element of futurity. Langacker (2008a: 306–7) draws out the nature of *potential* and *projected reality* which underlies these expressions, and they are particularly iconic and effective as part of this opening to a speculative 'scientific romance' (Wells' own term for the genre). It is clear that the readerly impressions of foreboding and anxiety, as well as the capacity of this opening passage for drawing the reader into the science fictional world, have been effected by a skilful combination of deflected agency, balanced action chain structure, and rich forms of modalisation. It is worth observing that these different forms of deflection from a straightforward and consistent transfer of energy across the passage represent at the grammatical level the causes of world-switching at the level of mental representation (Werth 1999; Gavins 2007). The rich resonance of the novel's opening and the rapid absorption which many readers appreciate in the novel as a whole are partly explainable in terms of the rich worlds that are set up in this way.

3.   The grammar of action

By contrast, where the opening passage is contemplative and anticipatory, cerebral and considered, events described later in the novel are direct, active and violent. It is easy to suggest from the opening passage above that the artistic technique of latent force generates a sense of suspense that is all the more strongly available later on in the reading. The reader's first direct encounter with the Martians is described in this passage:

Ch. 5 The Heat-Ray

[…]

Beyond the pit stood the little wedge of people with the white flag at its apex, arrested by these phenomena, a little knot of small vertical black shapes upon the black ground. As the green smoke arose, their faces flashed out pallid green, and faded again as it vanished. Then slowly the hissing passed into a humming, into a long, loud, droning noise. Slowly a humped shape rose out of the pit, and the ghost of a beam of light seemed to flicker out from it.

Forthwith flashes of actual flame, a bright glare leaping from one to another, sprang from the scattered group of men. It was as if some invisible jet impinged upon them and flashed into white flame. It was as if each man were suddenly and momentarily turned to fire.

Then, by the light of their own destruction, I saw them staggering and falling, and their supporters turning to run.

I stood staring, not as yet realising that this was death leaping from man to man in that little distant crowd. All I felt was that it was something very strange. An almost noiseless and blinding flash of light, and a man fell headlong and lay still; and as the unseen shaft of heat passed over them, pine trees burst into fire, and every dry furze bush became with one dull thud a mass of flames. And far away towards Knaphill I saw the flashes of trees and hedges and wooden buildings suddenly set alight.

It was sweeping round swiftly and steadily, this flaming death, this invisible, inevitable sword of heat. I perceived it coming towards me by the flashing bushes it touched, and was too astounded and stupefied to stir. I heard the crackle of fire in the sand pits and the sudden squeal of a horse that was as suddenly stilled. Then it was as if an invisible yet intensely heated finger were drawn through the heather between me and the Martians, and all along a curving line beyond the sand pits the dark ground smoked and crackled. Something fell with a crash far away to the left where the road from Woking station opens out on the common. Forthwith the hissing and humming ceased, and the black, domelike object sank slowly out of sight into the pit.   (H.G. Wells 1898: 23–4)

The first thing to notice here is the almost complete absence of modalisation, and instead the prominence of perception. Throughout, there is a sense of detached reportage, a simple relaying of the facts of the event in all its horror: this is an eye-witness account, and this impression is carried largely by the prominence of *subjective construal* across the whole passage (see Langacker 2008a: 295). There is a strong experiencer participant role in the first-person account with a high occurrence of verbs of experience and perception: 'I saw them', 'I stood staring', 'All I felt',

'I saw the flashes', 'I perceived it', 'I heard'. Even where an event is described without the explicit first-person experiencer trajector, it is expressed by analogy or in a way that draws attention to the perceived appearance: 'seemed to flicker', 'It was as if some invisible jet', 'It was as if each man', 'It was as if an invisible…' These last three 'as if' comparisons merit some further comment, since they echo the passage's coding of agency that I will address next.

The 'as if' expressions direct the reader's attention away from the current scene description and into a metaphorical world in which the properties then articulated are to be drawn down into the matrix world. It is noticeable that it is the most horrific events that are so metaphorised. However, the detail of each of these is rather odd, and the fact that they are the only fleeting departures from the matrix world makes their oddity even more prominent. The embedded clause that is set up as an analogy is in fact literally true: it really is an invisible jet; each man really is suddenly turned to fire. It is as if the observer can only gesture towards the horror by framing it as a metaphorical deflection, even though it is really true: in this respect, the technique might be understood as being similar to the notion of latent force outlined in relation to modalisation above. The last of the three is more truly metaphorical: it is not literally an invisible yet intensely heated finger – but even here, and with the only other metaphors ('death leaping' and the 'inevitable sword of heat'), there is a human-scale perception that further magnifies the horror.

The coding of agency in the passage mirrors this deflection in that it diminishes the activity of the humans in favour of the Martians. Humans have very little or diminished agency in this scene. In the first paragraph, the humans are described as a 'little wedge of people', and 'a little knot' and as 'small vertical black shapes'. The perceptions of the humans as little and insignificant is an iconic placement of the Martians' perception. In the first sentence, although the 'little wedge of people' is the agentive trajector in the clause, it/they are defocused by the inversion of the word-order that begins with the grounding 'Beyond the pit' and then has the (static) verb 'stood'. The entire trajector becomes part of a passive construction 'arrested by these phenomena', to the point at which the people become grounded and indistinguishable from the landmark material: 'black shapes upon the black ground'. At the same time, viewed in terms of attractors, the humans are made smaller and darker and motionless, so that the Martians' size, brightness and action that is about to come can be regarded contrastively even more vividly (see Stockwell 2002b, 2009b). First the humans' faces 'flashed' and 'faded' and 'vanished'.

Throughout the passage, the humans are diminished both as attractors and as *proto-patients* (Dowty [1991] suggests that proto-agency and proto-passivity can be regarded as a spectrum on which Langacker's participant roles of agent, experiencer, mover, patient, instrument and so on can be specified). The humans' agentive potential is deflected by passivisation and grounding, and as the passage progresses they become subordinated to the experiencer 'I'. There is a great deal of non-specificity and vagueness in the narrator's descriptions, and a preponderance of proximal deictics of various types. The 'as if' constructions can be associated schematically with an inarticulate grasping after precision, but vagueness is particularly carried in the indefinites: 'a humming', 'a long, loud, droning noise', 'a humped shape', 'a bright glare', 'the ghost of a beam of light'. Phenomena that are too terrible to comprehend are similarly expressed by vague underlexicalised phrases: 'it was something very strange', 'something', and paradoxical negation in 'An almost noiseless' and 'unseen shaft of heat'. The metaphorical analogies can also be seen as attempts to capture the incomprehensible mechanism of the heat-ray. These narrative techniques cleverly combine the sense of reporterly detachment and objectivity with the sense of humanity in the narrating voice.

Similarly, the highly descriptive account is characterised by a great deal of vivid adjectival modification. In Cognitive Grammar, these adjectives are not selected by the nominal headword (as in traditional grammars), but are understood as schematic trajectors which are specified by their nouns (Langacker 2008a: 116). For example, the set of adjectives in the passage tend to cluster around light and colour, size and shape, but the nouns to which they are attached are defamiliarised and unexpected. So people are a 'little wedge', a 'small knot' or are 'vertical black shapes'. There is 'green smoke' and faces are 'pallid green'. There is an 'invisible jet' and an 'intensely heated finger'. The overall effect is of unsettling estrangement. At the same time, this strangeness is presented in deictically proximal terms: 'the pit' (I think the definite article can function deictically here), 'these phenomena', 'this was death', 'that little distant crowd', 'far away', 'this flaming death, this invisible, inevitable sword of heat'. The spatio-temporal deixis is also carried in the directionality of the verb-choices ('arose', 'rose', 'turning to run', 'coming towards me'), which position the reader's perspective alongside the participating narrator. The prepositions and prepositional phrases throughout the passage also echo the relative positions of the human and narrator on the one hand and the Martians on the other. The humans are grounded by being associated with prepositions in which the landmark end of the image-schema is profiled: 'beyond', 'upon', 'turned to fire'. By contrast, the Martians and their activities are prominently figured, with prepositions associated image-schematically with the trajector end of the relationship: 'out of the pit', 'flicker out from it'; even at the end when the heat-ray mechanism retracts back into the landscape, the prepositional choice manages to sustain this pattern 'out of sight' even as the object sinks 'into the pit' to signal the end of this period of destruction.

By contrast with the diminished humans, the Martians and their associated objects are increasingly placed in strongly proto-agent positions, and as instruments and movers. They are the ellipted agent of the defocused 'by these phenomena'; they are the green smoke that 'arose'; they are the hissing noise that 'passed into' a drone which is also them; and they are the 'humped shape' that 'rose out of the pit'. Note, however, that these descriptions and the tone of the rest of the passage represent the Martians indirectly. They are described variously in terms of brightness and heat and noise, but mainly by the effect of their actions rather than by their inherent properties. So, instead of the Martians firing flashes of flame at the people, the clause is structured to profile the 'flashes of actual flame' which 'sprang from the scattered group of men', the jet 'flashed into white flame', and 'each man' (in a passive role) is 'turned to fire'. This stylistic codification serves to focus on the horror, and enacts the human incomprehension that the Martians in the fighting machine can somehow be causing the destruction. Indeed, the framing of the clause presents the humans' deaths as being somehow reflexive and self-generated 'by the light of their own destruction'. Similarly, the causal element is ellipted or defocused: there is 'the crackle of fire', there is 'the sudden squeal of a horse that was as suddenly stilled', and 'the dark ground smoked and crackled' as if by itself. 'Something fell' apparently causelessly, but the underlying cause of all of this violence is clearly understood because of the strong agency attached to the juxtaposed Martian object. By contrast with human insignifance and their passivity throughout, Martian power seems to saturate the passage, even as it is understated.

4.   The grammar of ambience

There is also a tonal or atmospheric difference between the two passages that the foregoing grammatical analysis partly captures as well. This is not simply because the opening excerpt is a descriptive pause while the second is a description of an action scene. Each is written in stylistic patterns that iconically match the content which is being described. In Stockwell (2013) I distinguish the two different ambient effects: tone relates to the quality of the narrative or authorial voice and is a matter of diction and register; atmosphere pertains to the quality of the world being presented and is a matter of semantic priming. A reader can be encouraged by textual patterns to focus on the tone of 'voice' in the writing or to see through this mediation and feel as if they are experiencing the presented world directly. In this respect, tonal effects correspond with Langacker's (2008a: 77) notion of *subjective construal*, while atmospheric effects are associated with *objective construal*. Of course, to forestall a critical theoretical objection, I am not suggesting that an atmospheric perspective on the fictional world is actually objective – only that a reader feels that there is no sense of a mediating narrative voice and the world of the text is immersive and absorbing. It is a matter of focus which can be induced either way in the reader by stylistic patterning. As Langacker (2008a: 536–7) points out, all linguistic representations are *simulations* either of an actual reality or of a fictionally imagined putative reality, with different degrees of attenuation between language and experience; objective and subjective construal is one factor in attenuation.

The ambience of a literary passage can be explored systematically within cognitive linguistics. Evans (2009) sets out how lexical concepts instantiated by particular word-choices provide access points to more schematised conceptual models (following Langacker's [2008a: 167–8] understanding of lexical choice as an instance of the schematisation of grammar). For literary reading, the overall sense of ambience in a passage is a consequence of the rich schematic experiences that are drawn on by the singular instances of the passage's style. So, for example, the opening sequence in *The War of the Worlds* has tone as its prominent ambient feature: the tone of voice is that of an educated, balanced, rational mind. 'Scrutinise', 'transient' and 'infusoria' – among many other examples – are consistently instances of scientific register. The balanced subordinate syntax matches this tone, but it also has an antique feel to it perhaps carried by expressions such as 'those departed days', 'this globe' and 'missionary enterprise' that echo 19th century phrasing. There are a great number of evaluative elements that foreground the subjectivity of the narrative voice and encourage the reader towards a subjective construal: a foregrounding of verbs of belief, thought and curiosity, a self-conscious use of modalised phrases such as 'It is possible that', a deployment of lexis instantiating human feeling such as 'cool', 'unsympathetic', 'envious' and 'disillusionment'.

By contrast, the 'heat-ray' description later in the novel has relatively little evaluation. In spite of the reporting clauses 'I saw', 'I perceived' and 'I felt', the passage is predominantly focused on the presented world as an object of experience, rather than on the musings or self-regarding evaluations of the narrator. It is less tonal and more atmospheric, in the terms set out above. As I have noted, there is a great deal of adjectival modification: while of course the choices of these descriptive schemes are made by the imagined narrator, by contrast with the evaluative lexis of the opening passage, here they are construed as being attached to the fictional world being presented. In other words, the fact that vivid adjectives are deployed from the common schematic set of vivid descriptions serves to focus readerly attention on the specification being offered by the world in view, rather than as part of the idiosyncratic characterisation of the mind-style of the narrator.

The lexical choices throughout are consistently from the semantic fields of fire and draw on battle imagery. The sustained consistency of these choices builds

CHAPTER 3

Construal and comics

The multimodal autobiography of Alison Bechdel's *Fun Home*

Michael Pleyer & Christian W. Schneider

1.   Introduction

In December 2006, *Time,* like so many other periodicals, compiled a list of the best books of the year. Topping this list was Alison Bechdel's *Fun Home*, described as a 'stunning memoir' and 'masterpiece' (Lacayo & Grossman 2006). Yet *Time* also had to address an important fact regarding the book's format: 'Oh, and it's a comic book' (Lacayo & Grossman 2006). Indeed, *Fun Home* is a graphic novel, a book-length comic book – which is a surprising title to find on this list.

Comics have long been disregarded as an art form, as they are often associated with trivial fare for children and adolescents. However, this notion has begun to change: not only have the media and the reading public discovered that comics – and graphic novels in particular – may be rather mature and thought-provoking works, the form has also attracted extensive academic interest. This interest manifests itself in a wide array of disciplines and methodological approaches. Still, the medium's distinct forms of expression present academic observers with several challenges. The most prominent among these is its multimodality, the blending of diverse modes of expression – most notably both verbal and pictorial dimensions of meaning – which complicates traditional literary and linguistic approaches.

These challenges are especially evident with regard to *Fun Home*. Bechdel's graphic novel is an autobiographical text, detailing not only her life, but also the life of her father Bruce. This amalgamation of autobiography and biography becomes even more complex: Bechdel describes discovering her homosexuality; however, she finds out that her father is also a closeted homosexual – who is killed only a short time after her coming-out, in a roadside accident that may have been a suicide. She approaches the intricacies and unsolved mysteries of her account in a highly literary and self-referential manner, trying to understand her father and come closer to him, despite their complicated relationship and the traumas of her adolescence.

How to grasp this text and its multimodality? While there are certainly various different possible answers to this question, it is our opinion that the concepts of cognitive linguistics, especially the work of Ronald Langacker, may provide a particularly fruitful approach to *Fun Home* as a graphic novel. As we will argue in more detail below, Cognitive Grammar (Langacker 1987, 1991b, 1999, 2001, 2008a) is ideally suited to model the multimodal construction of meaning, as it sees visual processes of meaning construal as being founded on the same conceptual principles as linguistic construals of meaning and describes them with a common terminology.

We will proceed as follows. First we will summarise the ways in which *Fun Home* can be described as a distinctly Gothic text, which offers one of the most promising literary approaches to its elaborate structure. Then we will introduce Cognitive Grammar as a theory that promises to be a significant aid in explicating the complex shifts in perspective and alternative construal that mark *Fun Home* as a text in the Gothic mode. Here, we will first elaborate on the central concept of *construal* in Cognitive Grammar before turning to the first of three concepts that we think prove central in the analysis of the complex multimodal construal operations in Bechdel's graphic novel, namely *profiling*. After explaining the general concept, we will illustrate how it can be fruitfully applied to *Fun Home* and its multiple overlapping profile-base relations and the complex domain matrix it incrementally builds up. The next concept we will turn to is that of *viewing arrangement*. Again, we will first explain how the concept of viewing arrangement is used to model different construal configurations and assignments of prominence involving a conceptualiser and a conceived situation as well as their relation. Then, we will illustrate how the analysis of the multimodal construction of viewing arrangements in the text enables us to understand and model Bechdel's complex, self-reflective and ambiguous narrative perspectivisation on a cognitive level. Lastly, in a brief outlook we will argue that these kinds of analyses should be supplemented by, and ideally be integrated with, Langacker's *current discourse space model*, which can model the ongoing flow of discourse and changing construals in complex, multi- and monomodal narratives. In the conclusion, we will shortly take stock and summarise the overall results and key points of our analysis.

2.   *Fun Home* – a Gothic autobiography

There are several potential literary approaches to the evident complexity of Bechdel's perspective – its queerness (Spiers 2010), for instance, or its intertextual references (Freedman 2009). However, focusing on its gaps and ambiguities, it is also possible to read *Fun Home* as a Gothic text (McCallum 2009; Schneider 2010). At first glance, this approach is rather counterintuitive. On the one hand, it seems to restrict the novel's complexity unduly, confining it within a limited – and apparently far from relevant – genre designation. On the other hand, its autobiographical status appears to be at odds with the Gothic's imitative formalism and counterfeit constructions (Spooner 2006: 32). However, the Gothic must not be used in such narrow terms. In contemporary literary studies, the concept has not only left behind its air of disreputability and triviality; it is also commonly viewed as an overarching mode of expression 'that exceeds genre and categories, restricted neither to a literary school nor to a historical period' (Botting 1996: 14). This mode may appear even in autobiography, complicating the genre's supposedly 'simple' approach to life and reality.

Indeed, *Fun Home* has several distinctly Gothic traits. The dust cover of its first edition already promises its readers 'gothic twists' and 'sweetly gothic drawings' (Bechdel 2006). If one reads the graphic novel accordingly, there are several levels on which the Gothic mode manifests itself. Probably most obviously, it colours Bechdel's setting, as it appears in words and images. Her family owned a funeral home, or as the family called it, the 'Fun Home', giving the comic its name. Thus, it was not unusual for young Alison to play among graves, corpses or coffins. A similarly morbid environment is the Bechdel family home, a Gothic revival mansion, whose décor reminds Alison of the Addams Family (Bechdel 2006: 35).

Within these gloomy settings, the noted Gothic plot twists unfold. It seems as if Bechdel 'casts herself as the gothic heroine needing to be freed from paternal tyranny and the gothic revival mansion' (McCallum 2009: 312). She feels constricted by her father's duplicity, the air of secrets and lies that surrounds the family life. However, this artifice does not spare her disturbing glimpses into a 'striking convergence of death and sexuality' (McCallum 2009: 310), especially regarding her father's suicide. The Gothic trauma of her past distinctly shapes Bechdel's reconstruction of it.

Both setting and plot are expressions of an underlying general attitude, one that characterises most instances of the Gothic mode in more or less explicit form. It represents a general doubt regarding forms of representation, regarding order, stability and action. The Gothic 'threatens not only the loss of sanity, honour, property or social standing but the very order which supports and is regulated by the coherence of those terms' (Botting 1996: 7). It focuses on negativity and ambiguity. Indeed, Bechdel explicitly thematises such an attitude, as she constantly notes the limits of her narration, doubting the reliability of her memories and contrasting different versions of potential reality. She comments on 'heavy-handed plot devices'

(Bechdel 2006: 155) in her life story and criticises a seemingly obvious narrative correspondence as 'maudlin in the extreme' (Bechdel 2006: 124). Commenting on her first autobiographical writings, her childhood diary entries, she concludes that her 'narration had by that point become altogether unreliable' (Bechdel 2006: 184), a judgement that is also a warning to the reader of her current, more comprehensive autobiographical attempt. She also offers ostensibly invented conjectures about her father's life and actions: she imagines the milkman rather than the mailman rescuing him when he was stuck in the mud as a child (Bechdel 2006: 41) and envisages him having an affair with his psychiatrist (Bechdel 2006: 185). It is this constant shifting of perspective and the focus on its constructedness that makes *Fun Home* such a complex text. In order to tackle this complexity, one may turn to methodological ways to analyse the ambiguity in more detail: Cognitive Grammar promises to be such a way.

3.   Construal in Cognitive Grammar

One of the most central notions of Cognitive Grammar and of cognitive linguistics more broadly is that of *construal*. The notion directs attention to the central role that conceptualisation and dynamic meaning construction in interaction play in these frameworks. It refers to the fact that when conceptualising a scene for purposes of expression, conceptualisers always structure situations in a specific manner and in specific relations, and selectively assign salience to certain aspects of it (Croft & Cruse 2004; Langacker 1987).

Importantly, all acts of conceptualisation and meaning construction are tied to a particular vantage point, perspective, and construal. Whenever someone is conceptualising an event, they establish a construal relationship, or *viewing arrangement* between themselves and their conceptualisation involving a specific perspectival construal. That is, they highlight portions of the construal and background others.

As an example, take one type of construal difference that will be important throughout this chapter: different degrees of attention can be assigned to the object and the subject of conceptualisation and their relationship. For instance, talking about an upcoming big match, a football player can say about their team *The team are really looking forward to the derby*, thus focusing attention on the object of conceptualisation alone – the team as a whole – with the speaker or subject of conceptualisation being only implicit in the background. The player could also present a different viewing arrangement, in which the player as the subject of conceptualisation and his or her membership in the team is also made salient: *We are really looking forward to the derby.*

These different ways in which conceptualisations can be structured or con-strued are referred to as construal operations. They thus refer to the different ways in which conceptual content can be organised with respect to a particu-lar vantage point and perspective. Construal operations serve as prompts for the allocation of attention to a particular aspect of the cognitive representation evoked in the listener. Importantly, in line with the general theoretical commit-ments of cognitive linguistics and Cognitive Grammar, construal operations as employed in language are seen as instantiations of general cognitive processes and mechanisms (Croft & Cruse 2004; Evans & Green 2006; Langacker 1987, 2008a).

This also has important ramifications and implications for the applicability of Cognitive Grammar to the analysis of the processes of meaning construal in graphic literature. If 'Viewing in Cognition and Grammar' (Langacker 1999: 203) is based on analogous cognitive processes, we can use the terminology of this model to describe graphic and linguistic processes of construal and their interac-tion and interfaces. These strong parallels are the reason why in Cognitive Gram-mar, the terms *viewing* and *viewer* are used both for perception and conception, the former of which is treated as 'special case', of the latter (Langacker 2008a: 261). Moreover, Cognitive Grammar and cognitive linguistics recognise that the con-struction of meaning is intrinsically multi-modal in nature. Human interaction and communication is never just verbal or linguistic (see Forceville 2009: 21), but consistently multimodal and has to be processed as such:

> When people meet, they invariably communicate in multiple modalities: the eyes, gestures, and tones of voice merge with the perceived affordances of the surroundings into an integrated and partially shared experience. Multimodal communication predates and contextualizes language [...].
>
> (Steen & Turner 2013)

Despite its focus on grammatical categories, Langacker's account implicitly adheres to this observation, as it affirms that grammar 'reflects our basic experi-ence of moving, perceiving, and acting on the world' (Langacker 2008a: 4).This multimodal aspect of Cognitive Grammar manifests itself in its visual bent: many of its categories are 'pictorial by nature, however abstract, and are often granted pictorial representation in analysis' (Gibbons 2012: 29). Langacker's 'use in CG of semipictorial diagrams' (Langacker 2008a: 11) does not mean his theory is entirely visual, as he warns (2008a: 12). Yet, he concedes that it may be 'hard to resist the visual metaphor, where content is likened to a scene and construal to a particular way of viewing it' (2008a: 55). While 'CG does *not* claim that all mean-ings are based on space or visual perception, [...] the visual metaphor does sug-gest a way to classify the many facets of construal' (Langacker 2008a: 55).

Applying categories of Cognitive Grammar to multimodal narratives, David Herman notes that this means that

> in multimodal narratives exploiting more than one information track, cognitive capacities and constraints associated with what Langacker terms the parameter of focal adjustment […] can be distributed across more than one semiotic channel, requiring interpreters to integrate these reflexes of perspective-taking processes into a more or less coherent mental representation of a given time-slice of the storyworld.   (Herman 2009a: 139)

This all speaks in favour of Cognitive Grammar being ideally suited to capture multimodal processes of dynamic meaning construal (Gibbons 2012; Herman 2009a, 2009b).

4.   Construal in *Fun Home*

Given that it features complex multimodal construal configurations arising from the interaction of graphic and linguistic dimensions of meaning, we submit that Alison Bechdel's graphic novel *Fun Home* is an ideal testing ground for a Cognitive Grammar approach to multimodal literature. This is why in the next section we will first briefly elaborate on some key concepts and categories used in Cognitive Grammar to analyse different forms of construal and then illustrate their usefulness by applying them to selected examples from *Fun Home*.

4.1   Profiling

Profiling is one of the most fundamental construal operations (Evans & Green 2006: 41–3; Ungerer & Schmid 2006: 163–206; Langacker 1987: 183–9). As outlined in the *Introduction* to this volume, it is associated with the assignment of prominence and makes use of the principle of figure/ground segregation. When we focus our attention on something, our perception singles out this entity as a salient figure standing out from the non-salient ground. Analogously, in Cognitive Grammar, profiling relates to the relationship between a conceptually foregrounded entity, or *profile*, and its conceptual *base*, from which it in part derives its meaning. The base forms the general locus of general viewing attention, whereas the profile is singled out as the focus of attention. The broader configurations of knowledge that provide the context for a conceptualisation are called *domains*. To illustrate, when speaking of 'Friday', it can be said that this day is profiled relative to the conceptual base *week*. The relevant domains providing the context for the conceptualisation are concepts like the calendar and human measurements of time (Langacker 2008a: 66–7; Radden & Dirven 2007: 30). The concepts of base and profile can also be illustrated using a theatre metaphor. If we compare the way conceptualisation works to the way a play is performed on stage, we can say that the base refers to what is 'onstage' – the foregrounded general locus of viewing attention – and that the profile is the specific focus of attention within the 'onstage' region (Langacker 2008a: 63).

What is especially important for the relevance of the notion of profiling for questions of perspectival construal is that conceptualisers can choose to profile different aspects of a conceptual base. For example, when conceptualising a wheel, different segments or aspects of this conceptual base can be profiled. So 'hub', 'spoke', and 'rim' all represent different profiles against the same conceptual base of *wheel*. In addition, the profile and the conceptual base can of course also be coextensive, as in the expression 'wheel' which profiles the whole conceptual base of the *wheel* (Langacker 2008a: 67). Similarly, a certain profiled aspect can be characterised by multiple bases and overlapping domains. Take the profile of 'father' as an example. One conventional conceptual base for this profile is the father-child relation, but beyond that it can be contextualised and characterised by a number of domains or knowledge configurations which can also overlap. To pick just a few, fatherhood and the father-child relation can be related to the domain of *kinship* or *genealogical relations*, the domain of *biological relations*, or even more generally to the conceptual domain of *living thing*. If they are explicitly activated and accessed, these domains are then said to be in the expression's matrix.

In fact, *Fun Home* is an ideal example of how multiple overlapping bases and domains are used in trying to characterise and construe complex conceptual situations and their underlying meaning, which is why in the next section we will turn to how profiling can be used to illustrate the dynamic meaning construal in Bechdel's graphic novel.

4.2   Profiling in *Fun Home*

Of course, profiling processes may occur whenever an object is conceptualised and imbued with meaning. What makes *Fun Home* particularly apt for illustrating profiling in multimodal texts is that Bechdel explicitly thematises the ascription of identity and the construction of meaning from different perspectives. She constantly looks for the most suitable comparisons to understand her father and his role in her life. Frequently, she does so by using literary references, likening her father to both authors and their characters, for example to both James Joyce (Bechdel 2006: 228–30) and Leopold Bloom (Bechdel 2006: 221). As she confesses, Bruce Bechdel seems to be 'most real to me in fictional terms' (Bechdel 2006: 67), as they promise to imbue his life with more meaning than a purely factual biographical account.

One of most prominent and layered literary analogies in *Fun Home* posits Bechdel's father as Daedalus, an association based on his passion for architecture and restoration, creating 'dazzling displays of artfulness' (Bechdel 2006:9). This extended correspondence can be described as a profiling process that Bechdel reveals to the reader. When she conceptualises her father as Daedalus, it can be argued that she profiles the concept *my father* on the base of *Daedalus as constructor*, highlighting the similarities to Bruce Bechdel within the conceptual content connected to the mythical figure.

This profile-base relation *My father as Daedalus* may be construed within distinct, if connected, domains. On the one hand, it can be defined with regard to the Minotaur myth, in which Daedalus appears as the constructor of the labyrinth that confines and conceals the Minotaur. On this background, Bruce Bechdel is profiled as the constructor of a confining structure 'from which, as stray youths and maidens discovered to their peril … escape was impossible' (Bechdel 2006:12). The family home becomes a labyrinth, hiding a monstrous secret.

Yet, *My father as Daedalus* can also be construed within the domain of the Icarus myth. Here, Bruce Bechdel's obsession with artifice lets him appear as someone who, like 'Daedalus, too, was indifferent to the human cost of his projects' (Bechdel 2006:11), especially with regard to his children. This conceptualisation also carries connotations of tragic transgression, i.e. Icarus' fall into the sea. In *Figure 4.1*, the overlapping domains of the Minotaur myth and the Icarus myth provide the context of the profile/base-relationship.

This already hints at how Bechdel further complicates the profile-base relationships and construal of *my father* and *Daedalus*. In the narrative, Bruce Bechdel

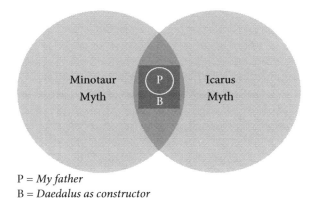

P = *My father*
B = *Daedalus as constructor*

Figure 4.1. The conceptual entity *My father* is profiled against the conceptual base *Daedalus as constructor* (after Taylor 2002:197)

Figure 4.2. The father as a monster (Bechdel 2006: 12)

does not figure solely as a tyrannical constructor; he is simultaneously the victim of his own artifice. Thus, it is no surprise that his daughter offers further construals of him that profile different aspects within the overlapping domains of the Daedalus mythology. On the one hand, she notes that it was her father 'who was to plummet from the sky' (Bechdel 2006: 4), thereby equating him with Icarus, the victim of artifice and transgression. On the other hand, she also conceptualises him as the Minotaur, a 'half-man monster' (see *Figure 4.2*) that haunts the labyrinth. In this case, it is indeed the multimodal connection of casually informative text and threatening image which makes the analogy clear.

Thus, Bechdel introduces different conceptualisations of her father; in terms of profiling, she creates a complex domain matrix of overlapping profiling processes in connected semantic domains. This illustrates how intricately her father's identity is portrayed, especially since it implies how she may conceptualise herself within her matrix: if her father is Daedalus, is she Icarus? If he is the Minotaur, is she Theseus – or one of his young victims that cannot escape? This intricate construal of identities also highlights the dynamic nature of shifting meaning: Bechdel does not – and cannot – choose only one conceptualisation, construe only one stable profile-base relation and thus interpretation of her father's role. Thus, while the concept of profiling can offer important insights into the way Bechdel employs multiple construals to conceptualise her father and their relationship, in order to properly grasp the dynamic nature of construal and perspectivation, this analysis needs to be supplemented by other concepts within Langacker's methodological apparatus that explicitly address changes in perspective.

4.3   Viewing arrangements

The second construal category that is of fundamental importance both in Cognitive Grammar and also in the conceptualisation processes employed and made salient in *Fun Home* is that of the *viewing arrangement*, which has already been mentioned above. To reiterate, the viewing arrangement refers to the 'overall relationship between the "viewers" and the situation being "viewed"' (Langacker 2008a: 73). In other words it refers to the following questions: in a given conceptualisation, to what degree does a conceptualiser focus exclusively on the external situation, that is to what extent does the conceptualiser try to adopt a perspective on the situation the conceptualiser is not part of? Alternatively, to what degree does the conceptualiser make his or her own involvement in the act of conceptualising explicit, to what degree does she or he adopt a perspective, or 'viewing arrangement', that involves both him or her as conceptualiser and the situation being conceptualised? When talking about viewing arrangements, we are thus talking about the relation between the object of conceptualisation and the subject(s) of conceptualisation, or ground. (Note that this use of the term *ground* as indicating the subject(s) of conceptualisation, and the immediate circumstances of the conceptualisation event is distinct and has to be distinguished from the use of 'ground' in the cognitive principle of figure/ground segregation mentioned in 4.1 above; see Langacker 2008a: 58).

As with profiling, this can again be illustrated with the help of the stage metaphor (Langacker 2008a: 77). If we think of an audience watching a play, in one type of viewing arrangement the attention is focused on what is onstage. What is offstage is accessible in principle and is implicit but it is not in the centre of attention. For example, the viewers in the audience normally do not pay much attention to other people in the audience, or to other 'irrelevant' parts of their surroundings that don't pertain to what is happening in the play. But the audience can also be profiled as part of the viewing arrangement so that their reception of and relation to what is happening onstage also becomes part of the conceptualisation.

Following Verhagen (2005), the viewing arrangement or construal configuration of a conceptualisation (that is, the relationship between the object and the subject of conceptualisation, or the conceptualiser and the situation being conceived) can be illustrated in the diagrammatic representation of viewing arrangements of the following utterances (in *Figure 4.3*):

a.   *Bruce is sitting across the table from me*
b.   *Bruce is sitting across the table from Alison*
c.   *Bruce is sitting across the table*

In the diagram, the object of conceptualisation for each utterance is represented by the two circles on the top, the subject of conceptualisation, or viewer – also called *ground* – is represented by the bottom circle, and the construal relation between conceptualiser and the conceived situation is represented by the line connecting the two. The bottom circle denotes the subject, the upper circles the object of conceptualisation. The connecting line denotes the construal relation (adapted from Verhagen 2007: 59–71). This kind of diagram also enables us to represent the different degrees of explicit or implicit involvement in the conceptualising process expressed in different viewing arrangements. For instance, the situation of people sitting at a table can be conceptualised using different viewing arrangements (Langacker 2002: 326–8; Verhagen 2007: 63–4).

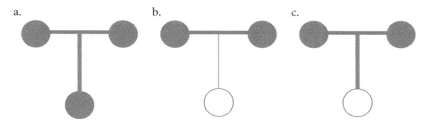

Figure 4.3. The viewing arrangements for three variant utterances

The viewing arrangement of utterance (a) ('Bruce is sitting across the table from me'), represented by the diagram on the left, explicitly directs attention to the whole of the viewing arrangement, that is to both the conceptualised situation and the subject of conceptualisation (*me*). Here both object and subject of conceptualisation, which is also called the *ground* in this context, are put onstage and become the focus of attention. In Langacker's (1987: 128–31, 2008a: 260–61) terminology the object of conceptualisation and the subject of conceptualisation are both *objectively* construed, as they are both explicitly mentioned (*Bruce* and *me*) and profiled and thus put onstage as the focus of attention. In terms of conceptual perspective, according to Langacker, it can be said that in this utterance the conceptualiser treats their 'participation as being on par with anybody else's' (Langacker 2002: 328). Following Verhagen, in the figure this is indicated by the whole of the construal configuration being represented in bold lines. The process of explicitly making the conceptualiser an overt, salient part of the viewing arrangement is called *grounding*.

In utterance (b) ('Bruce is sitting across the table from Alison') there are no grounding elements directing attention to the subject of conceptualisation, or viewer of the conceived situation. The ground, that is, the perspective and role of the conceptualiser, is 'offstage' and is not made explicit, but is only minimally present, covertly and tacitly, at the fringes of attention. As Langacker puts it: 'It inheres in the conceptual substrate supporting [the expression's meaning] without being put onstage as a focused object of conception' (Langacker 2008a: 260). In this maximally distinct viewing arrangement, the object of conceptualisation is thus construed with maximal objectivity as the onstage focus of attention, and the subject of conceptualisation is construed with maximal subjectivity as it only functions 'as a tacit conceptualising presence that is not itself conceived' in this utterance and only has the role of an implicit, conscious locus of the act of conceptualisation (Langacker 2008a: 77). This is indicated in *Figure 4.3* by the faint circle representing the subject of conceptualisation/ground and the faint line connecting ground and the object of conceptualisation.

Finally, there are also construal configurations in which the ground or subject of conceptualisation is not overtly mentioned, but is still evoked indirectly, as an implicit reference point. An example of this would be utterance (c) ('Bruce is sitting across the table'). Here, there is no explicit grounding, but the prepositional phrase *across the table* still evokes a connection between the conceptualiser and the object of conceptualisation, that is stronger and directs more attention to the perspective of the conceptualiser in the construal of the viewing arrangement than does utterance (b). In utterance (c), the subject of conceptualisation is also left covert, but *across the table* construes Bruce's location with respect to the spatial perspective and point of view of the conceptualiser, and thus also directs attention to and establishes a connection between the object of conceptualisation and the ground (see Langacker 2002: 328–9; Verhagen 2007: 63–4). In Verhagen's (2007: 64) terms, the viewing arrangement can be said to be 'minimally perspectivized' due to its implicit reference to the ground. In *Figure 4.3*, this is indicated by the line connecting object and subject of conceptualisation being solid.

As it will be important for the analysis of viewing arrangements in *Fun Home* it should be noted that spatial perspective is not the only implicit element with the effect of more or less implicitly evoking facets of the ground and the role of the conceptualiser in the viewing arrangement or construal configuration. More generally, all expressions that indicate or give access to the attitude or relation of the conceptualiser/viewer, on the one hand, and the object of conceptualisation, on the other, can evoke a connection to the ground and thus might direct attention to or put onstage the perspectival nature of a construal (Langacker 2008a: 262).

4.4   Viewing arrangements in *Fun Home*

Obviously, when applying the concept of viewing arrangements to *Fun Home*, 'viewing' has to be taken literally; it is after all a graphic novel and thus a visual text. Bechdel's visual perspective on her diegetic world is always obvious. Thus, it could be argued, a certain form of perspectival grounding is always present in the text. Furthermore, since it is also an autobiography, Bechdel's view usually includes herself both as narrator and as subject, a duality which characterises the entire narrative perspectivisation. A rather morbid scene (see *Figure 4.4*) from the Bechdels' family life, where young Alison walks into the embalming room of her father's funeral home and sees him working on a naked corpse, may function as an example for the complexity of this perspective.

Figure 4.4. The disturbing aspects of the 'Fun Home' (Bechdel 2006: 44)

At first glance, this seems to be a straightforward representation of Alison's view, in both words and image. Yet, there are subtle differences regarding the perspectivisation in the respective modal channels. If one were just to consider the narrative comment *sans* image, this would represent Verhagen's 'minimally perspectivized' viewing arrangement (see *Figure 4.5*). Alison Bechdel as the conceptualising subject is not explicitly present in her statement, but her usage of the word *dad* alerts the reader to her subjectivity within this perspective.

Figure 4.5. A minimally perspectivised viewing arrangement (cf. Verhagen 2007: 64)

However, the actual panel image (*4.4*) presents us with a different viewing arrangement. Here, one can identify a case of grounding, as Alison is clearly part of the visualised scene; thus, as the scene's conceptualiser, she is explicitly objectiv-ised within the perspective construction (see *Figure 4.6*).

Figure 4.6. A viewing arrangement in which both subject and object of conceptualisation are objectively construed and put 'on stage' (cf. Verhagen 2007:65)

In Langacker's nomenclature, this is also called an *egocentric viewing arrangement*, 'in which the objective scene is expanded beyond the region of perceptual optimality to include the observer and his immediate surround-ings' (Langacker 1987:488–9). This egocentrism is practically the norm for *Fun Home*, in which a majority of the panels feature Bechdel's graphic representa-tion of herself. Interestingly enough, in this example, she chooses to portray her younger self only in silhouette, keeping the visual focus clearly on the corpse as object of the viewing arrangement. While she acknowledges her objectivised presence, the main focus of the panel seems to be on the grisly sight and its emotional effect on young Alison, while she 'studiously betrayed no emotion' (Bechdel 2006:44). According to Langacker, an egocentric viewing arrange-ment 'suggests a detached outlook' (Langacker 2002:328); this seeming detach-ment on Alison's part clashes with the emphasis on the corpse and the more subjective perspective of the caption.

As mentioned, Bechdel's perspective does not only concern her own biogra-phy; *Fun Home* is also an account of her father's life. Thus, she represents several scenes from it, including an example from Bruce Bechdel's days in the US Army (*Figure 4.7*).

At first glance, the viewing arrangement here seems to put a much greater distance between subject and object. Indeed, the image alone presents us with an *optimal arrangement*, a 'situation in which the roles of the observer and the observed are maximally distinct' (Langacker 1987:491) and the ground is not part of the viewing arrangement. Bechdel as the conceptualising subject is only objec-tivised if one regards the basic visual traits of her drawing, her linework and artis-tic style, as traces of its presence (see *Figure 4.8*). Still, using the stage metaphor, the reader's attention is directed practically exclusively on the action 'on stage', the maximally objectivised objects of conceptualisation.

Figure 4.7. Bruce Bechdel's past – from his daughter's perspective (Bechdel 2006: 62)

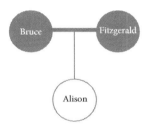

Figure 4.8. An optimal – or maximally 'objective' – viewing arrangement, in which the subject is construed with maximal subjectivity and the object with maximal objectivity (cf. Verhagen 2007: 61)

Yet, it is again the graphic novel's multimodality which complicates such a simple perspective. In the accompanying narrative comment, it is once more the little word *Dad* which implicitly includes the ground with Bechdel as conceptualising subject and thus represents a minimally perspectivised viewing arrangement.

This implicit presence of the subject of conceptualisation, at odds with the ostensibly maximally objective construal of the object of conceptualisation in the image's viewing arrangement, reveals an important aspect of *Fun Home*'s narrative point of view: many of the scenes described by Bechdel, including this one, are actually outside her subjective grasp; they have taken place without her witnessing them – in this case, even before she was born. Thus, the multimodal clash of viewing arrangements explicates the noted unreliability of Bechdel's account.

In consequence, analysing the intricate viewing arrangements in *Fun Home*'s multimodal account helps us in understanding the complexity of Bechdel's narrative perspective and the ambiguity and the self-awareness of her construction. However, this is not the end to the applicability of Cognitive Grammar's apparatus with regard to multimodal texts.

5.   The current discourse space model

Although the inclusion of the concept of viewing arrangement into our analysis already goes a long way in explicating the dynamic, multimodal processes of meaning construal in *Fun Home*, at the end of this chapter we want to present a brief outlook on another theoretical concept in Cognitive Grammar whose application to the study of complex monomodal and multimodal texts promises to be very fruitful: the *current discourse space* model. The CDS model was originally developed to capture the intricacies of the dynamic co-construction of meaning in interactive settings through ongoing chains of connected usage and construal events arising from the interaction of speaker(s) and hearer(s). The *current discourse space* can be defined as '[t]he mental space comprising those elements and relations construed as being shared by the speaker and hearer as a basis for communication at a given moment in the flow of discourse' (Langacker 2001: 144). Any conceptualisation includes an apprehension of the CDS and the ground, which serve as the basis for the construction of meaning. In addition, in the CDS model, conceptualisations are also built on the foundation of contextual knowledge. On the one hand, this includes stable knowledge such as knowledge of the language, general knowledge about the world, social knowledge, and cultural knowledge, which in a literary text also would include knowledge of text types, literary reception, intertextual and intermedial knowledge and so forth. On the other hand, this contextual knowledge also includes transient knowledge such as currently shared knowledge, the current discourse record, i.e. knowledge of previous conceptualisation events, and knowledge about the immediate circumstances of the conceptualisation event (Langacker 2008a: 463–7, 2001: 144–6).

For the analysis of complex literary texts, two things are important here: first of all, the CDS model can of course also be adapted to feature only one subject of conceptualisation. Second, it can be used to model the change in construals in complex texts featuring changing, unfolding perspectives. Each utterance updates the CDS and then serves as the basis for a new construal, which then updates the CDS again, and so forth. What is even more interesting from a multimodal perspective is that the individual contributions of the different modalities to the conceptualisation as a whole can be modelled as incremental updates of the CDS.

In Cognitive Grammar, it is explicitly acknowledged that on the expressive side, usage events not only include the dimension of speech or writing, but also other kinds of signals in other modalities. Langacker speaks of multiple expressive and conceptual *channels* that enter into the representation of a usage event. These channels include factors like information structure, intonation, and gesture (Langacker 2008a: 457–63, 2001: 146–7). From a multimodal perspective, it would be a rewarding enterprise for the future to model the contributions of channels in other modalities more explicitly, including the visual-imagistic dimension of meaning construal. Specifically, a multimodal extension of the CDS promises to be a very fruitful heuristic and hermeneutic tool for capturing the dynamic unfolding of complex meaning construal found in graphic novels like *Fun Home*.

This general point can be briefly illustrated by coming back to the example above of the conceptualisation of Bruce Bechdel's time in the army. In comics, a storyworld is unfolded multimodally panel by panel. With each panel, the graphic narrative and its complex configuration of meaning changes and extends, and this is represented by the changing discourse spaces in the CDS model. (For an outline, see *Figure 1.4* in *Chapter 1: Introduction* of this volume). In the CDS model, the boxes designate, from left to right, the continuous, unfolding flow of complex meaning construals from a previous usage event, to a current usage event, and a dashed anticipated usage event, which can be equated with instances of acts of conceptualisation within the graphic novel. In Section 4 above, we encountered the viewing arrangement of the visual scene, in which the object of conceptualisation is construed with maximal objectivity and the subject of conceptualisation is construed with maximal subjectivity. Now, in a next step of conception, we can take into account the text above the image in *Figure 4.7* which includes the word *Dad,* and leads to a minimal evocation of the ground and a minimally perspectivised viewing arrangement. This current usage event reflects an updated current discourse space featuring this updated viewing arrangement. In principle, the CDS model can be used to explicate and represent every act of conceptualisation and the multimodal interaction of different channels of meaning, which yield construals that are currently updated and modified in the proceeding discourse of the graphic novel.

To conclude, then, we propose that the CDS model can serve as a fruitful tool for the analysis of shifts and changes in construals in both monomodal and multimodal complex literary texts. A further elaboration and application of the model for literary analysis seems to be a promising avenue for future interdisciplinary work.

6. Conclusion

This chapter was a first attempt to demonstrate that the categories of Cognitive Grammar can be fruitfully applied to the analysis of a multimodal literary text, Alison Bechdel's *Fun Home*, yielding new perspectives, new insights and new ways of modelling and explicating the multi-faceted and multi-layered web of meanings and representations woven in the graphic novel.

In terms of literary interpretation, what we have shown is that in *Fun Home* multiple construal operations interact, intertwine and overlap in Bechdel's attempt to understand her father. However, these processes of dynamic construal do not yield satisfying explanations. Much of the novel's complexity and multiplicity of construals result from this difficulty in grasping and understanding her father and her relationship to him, without, however, ever coming to any form of conclusion or answer. This lack of closure and the connected sense of loss mark *Fun Home* as a work in the Gothic mode. Within this mode, which focuses on the horribly unspeakable, any attribution of meaning is at least doubtful, if not impossible, as *Fun Home* demonstrates. Thus, our cognitive operations of constructing meaning are always complicated, disturbed or denied.

We also hope to have demonstrated that Cognitive Grammar is ideally suited to capture the cognitive dimension of these processes. This holds especially for their multimodal nature. Cognitive Grammar seems ideally suited to capture the dynamic nature of multimodal meaning construal, something which we have illustrated using the concepts of profiling and viewing arrangements. However, many other construal operations and concepts from this framework could surely be applied profitably to *Fun Home* and graphic novels in general, and this seems like a very promising enterprise for future work. Specifically, we have suggested that these analyses should be integrated with Langacker's current discourse space model. Indeed, the capacity of Cognitive Grammar to model multiple, overlapping layers of meaning in a dynamic fashion and also to model complex discourse sequences involving shifting construals to us seems one of its most promising advantages. It is surely one of the most exciting avenues for further exploration of the potential of Cognitive Grammar in literary analysis.

CHAPTER 4

Attentional windowing in David Foster Wallace's 'The Soul Is Not a Smithy'

Chloe Harrison

1.   'The Soul Is Not a Smithy'

This chapter looks at the specific linguistic choices made by the producer of liter-ary language; how he has chosen to represent the narrative, and the effects elic-ited by these choices. As Langacker's (2008a) Cognitive Grammar model lacks a specific counterpart for linguistic gapping, this analysis applies the CG notion of *profiling* alongside Talmy's (2000) theory of the *windowing of attention* to David Foster Wallace's short story 'The Soul Is Not a Smithy', which appeared in his short story collection *Oblivion* (Wallace 2004: 67–113). 'The Soul Is Not a Smithy' is pri-marily concerned with the windowing of attention – often quite literally.

The story focuses on an unnamed narrator, who recounts a traumatic event from his childhood. The event in question was a 'hostage situation' at compre-hensive school, which involved a substitute teacher (Mr Johnson) experiencing a mental breakdown which caused him to write '*KILL THEM*' (Wallace 2004: 87) repeatedly on the board. However, the narrator's account describes in greater *specificity* the daydream he was having at the time, which was centred on a blind girl Ruth, her dog Cuffie, and her life with her family. The story concludes by describing through a newspaper account how Mr Johnson was shot by police troops, and finally finishes by outlining the fact that, ultimately, the narrator wanted to recount his relationship with his father, and his fear of entering the workplace as an adult.

> This is the story of how Frank Caldwell, Chris DeMatteis, Mandy Blemm, and I became, in the newspaper's words, the 4 unwitting hostages, and of how our strange and special alliance and the trauma [...] bore on our subsequent lives and careers as adults later on.   (Wallace 2004: 67)

Although supposedly about a hostage situation in a primary school, like many of the other stories in the collection and indeed in Wallace's other works in general, 'The Soul Is Not a Smithy' seems to focus on the peripheral events of the story – and so digresses almost immediately from the purported narrative arc as outlined in the above abstract (Phillips 2005). What could be termed the main events of the narrative – the shocking events in the classroom – become marginalised as the story of the narrator's childhood relationship with his father takes centre stage, alongside the projected imaginary story unfolding through the window panes of a blind girl called Ruth and her family. Despite the terrifying events occurring in the classroom, the narrator recalls the daydream he was having at the time in much greater depth of detail than the events of the hostage situation itself.

It is this process of displaced attention which leads critics to label Wallace's work as post-postmodernist fiction. Post-postmodernist texts are said to aim to disassemble constructed representations of the world in order to represent reality (McLaughlin 2012: 218, McHale 1989, 1992). This is achieved in 'The Soul Is Not a Smithy' through its treatment of attention – how it is directed, where it is directed, for how long, and to what effect.

This particular story is thus in line with the general critical view of Wallace's writing style, such as that in his works often 'major plot points are deferred, held out of frame, or ignored altogether' (Phillips 2005: 677), focusing instead on the 'peripheral tableaux' (Wallace 2004: 94), and that consequently the main narrative can constitute a 'jamboree of distraction' (Mason 2004: 17). This 'jamboree of distraction' is apparent in Wallace's other works (1989, 1997: 231–375, 2004), and is often manifested through an extremely high level of world-building information used to describe a particular scene. Frequently there is so much world-building information described and with such a high level of specificity that it can be difficult for a reader to decide which elements require the most attention (Langacker 2008a, Werth 1999; Gavins 2007).

Although the prominence of actual windows in this story arguably means that the framework chosen is particularly well suited, it was chosen for analysis here because of its challenging nature; because the continual shifting of attention constitutes its overarching structure – rather than for the coincidence of windows. The link between visual and cognitive processes is one which has been long established, and represents a close connection between the two modes which is enforced by Langacker's metaphor for construal processes (Langacker 2008a, Chafe 1994: 53). The nature of 'The Soul Is Not a Smithy' means that the relationship between the narrator's consciousness and the represented visual scene is one which is closely connected. At the production end of construal, the narrator has the power to encode a scene in a particular way. Elsewhere I expand upon this, and apply the framework to a text which windows and gaps information using more than one semiotic channel (Harrison 2013). In this wider research, I argue that particular components of Cognitive Grammar (namely, the reference point model, the current discourse space, force dynamics and the compositional path) can be scaled up from their original clausal application to be adapted as a discourse framework of literary narrative (Langacker 1987, 1991a, 1991b, 1999, 2008a, 2009; Evans & Green 2006; Croft & Cruse 2004; Taylor 2002). Often this involves scaffolding CG concepts onto existing cognitive, narrative or stylistic models (see Harrison & Stockwell 2013), or providing a cognitive turn to more formalist approaches (Herman 2009b; Doloughan 2011; Dancygier 2012).

2.   Windows, profiles, splices

Talmy (2000: 255–309) describes the windowing of attention (hereafter termed *attentional windowing*) as the process where one or more portions of a referent scene – where each portion has internal continuity but is discontinued from any other selected portion – will be placed in the foreground of attention while the remainder of the scene is backgrounded (Talmy 2000: 258).

Langacker (2008a) applies attentional frames differently to Talmy, using the term instead to refer to marking boundaries of conceptual units in phonological processing specifically, following Chafe's (1994: 482) notion of *intonation units*. Talmy, however, refers to this intonation delineation as just one facet of attentional windowing (2008). Perhaps the closest point of contact between Talmy's Cognitive Semantic application of windowing and CG relating to attention is Langacker's (2008a) reference to profiling, which comes under his rubric of construal. This latter organisational structure can be linked to Talmy's *conceptual alternativity*, which is perhaps a more neutral term than construal. It gives equal autonomy on the part of the language producer (P) as well as the language receiver (R), whereas construal arguably prioritises the conceptualiser.

Although following Langacker's framework as the organising structure for this discussion overall, I will be using Talmy's attentional windowing alongside the concept of CG profiling. This is largely because Talmy's framework of attentional windowing is a somewhat more comprehensive version of profiling, not least because of the inclusion of gapping which has no conceptual equivalent in Langacker's scheme.

Table 5.1. Attention in Langacker and Talmy

	Directed attention	*Omitted attention*
Talmy (2000)	Windowing	Gapping
Langacker (2008a)	Profiling	X

Langacker maintains that a negative expression also evokes profiling, which involves the drawing of attention to a profile of a conceptual base. The former relates to the substructure which holds our attention and the latter the particular 'body of conceptual content', which may be broad or immediate depending on its contextual use (2008a: 66); and an 'expression can profile a thing or a relationship' (Langacker 2008a: 67). In this way profiling is used as one facet of prominence alongside the alignment of trajector and landmark. However, although both Talmy's windowing and Langacker's profiling are conceptually very similar, Talmy's attentional system provides a more detailed framework for what occurs in 'The Soul Is Not a Smithy', particularly with regard to what is not said (gapping), and the ordering of events (splicing).

In a sentence or an event frame there can exist initial, medial or final gapping or windowing. This means that some of the sections of the scene are included (*windowed*) or excluded (*gapped*). Typically, the medial section of a sentence is often not as attentionally foregrounded as the other two sections, which can result in conceptual *splicing* (Talmy 2000: 270). In this instance, rather than a sentence delineating the entirety of a concept (A>B>C), the medial portion is instead omitted (A>C). There are different kinds of windowing depending on the inclusion, omission or change of various pieces of textual information. For instance, an event frame, which is 'the coherent referent situation with respect to which the windowing must take place' (Talmy 2000: 257), can have clearly demarcated boundaries between itself and another event frame depending on whether information included is said to lie inside or outside of the frame. Boundaries can also be drawn between and across frames, and to describe this phenomenon Talmy discusses the connectivity versus the disjuncture of a particular concept. These links or disjunctures may be 'spatial, temporal or causal' in nature (Talmy 2000: 161). Essentially, then, this windowing of attention outlines how our attention can be drawn from point A to point B (which represent particular locations), and the means by which we get there. Furthermore, it is sometimes possible for the event frame to both begin (named the departure) and end (the return) in the same location. This constitutes what Talmy terms a *closed path*.

A>B>C here label specific locations, or as Evans and Green (2006) point out, correlate directly with the notions of

Initial	SOURCE	
Medial	PATH	
Final	GOAL	(Evans & Green 2006: 199)

All of the definitions outlined above are applied by Talmy solely to the sentence-level of language. This means that much of his original discussion of the effects of attentional windowing also centres on the problems caused by those elements of syntax such as complements and adjuncts (2000: 262). In line with my general discussion, I shall be applying these Cognitive Semantic terms to linguistic units above sentential level.

Attentional-, or path-, windowing is therefore 'a way of focusing attention on a particular subpart of a path of motion', and falls within Talmy's broader attentional system (see Evans & Green 2006: 198). That it specifically 'allows language users to window (focus attention on) sub-parts of the trajectory associated with the motion of an object' is important to consider when discussing narrative or discourse trajectory (Evans & Green 2006: 198). In relation to this analysis, I will be exploring motion with regard to the development and progression of the narrative.

Discontinuous windowing occurs when we move from location A>C, with a windowed agent and result, and a gapped path. This is also referred to as conceptual splicing, which is where 'the medial portion of the path in some hearers' cognitive representations may reduce to so minimal a state in conscious conceptualization that the discontinuous initial and final phases may seem to run together contiguously, perhaps even seamlessly' (Talmy 2000: 270). This will be looked at in more detail in the analysis here. In terms of the attentional windowing at the discourse level of this particular short story it can be said that most of the main plot elements are gapped, whereas what we would perhaps term the less significant elements of the story are windowed. This has the unusual effect of foregrounding backgrounded elements and vice versa, creating a somewhat unsettling reading experience. For instance, although we receive brief snapshots of the 'hostage situation' in the classroom, we are not offered much information as to the 'resolution' (Labov 1972) of the event. Ironically, however, although much of the 'real incident' is gapped, in terms of the amount of information and full disclosure for many physical descriptions included, frequently the initial, medial and final portions of many viewing frames are fully windowed at the sentential, if not the discourse, level (Wallace 2004: 84). This analysis will focus on how the differences between sentential and discourse-level windowing function in this narrative, and to what effect.

3.   The cognitive turn vs. structuralism

Moving on from classical and structuralist narratological studies (Barthes 1974, 1977; Culler 2002; Propp 1968; Todorov 1977), Doloughan (2011: 8) describes how post-classical narrative research places 'the focus on process rather than simply on product'. This new approach to structuralist accounts is supported by Dancygier (2007), who describes how the construction of contemporary literary narratives necessitates a rethinking or extension of key narratological concerns. Arguably, the kind of analysis used in this chapter is a cognitive extension of Genette's (1980,

1988, 2002) structuralist work on story, narrative and narrating, and the ordering of events in narrative. Some of the fundamentals are undoubtedly similar: Genette's (1988: 13) work concerns mapping the locations and events of a narrative in chronological order ('story'), which he terms the 'totality of narrated events', and then observing how the particular narrative structures the representation of the events ('narrative'), which, as stated, I will also be observing in this analysis.

However, I argue that scaling up a sentential framework using a cognitive approach is particularly beneficial. Firstly because whereas Genette's original work focuses on plot points and their ordered representation, using Langacker and Talmy's structuring systems here allows for a more fluid scheme. Through observing the cognitive mechanisms of the text we can look at how these events and locations are structured on both a micro- and macro- level in a literary discourse, and the relationship between the event frames of these different levels. Such an analysis should conceptually account for how attention is directed to a particular event or location. Secondly, Genette maintains that 'the sole specificity of narrative lies in its mode and not its content' (1988: 16). Here, I hope that a more cognitive-linguistic approach to these structures will pertain more to the effects that the different attentional windowing has on the reading process itself, and the effect created by profiling different elements of the narrative content.

Although building upon these formalist foundations, the kind of event frame oscillation in 'The Soul Is Not a Smithy' parallels Genette's (1980: 52) notion of 'paralipsis', which he calls a 'kind of lateral ellipsis', or a 'type of gap', of a less strictly temporal kind, created not by the elision of a diachronic section but by the omission of one of the constituent elements of a situation in a period that the narrative does not generally cover'. Paralipsis differs from ellipsis in this way in that it concerns parallel time development; rather than omitting an event or location, the process 'sidesteps a given element' (Genette 1980: 52).

Despite being conceptually rather similar, I suggest that Talmy's conceptual splicing (movement from A>C within an event frame, with a gapped medial path) differs from paralipsis in that it does not necessarily concern a 'sidestep' in time; splicing can account for a jump to location C in event frame 2, from B in the first event frame, which is a displaced temporal domain. It is not a mere shift in focus within the same temporal frame, but rather a shift in frame, and fundamentally, location – albeit temporal or spatial in essence. Arguably splicing is a more encompassing term than paralipsis because it better accounts for the disruption of the anticipated narrative arc, and better explains discontinuity by extension. Whereas paralipsis 'sidesteps' from the location of the first event frame to the location of a parallel event frame, retaining the same temporal parameters, I argue that conceptual splicing instead accounts in a more general way for the movement between locations of different frames. This movement is not strictly lateral; the process can account for movement backwards, forwards, or parallel to the current time.

It could perhaps be argued that this temporal jumping about may be closest to the process of interpolated narrating style, which is described as a 'complex' mode of narrating denoting causality between different points of different event frames, different temporal locations (Genette 1980: 217). Although this is not what happens in this story, the 'entangling' which Genette describes as being central to this latter process does occur in splicing. While Talmy (2000) simply describes conceptual splicing in terms of A>C and gapping in the medial path, I think that applying the term more widely and in a more multidirectional manner is of benefit, particularly in literary applications such as this where the literary text in question challenges the structuring of story and discourse.

4.   Discourse event frames

The discourse event frame of the 'hostage situation' is the central event frame: all the other narrative strands are grounded in and developed around it, as the 'real incident' (2004: 84) of the story. It seems to be the most *tellable* (Labov 1972) part of the story, in that it involves a terrifying event. It is not represented as a fully windowd path, however. As a profiled participant in this event frame, the supply teacher Mr. Johnson is frequently established as a referent: 'MR. JOHNSON [...] WAS LATER REVEALED TO HAVE NO RECORD OF MENTAL DISTURBANCE' (p. 73). Conversely, the path and goal of the frame are gapped until a conceptual splice fills in the gapped information by way of a discontinuous path: 'IT WAS CLEARLY MR. JOHNSON'S FACIAL EXPRESSION [...] WHICH PROMPTED THEM TO OPEN FIRE' (pp. 99–100).

Including this central discourse event frame, the various nested narratives of this short story can be grouped into five main narrative strands or discourse event frames (i.e., events which appear throughout tha entirety of the story), elements of which are windowed at various points in the narrative.

- the hostage situation – 'the real incident' (Wallace 2004: 84)
- the immediate aftermath of the event
- the present day and 'subsequent lives and careers as adults later on' (Wallace 2004: 67)
- the narrator's childhood more generally and his relationship with his father
- the nested 'split narrative' (Wallace 2004: 79) which details the lives of a blind girl named Ruth, her mother and father, and her dog.

These interrelated strands form a chain of nested narratives (Talmy 2000: 84). The main narrative is the embedded yet predominant daydream: embedded because it is clearly tangential to the narrative trajectory as promised at the beginning, and predominant due to its prevalence in terms of its monopoly on the physical length of the story – or in Genettean terms, the frame has a long duration (1980, 1988, 2002). The nested narrative is an open path event frame because the resolutions of each of the character's narrative strands progress in terms of location, from the daydream's starting point. The backstory to this embedded narrative is very detailed: the daydream has different narrative levels itself, and often portions of the nested narrative which we assume are gapped entirely become windowed during flashbacks or through the inclusion of elements of the backstory of one of the nested characters.

It is important to consider that the chronology of the event frames is problematic in relation to the domain of time.

> Profile-base distinctions also exist in the domain of time. The flow of time constitutes (part of) the base of the meaning of verbs. Different lexical verbs may profile different 'slices' of time, backgrounding and foregrounding different features (thus producing different 'aspectual' profiles).   (Verhagen 2007: 50)

With this in mind, we can assign a different spatiotemporal base to each of the above frames. This means that, as well as splicing between locations, the story also splices between temporal bases. However, this often causes confusion in this story; although we can anchor these discourse event frames according to (largely) distinct spatiotemporal domains, at the sentential level there is some disjuncture as to whether the aspectual profile of the speaker is based in the discourse event frame currently being profiled, or whether the profile is anchored elsewhere. This will be explored in more detail in the next section.

Despite the insistence of the narrator to tell us about his daydream, we do see the occasional splice to 'the real incident' (Wallace 2004: 84): 'Meanwhile, in the inception of the real incident, Mr. Johnson had evidently just written KILL on the chalkboard' (2004: 84), as well as capitalised interjections which continue to revert to the main event. These insertions create temporal disjuncture with regard to the main narrative, but are linked thematically with elements from the other event frames. In this way, rather than creating structural or grammatical disjuncture or connection, this narrative uses semantic domains and themes as a cohesive device. As the narrative progresses, the separation between the discourse event frames and the cohesive ties become easier to discern. The demarcation of scope is often marked by a graphological boundary (i.e. by new paragraphs, or the insertion of capitalised passages); or in terms of the internal content of each frame, as we learn to recognise which characters belong to which event frame.

This means that as the story progresses we can increment world-building information from the particular discourse event frames into a central directory of world-identifying components (Emmott 1997); or, in CG terms, into the ground of the discourse event.

5.   Micro- and meso-windows

Intuitively, however, it feels as if the narrator of 'The Soul Is Not a Smithy' wants to disrupt the creation of a coherent *central directory* of world-building information, and does so by frequently and somewhat self-consciously making self-reflexive references to the problem of attention at the sentence-level of the text:

> In testing, many schoolchildren labeled as hyperactive or deficient in attention are observed to be not so much unable to pay attention as to have difficulty exercising control or choice over what it is they pay attention to.   (Wallace 2004: 97)

Like the narrator, we have little choice over which elements of the story we can pay attention to. In this way we are very much presented with the mind style of the narrator: we are in his head, and are presented with the events as he processed them at the time (Semino 2008; Fowler 1977; see also Stockwell 2009a). Mind style is a useful label for the stylistic representation of the narrative here, for as Semino (2008: 269) highlights, the term captures 'those aspects of world views that are primarily personal and cognitive in origin, and which are either peculiar to a particular individual, or common to people who have the same cognitive characteristics (for example, as a result of a similar mental illness or of a shared stage of cognitive development, as in the case of young children)'; and, furthermore, how this world view is represented becomes representative of 'an individual's characteristic cognitive habits, abilities and limitations'. The narrator's mind style makes the reading of the story a somewhat frustrating experience; the tangential nested narrative of the daydream takes centre stage, while the option of shifting focus onto the unfolding events inside the classroom becomes impossible. Ironically, the narrator talks about deprivation of the senses in the daydream in relation to the characters, in that Ruth's classmates comprise blind and deaf children. The readers of this story are placed in this same discourse situation: in reading, I felt a constant desire to change the viewing frame, to see the events in the classroom.

The narrative strand which constitutes the main attentional windowing in the story is the daydream imagined by the narrator. Much of the framing of this narrative is outlined literally, as the narrator frequently describes the physical frame of his daydream:

> The wire mesh, which divided the window into 84 small squares […], was designed in part to make the windows less diverting and to minimize the chances that a pupil could become distracted or lost in contemplation of the scene outside.
> (Wallace 2004: 70–71)

The story is graphologically interspersed with capitalised paragraphs or sentences, which act to summarise what is going on, often splicing to the present in which the narrator is reflecting on what happened. For instance,

> ESSENTIALLY, I HAD NO IDEA WHAT WAS GOING ON. (Wallace 2004: 80)

This occurs after a 3½ page-long paragraph outlining the narrator's segue into his daydream, or rather, the nested narrative (Talmy 2008: 84). This quotation also influences literary critical responses to the collection. For example, Mason (2004) states of Wallace's *Oblivion* that,

> Perhaps more than anything, the defining quality of these fictions is the degree to which they leave the reader unsure about very basic narrative issues: who is telling this story? Where are we? What exactly is happening?   (Mason 2004: 17–19)

I think it can be argued that the defining quality of 'The Soul Is Not a Smithy' is that the narrator himself, by his own admission, 'had no idea what was going on' (Wallace 2004: 80). Although piece by piece, event frame by event frame, we find out more about the full narrative, much of this information is provided by a retrospective account which has been produced by reconstruction through conversations in the aftermath and through the newspaper reports of the event. This makes us question both the reliability of the narrator, and what he considers to be the main point of narrative *tellability* (Labov 1972). What story are they trying to tell? Which story should we pay the most attention to?

6.   Conceptual splicing

Essentially what occurs in this story – creating the sense of oblivion – is conceptual splicing. Rather than complete each event frame discretely, the splicing between the event frames in this story is not straightforward. Rather than omitting B entirely, the location frequently jumps from A and continues elsewhere – splicing instead where we would expect to read B to a new location: often the A/B/C locations of another event frame. We see this in the following sentences:

> […] later on that day Christ DeMatteis' sled had tripped to one side and struck a tree, and his forehead had had blood all over it while we all watched him keep touching his forehead and cry in fear at the reality of his own blood. I do not

remember what anyone did to help him; we were all likely still in shock. Ruth Simmons' mother, whose name was Marjorie and had grown up admiring herself in different dresses in the mirror [...]   (Wallace 2004: 81)

Graphologically, it seems that the relationship between each narrative frame is one of disjuncture: the narrative consists of numerous capitalised insertions (67, 70, 73, 75, 80, 85, 89, 99, 103, 110–111), and often there are no new paragraph demarcations between two event frames, as discussed below. The lack of formal marking between narrative event frames means that there is frequent conceptual splicing (as outlined above, where the medial part of the frame is missing and the path is presented as A>C in a (near-)fluid conceptualisation – Talmy 2000: (270). The role and transparency of boundaries between and across frames has a direct bearing on the connectivity or disjuncture of the narrative. As also discussed, Talmy identifies these boundaries as being spatial, temporal or causal in nature (2000: 261). The temporal disjuncture is not entirely clearly delineated or signposted at the discourse level of the text: these conceptual splices appear through internal stylistic markers, such as a change in previously established characters as in the above passage. For instance, both Chris DeMatteis and Marjorie Simmons have been introduced prior to this point in the narrative, and therefore we already know they belong to different spatiotemporal frames. Furthermore, there are also some elements of connection across the discourse frames in relation to the particular 'world builders' of the scene: for instance, small details such as the 'burled walnut' table appear as a description the nattator remembers from his childhood home (p. 76) and also as a description of the home in the daydream narrative (p. 81). In this way, the graphology and the minutiae of the world-building details combine to create, as Talmy says, a 'near-fluid conceptualisation'; the boundaries between the ontological levels of the story become weakened, and the discrete event frames appear to blend together.

Thus we can say that in this story, as in most literary narratives, the more the event frames are developed, the more continuities and cohesion can be seen across and between frames. However, whereas perhaps elsewhere in other literary texts these cohesive devices are more immediately apparent, it takes a close reading to observe these connections here.

7.   Quantitative/ qualitative specificity

Despite the sense of vagueness in relation to the events of the story, Wallace's style has been described as 'inexhaustibly mimetic' (Phillips 2005: 677). It comprises sentences which can span pages at a time, and frequently barrages the reader with descriptions of the minutiae of the scene in such high-grained detail that it becomes problematic to discern which elements of the narrative can be deemed as particularly significant. In other words, elements which are usually back-grounded or schematised in this discourse become foregrounded to the extent that it becomes unclear which of the figures are salient in the narrative trajectory. The levels of *specificity* become upset and unbalanced.

This is particularly true in 'The Soul Is Not a Smithy', in which we encounter a narrator who by his own admission is more concerned with the quantitative details of a text or a scene. Although he cannot read, he points out how he could 'supply a certain amount of specific quantitative information, such as the exact number of words per page, the exact number of words on each line, and often the word and even the letter with the most and fewest occurrences of use' (Wallace 2004: 72).

As a result of this, although we receive a lot of very exacting information as to the placement of world builders in the scene ('the total number of words on the chalkboard after erasures was either 104 or 121, depending on whether one counted Roman numerals as words or not' – 2004: 88) we receive very little quali-tative response to the events themselves. The only emotional response appears when the narrator discusses his father, and his fear of entering the workplace as an adult (2004: 106–9). Indeed, the resolution of the story is told by a capital-ised summary which is spliced from the narrator's current text world (Wallace 2004: 99–100). This demonstrates gapping of the final portion of the discourse event frame, as we do not find out what happened to Mr. Johnson as the police troops arrived directly from the main narrative; rather we receive the resolution through a shift in perspective from the news report which summarised the facets of the scene:

> WHICH PROMPTED THEM TO OPEN FIRE. THIS WAS THE ONLY REAL TRUTH – THEY WERE AFRAID.   (Wallace 2004: 99–100)

The act of having conceptual gapping in one event frame but windowing in another displaces the evaluation or emotional response we would perhaps expect to see this event of which the narrator is an eye-, if admittedly oblivious-, wit-ness. Genette terms this kind of retrospective narrative completion as 'completing analepses' (1980: 52). However, it could be argued that the resolution regarding the content of what happened (i.e. that Mr. Johnson was shot) is also a kind of anticipatory viewing frame (Langacker 2001). Although Genette likes to work pre-dominantly on the form of a text and not the content, here it is the content which acts in a similar cohesive way to the completing constituent element. That is, from the very beginning of the story we know what the resolution, the resulting effect, of the story is; we are given a clear abstract in the opening sentence, detailing that the story is about a hostage situation, and that what becomes foregrounded and backgrounded depends greatly upon which event frame is currently profiled, and the locations involved and outlined. 'In The Soul Is Not a Smithy' the conceptual base (maximal scope) of the literary discourse in terms of the physical location is the classroom itself – or, specifically, '4th grade Civics class, second period, at R.B Hayes Primary School here in Columbus' (Wallace 2004:67). Through this specific world-building information, point A of the classroom event frame, or the SOURCE, is windowed in great detail, and establishes a proximal dual location of the story being recounted and the location of the current speaker. This is encoded in the deictically proximal 'here in Columbus'.

The daydream and classroom events are profiled from the same temporal base. For instance, the window narrative takes a negative turn when the atmosphere in the classroom does, and the narrator describes the events of the nested narrative as though they are unfolding out of his control. In this way it can be seen as some sort of psychological coping mechanism, which indeed is acknowledged as a possibility by the narrator himself: 'I believe that the atmosphere of the classroom may have subconsciously influenced the unhappy events of the period's window's mesh's narrative fantasy, [...] which required tremendous energy and concentration to sustain' (Wallace 2004:92). This influence between frames progresses throughout the story, and eventually the conceptual overlap of the classroom events over the daydream becomes 'so traumatic that this narrative line was immediately stopped and replaced with a neutral view of the pipe's exterior' (Wallace 2004:94). Here a conceptual override occurs, which we can label as a sort of act of self-preservation. Ironically, however, it is the daydream that becomes more traumatic than the events of 'the real incident' in the classroom – which, arguably is more traumatic, being that it is, ontologically speaking, one level more 'real'.

The blurring between boundaries of the event frames can also be seen at other times in the narrative discourse, where there seems to be a compression of the narrator's fictional reality of the daydream and that of his 'real' fictional reality:

> and even though Cuffie was just a dog and didn't have thought bubbles as you or
> I do...   (Wallace 2004:83)

In this example, the ontological barriers have become broken down for the narrator so much that he superimposes features of the daydream into his (fictional) reality; or, rather, he self-implicates to such an extent that he does the opposite. By this, I mean that he is so absorbed in his fabricated reality as to situate his *origo* (Green 1995) as belonging there. As in previous quotations, there is no clear signposting to suggest that even the narrator can differentiate between the events.

8. Conclusion

The technique of distraction in 'The Soul Is Not a Smithy' is signposted in the very first paragraph. Although comprising multiple narrative strands, the story does not focus on the 'subsequent lives' of the '4 unwitting hostages' – rather, reading this story becomes an exercise in trying to ascertain the main point of *tellability* (Labov 1972) from the perspective of the narrator, of trying to decide where our attention should be directed. Ultimately the narrative profiles a particular macro event frame, but not the one which is expected. Instead, the scope of the story comprises a wider narrative arc than necessarily anticipated. The representation of the discourse in this text demonstrates strong cohesion, or *symbolic correspondence* (Langacker 2008a), between form and effect. This digression and complicated plot structure in the form of Wallace's writing reflects the internal themes, and means that 'spectators are discouraged, and active readers rewarded' (Mason 2004: 17–19).

In this way Wallace's writing involves an interaction between writer and reader, and Stockwell's (2009a) READING AS INVESTMENT metaphor certainly has a direct bearing on how we construe this particular story. READING AS INVESTMENT indicates that when you invest in a story, you prime feelings of sympathy or empathy with a particular character. However, because much of 'The Soul Is Not a Smithy' comprises comments or asides which remind us of the fact that we are reading a book, arguably the investment becomes difficult to make, and we are therefore recast in the role of spectator:

> You move, gradually, from merely thinking about something to experiencing it as really there, unfolding, a story or world you are part of, although at the same time enough of you remains awake to be able to discern on some level that what you are experiencing does not make sense, that you are on the cusp of true meaning.
> (Wallace 2004: 107)

Through these self-reflexive references, the themes of this story are continually foregrounded: we are forced to think about attention, about the reading process, and the impact this has on our interpretation of the events. Similarly to the narrator in the above quotation, we feel that we remain 'on the cusp of true meaning'. What is this story actually about? The 'real incident, the daydream, the narrator's adult life, or his relationship with his father? Each event frame jostles for space and attention here, but the complex windowing and splicing between the frames means that we become close to 'the true meaning' of the strand of one story, before our attention is directed to another window.

The analysis has shown that firstly such a framework opens up possibilities for contemporary texts which are complexly structured in terms of relationships between multiple discourse event frames. Secondly it has been observed that conceptual splicing and notions from cognitive semantics work successfully alongside CG in application to a literary text, as well as pertaining to wider conceptual processes. Finally, such a cognitive approach to the attentional system extends traditional structuralist approaches to event frames, and allows us to discuss and explore the effects that the particular narrative form has on how we interpret it, as well as how we can characterise the narrator and respond to the linguistic cues as construed by the linguistic producer. In the wider application of CG as a literary discourse framework, I argue that such a cognitive discourse grammar can offer new insights into how we can think and talk about contemporary literature, and because CG models language 'in terms of well-attested mental capacities that are not unique to language' (Nesset 2009: 477), this has allowed an exploration of language which is essentially a disassembling of intuitive processes. Consequently, this analysis gestures towards a holistic cognitive discourse grammar for literary texts.

CHAPTER 5

Resonant metaphor in Kazuo Ishiguro's
Never Let Me Go

Sam Browse

1.   Text-driven cognition

In this chapter, I outline the ways in which Cognitive Grammar can enrich an analysis of the conceptual mappings involved in metaphor and simile. Using an example from Kazuo Ishiguro's (2005) *Never Let Me Go*, I highlight the importance of the linguistic dimension of metaphor in 'texturing' these mappings.

In a recent article, Gavins and Stockwell (2012) argue the following:

> Within what is fast becoming a paradigm-shift towards a cognitive-science approach to literature, we have observed an eagerness amongst literary scholars and linguists to contribute to other fields in the social and natural sciences, and to adapt their insights in the field of literary scholarship. However, the centrality of textuality has not always been maintained in the rush for progress.
>
> (Gavins & Stockwell 2012: 34)

Research into cognition and literature has tended to emphasise the analysis of conceptual structures rather than the detailed linguistic exploration of the text usually associated with traditional approaches in stylistics (e.g. Leech & Short 1980; Weber 1996). To remedy this imbalance, Gavins and Stockwell (2012: 34) suggest that 'approaches within cognitive poetics are best developed with a stylistic analysis embedded within them, rather than "bolted on" to a schematic, idealised, purely psychological or conceptual model'.

Similarly, the starting point of this chapter is the text. It is the text that prompts the creation of mental representations in the minds of readers (Werth 1999; Gavins 2007). Readerly cognition is therefore cognition cued by the text. An analysis of conceptual structures is predicated on a concern for the language prompting the creation of those conceptual structures. A linguistic description and analysis of the text, then, is not an optional 'bolt-on' (see Gavins & Stockwell 2012), but fundamental to any description or explanation of readerly cognition.

One of the largest areas of research in contemporary cognitive linguistics and psychology is metaphor. The cognitive turn in metaphor studies, beginning in the late 1970s with Ortony's (1979) edited collection, *Metaphor and Thought*, followed closely by Lakoff & Johnson's (1980) seminal work, *Metaphors We Live By*, signalled a fundamental shift in the ways scholars talked about figurative language. Metaphor, and by extension, simile, were re-described as not simply 'figures of speech', but figures of thought that structure human thinking about abstract concepts (Lakoff & Johnson 1980; Gibbs 1994). I argue that just as work on cognition and literature has, according to Gavins & Stockwell (2012), favoured schematic, psychological description and explanation over close stylistic analysis, the cognitive turn in metaphor studies has meant a neglect of the ways in which metaphor and simile are textually manifest. I emphasise the importance of this textual aspect of metaphor with reference to Kazuo Ishiguro's *Never Let Me Go*.

Published in 2005 and nominated for the Man Booker Prize, the novel has since been made into a feature length film. It is set at some time in the future and tells the story of three students who, the reader discovers, are clones, bred for the sole purpose of harvesting their organs for medical research. I concentrate on one particular passage of the text and use this passage to explore the important relationship between the linguistic dimension of metaphor and simile and their conceptual dimensions in reader cognition. My primary analytical framework in examining this relationship is Cognitive Grammar (see Langacker 1987, 1991a, 2008a). However, before proceeding to implement a CG analysis of metaphor and simile in a passage from *Never Let Me Go*, an outline of the prevailing theory of metaphor, Conceptual Metaphor Theory (CMT, see Lakoff & Johnson 1980; Lakoff 1993), is first required.

2.   Metaphor, cognition and text

Since the early eighties, CMT has dominated studies of metaphor. Its influence can be seen in work in cognitive linguistics, discourse analysis in both its more political (e.g. Charteris-Black 2004; Koller 2005; Koller & Davidson 2008) and non-political forms (e.g. Cameron 2007; Low et al. 2008; Steen et al. 2011), and in stylistics (e.g. Badran 2012; Crisp 1996; Wallhead 2003). Indeed, Lakoff's (1993) article outlining the theory is boldly titled (note the definite article) *The Contemporary Theory of Metaphor*.

According to CMT, the metaphors we use to understand and talk about the world are motivated by correlations in our embodied experience (Lakoff & Johnson 1980: 244–5). We recruit concrete aspects of our experience to conceptualise and communicate to others our more ineffable subjective experiences (e.g. TIME, LOVE, HATE, ANXIETY, our sense of SELF), or the abstract concepts that cannot be directly experienced by human beings (e.g. DEMOCRACY, FEMINISM, ECONOMY) (see Grady 1997, 2004; Lakoff & Johnson 1999). For example, we regularly talk about TIME in terms of SPACE (e.g. one can be 'coming closer to the holidays', or, conversely, one could say that 'the holidays are descending upon us'). CMT argues that this metaphorical language is evidence for a spatial conception of TIME. Aside from numerous examples in all languages of regular, conventional metaphorical expressions, one of the more compelling pieces of psychological evidence suggesting that metaphor is a ubiquitous aspect of human thinking is that there is no statistically significant time difference in the way that people process equivalent metaphorical and literal statements (Gibbs 2002b). In cognitive psychology, there is mounting evidence suggesting that metaphor is a routine aspect of human cognition (e.g. Boot & Pecher 2010, 2011; Casasanto & Dijkstra 2010; Schubert 2005; Zanolie et al. 2012).

CMT defines metaphor as 'a cross-domain mapping in the conceptual system' (Lakoff 1993:203) from one familiar, concrete domain of human experience, called the *source domain*, onto a less familiar or more abstract and intangible domain, called the *target domain*. Lakoff (1993:215) explains how source domains are mapped onto target domains by way of the 'invariance principle'. According to this principle, mapping structures is not only a question of mapping shared attributes, but of shared structural relations between different aspects of source and target domain topology. It is this mapping of shared topological relations that allows for extended metaphor and allegory because structure mapping is analogical (Gentner 1983; Gentner & Markman 1997). Gentner & Markman (1997:51) suggest that such mappings provide a means of creative reasoning. Cognisors reason by reference to the source domain thereby inferring, by analogy, new things about the target domain. Gibbs (2006) provides empirical evidence of such analogical reasoning in the case of the conventional metaphor, ROMANTIC RELATIONSHIPS ARE JOURNEYS.

With some exceptions (e.g. Evans 2006, 2010; Pragglejazz 2007; Steen 1999, 2004, 2008, 2009; Steen et al. 2011), the turn from metaphor as figure of speech to metaphor as figurative thought has corresponded with a shift in the emphasis of research on the subject. Whilst emphasis on the conceptual pole of metaphor has increased since the eighties, its linguistic aspects have become less and less the focus of contemporary study. A good example of this shift is the relationship between simile and metaphor. Obviously, simile and metaphor are linguistically distinct insofar as similes require a marker of comparison whereas metaphors do not. However, in the literature on structure mapping the cognitive processes underlying the two distinct linguistic tropes are seen as identical. Bowdle & Gentner (2005) write: 'metaphors can be understood as figurative comparison statements' (Bowdle & Gentner 2005: 197) and 'like literal comparisons and categorisation statements […] metaphors convey that certain aspects of the [source] also apply to the target' (Bowdle & Gentner 2005: 193). Here, metaphor is seen as implicit simile; an instruction to compare. This neglect of the linguistic pole of metaphor and simile is not shared by all metaphor scholars. The debate in this area has centred on the cognitive effects of 'deliberate' metaphor (Steen 2008, 2011a, 2011c; Gibbs 2011a, 2011b). Deliberate metaphors 'involve mandatory attention to the fact that they are metaphorical' (Steen 2011a: 84). They are metaphors that, by virtue of the language in which they are manifest, explicitly signal their own metaphoricity. Under this rubric, simile constitutes a form of deliberate metaphor. The principle processing difference between deliberate and non-deliberate metaphors is that, according to Steen (2008, 2011a, 2011b), deliberate metaphors are processed as mapped structures (c.f. Bowdle & Gentner 2005; Gentner 1983; Gentner & Markman 1997), whereas non-deliberate metaphors are processed as class inclusion statements (c.f. Glucksberg 2003; Glucksberg & Haught 2006; Glucksberg & Keysar 1990).

Despite legitimate criticism of his use of the word 'deliberate' to describe the phenomenon identified by deliberate metaphor (Gibbs 2011a, 2011b), the refocus on the interrelation between language and conception in Steen's (1999, 2004, 2008, 2009) work is welcome. The debate around deliberate metaphor has largely focused on the types of cognitive processing at play in the production and reception of metaphor. Missing from this debate has been a thorough discussion of the quality of these processes, or of what Stockwell (2009a) might call the 'texture' of metaphor in readerly cognition. 'Texture' is 'the experienced quality of textuality (Stockwell 2009a: 191), it 'involves a rich sense of the world of literary experience' (Stockwell 2009a: 192) and concerns such issues as ethics, literary resonance and emotion. My own understanding of Stockwell's (2009a) use of the word is that texture relates to the felt experience of literary discourse; the felt experience and synthesis of verbal art and/as representation. Texture, then, is centrally concerned with the cognitive aesthetics of reading.

In the following section, following Stockwell (2009a), I use ideas from Cognitive Grammar (see Langacker 1987, 1991a, 2008a) to explore the texture of a simile in a passage from Ishiguro's novel, *Never Let Me Go*. The focus may seem narrow, but this is because I hope to demonstrate that even in a single simile there is more to talk about than whether the metaphor is 'on' or 'off' in reader cognition. The range of ideas I draw upon from CG is eclectic and includes Langacker's (2008a) notion of *grounding*, the *force dynamics* of simile and epistemic modals, and the *construal* and *dominion* of Ishiguro's pronominal choices. I also use ideas from Stockwell's (2009b) work on *resonance* and from the standard literature in CMT (e.g. Lakoff 1993, Lakoff & Johnson 1980). This eclecticism – which is certainly not alien to stylistics (Carter & Stockwell 2008; Jeffries 2000) – reflects the holistic enterprise of attempting to describe the nuances of literary experience. One cannot hope to talk about the texture of a simile without recourse to multiple frameworks from different areas within cognitive linguistics.

3.   'It seemed like we were holding on to each other because that was the only way to stop us being swept away into the night': analysing the texture and resonance of simile

The following is an extract from Ishiguro's novel, *Never Let Me Go*. It comes after Tommy, who is one of the clones, discovers he has not long to live due to the harvest of his organs. Kathy, the first person narrator and Tommy's 'carer' (she is also a clone who – significantly – is romantically involved with Tommy), takes Tommy out on a trip into the countryside where he flies into an unexplained rage:

> I caught a glimpse of his face in the moonlight, caked in mud and distorted with fury, then I reached for his flailing arms and held on tight. He tried to shake me off, but I kept on holding on, until he stopped shouting and I felt the fight go out of him. Then I realised he too had his arms around me. And so we stood together like that, at the top of that field, for what seemed like ages, not saying anything, just holding on to each other while the wind kept blowing and blowing at us, tugging our clothes, and for a moment, it seemed like we were holding on to each other because that was the only way to stop us being swept away into the night.
> (Ishiguro 2005: 269)

The section of the extract that is interesting to look at in terms of metaphor is the final part of the last sentence: 'for a moment, it seemed like we were holding on to each other because that was the only way to stop us being swept away into the night'. This final section is a figurative comparison in the sense that the target domain ('it'), which as I argue below acts rather like a dummy subject, is being compared with a non-literal situation ('we were holding on to each other because that was the only way to stop us being swept away into the night'). The gist of the conceptual mapping is that Tommy and Kathy behave as if the wind is capable of blowing them away (whilst the book is a somewhat original take on science fiction, this is beyond the ontological possibilities of the story-world). However, there seems more to the mapping than this alone. Indeed, in discussions with friends and colleagues, this passage of the book is described as particularly emotionally affective (Whiteley [2010] provides a detailed account of reader's emotional responses to the novel as a whole). The simile itself has a particular resonance and richness and acts as an emotional climax in the text. In what follows, I examine the reasons for this conceptual richness using ideas and concepts from CG as my starting point. One of the things making the simile so strange and non-prototypical is Ishiguro's use of the verb 'seemed', which gives it an uncertain, modal quality. It is for this reason that I begin my analysis with a discussion of CG, modality and grounding.

3.1   Cognitive Grammar and modality: fictionalising the ground

Nuyts (2006: 1) points out that modality is often defined broadly 'such as to refer to any kind of speaker modification of state of affairs, even including dimensions such as tense and aspect'. Modality can also encompass grammatical mood as well as a modal system of auxiliary verbs (Palmer 1986). Perkins (1983) broadens the scope of modality to deal with 'modal expressions' (e.g. 'it is obligatory that…') and Simpson (1993) goes further still in describing the ways narrative perspective, on the discourse level, can be 'modally shaded' using a combination of mood, modal auxiliaries and modal expressions. In fact, Ishiguro uses a modal expression, or what I will call a modal simile, in my example from *Never Let Me Go*; 'it seemed like', where *seemed* plays an epistemically distancing role (I will return to this simile in the next section).

On the other hand, Nuyts (2006) and Perkins (1983) have also suggested that linguists have used the term 'modality' to refer quite narrowly to the set of modal auxiliaries available in a language. Langacker (2008a) approaches modality in this narrower sense of the term, concerning himself with the way the five modal auxiliaries (*may, can, will, shall*, and *must*) ground finite clauses. *Ground* is used in the following sense:

> The term ground is used in CG to indicate the speech event, its participants (speaker and hearer), their interaction, and the immediate circumstances (notably, the time and place of speaking). A grounding element specifies the status vis-à-vis the ground of the thing profiled by a nominal or the process profiled by a finite clause […] grounding establishes a basic connection between the interlocuters and the content evoked by a nominal or finite clause.   (Langacker 2008a: 259)

'Grounding' language is about situating it with respect to some language event; about differentiating *types* ('ball') from *instances* ('this ball') (Langacker 2008a: 264–72). Modality, according to Langacker (2008a), defines the ontological status of the clause in relation to this ground. The fact that something 'shall' happen presupposes that it is not currently. Modals, then, in Langacker's (2008a) scheme, unlock a potential state of affairs from an actual one. It is notable, however, that modals need not always be grounded with respect to the 'immediate circumstances' in which an utterance or sentence is produced, but rather a fictional world. In fact, in leafing through the first few pages of my copy of *Never Let Me Go*, I can find

'I *can* understand how you might get resentful' (p.3), 'I still see things that *will* remind me of Hailsham' (p.6), and 'someone said we *shouldn't* be so obvious about watching' (p.7) (all my emphases). It is not anyone in the immediate context of the interaction between the author (Ishiguro) and his reader (me) that produces these examples. Rather, the words are placed by Ishiguro into the mouth of a fictive narrator, Kathy. It is for this reason that whilst Langacker's (2008a) notion of *modal grounding* is, as I shall argue, certainly useful in this discussion of modality and conceptual metaphor in *Never Let Me Go*, I prefer to say that modals can also be grounded in the fictive text-worlds, or mental representations, we create when we read. Indeed, this is the position taken in text-world theory (see Gavins 2005, 2007; Werth 1999). According to this perspective, modality engenders a world switch from one text-world representation to a modal world in which the modalised state of affairs is represented in reader cognition. Modals are thus responsible for the creation of new, ontologically discrete text-worlds in reader cognition.

In what follows, I retain Langacker's (2008a) notion of *grounding*, and agree that modals act as grounding elements. However, following Gavins (2005, 2007) and Werth (1999) I also expand Langacker's (2008a) concept of 'the ground' to mean either our face-to-face 'discourse world' or the text-world. Indeed, in my analysis of the passage from Ishiguro's novel, this latter type of text-world grounding is more important to the cognitive dynamics of the text. It is the cognitive *force-dynamics* of modality, and specifically the modalised simile used by Ishiguro, that I turn to in the next section.

3.2　Cognitive Grammar and the force dynamics of modal similes: 'seemed like' versus 'was like'

In CG, transitivity relations in the clause are seen as transfers of energy along an action chain. Langacker (2008a) notes that

> the English modals developed historically from lexical verbs with meanings like 'want to V', 'know how to V' and 'have the power to V'. The relationships profiled by such verbs have something in common. Namely, they ascribe to their trajector some kind of propensity, or 'potency' which – when unleashed – can lead to its execution of an action (V). While the situations described by these verbs are therefore stable [...], they do involve some kind of force tending towards V's occurrence.　(Langacker 2008a: 304)

Langacker (2008a) argues that whilst these lexical verbs have, through a process of language change, become grammaticized into the five modal auxiliaries, they have retained the 'force dynamic' and 'future-oriented' nature of their earlier, lexicalized counterparts (Langacker 2008: 304). As in all other action chain relationships in CG, this force dynamic consists of a trajector and a landmark. In modern grammaticized modals, Langacker (2008a: 304) represents this force dynamic as in *Figure 10.1*.

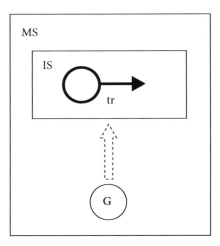

Figure 10.1. The force dynamics of a modal auxiliary

The two encompassing squares, marked MS and IS, represent the maximum and immediate scope of the modal auxiliaries. In CG, *scope* refers to a level of semantic organisation and hierarchy. Take, for example, the word 'wrist'. The immediate scope of the word 'wrist' is the joint at the end of one's arm. 'Zooming out' from this close up view of the wrist, we can see how the wrist is also a part of the arm which is itself a part of the body. 'Body' therefore constitutes the maximum scope of 'wrist'; we need to know about bodies to know about wrists (Langacker [2008a] uses the example of 'elbow'). Note, however, that although we need to know about the body in order for the concept, WRIST, to make any sense, this other knowledge is backgrounded. In the case of wrists, the focus of attention is on the joint at the end of the arm. As such, the immediate scope of an utterance can metaphorically be called 'onstage' because it is the thing that is occupying the conceptual 'spotlight', as it were. In the diagram, the modalised action chain is represented as being in the immediate scope – the 'spotlight', or focus – of the clause. It is profiled.

Recall that Langacker (2008a: 304) argues that modals 'involve some kind of force tending towards [the verb's] occurrence'. In the case of modal verbs, the action chain is grounded in some already existing state of affairs. In force dynamic terms, then, sentences employing modal verbs imply a transfer of energy from one existing state of affairs to another modalised state of affairs. The sentence, 'you *might sprain* your wrist', is 'grounded' – in the CG sense of the word – in a current situation, but implies a movement from this situation into a hypothetical text-world in which the wrist is sprained (see Gavins 2005, 2007). This 'evolutionary momentum' of our 'conceived reality' to a 'potential reality' (Langacker 2008a: 306), or from the ground (represented by a circle marked with a 'G') to the profiled process of spraining one's wrist, is represented in *Figure 10.1* by a dashed arrow. This dotted arrow represents the billiard ball-like transfer of energy from the ground to the profiled verb process. This also neatly represents the notion that epistemic modals are grounding elements. They ground the verb processes of *potential* (modal) text-worlds in relation to reality as it is perceived by the discourse participants.

Returning to the example from *Never Let Me Go*:

> It seemed like we were holding on to each other because that was the only way to stop us being swept away into the night.

Whilst the text does not use a grammatical modal auxiliary, it is what Simpson (1993) would call modally 'shaded'. The epistemic modal expression, 'it seemed like', throws into uncertainty the profiled processes that follow it. In his discussion of modality, Langacker (2008a) differentiates between *root* modality, and *epistemic* modality. The former relates to what others have called *deontic* modality (see Gavins 2005, 2007; Palmer 1986; Perkins 1983; Rescher 1968; Simpson 1993), or modals that have some kind of illocutionary force, whereas the latter – which is more relevant to this discussion – are modals which relate to knowledge. Langacker (2008a: 306) writes:

> Rather than tending to induce the profiled process, the modal force reflects the speaker's efforts in assessing its likelihood. The potency is directed at incorporating the envisaged process in the speaker's conception of reality (Rc). It represents the speaker's force-dynamic experience in mentally extrapolating the current reality conception – imagining its future evolution – in such a way that Rc comes to include it. Thus it bears on the grounded process not in terms of bringing it about, but rather in terms of accepting it as real.   (Langacker 2008a: 306).

The modal phrase, 'it seemed like', is particularly interesting to examine from this perspective of modality and 'potency'. 'It seemed like we were holding on to each other because that was the only way to stop us being swept away into the night' is not a straightforward simile, but rather a modal simile. It is epistemically modalised by the verb 'seemed'. If it were a straightforward simile (that is, if the clause began, 'it *was* like we were holding on to each other'), one could ground the clause in a text-world in which *it was not the case* that Kathy and Tommy 'were holding on to each other because that was the only way to stop them from being swept into the night'. The simile would simply create a scenario which could then be figuratively mapped onto the behaviour of Tommy and Kathy; they behave as if they will be blown away. However, rather than 'it *was* like', the past tense of 'be' is replaced with the epistemically weaker 'seemed': 'it seemed like'. 'Seemed' is a far more ambivalent grounding element than 'was' because it suggests an indeterminacy in what is actually the case. The claim here is that 'seemed like' is epistemically far less certain than 'was like' and is therefore a far worse grounding element. This is due to the fact that, in force dynamic terms, it is less potent. It only weakly departs from its grounding in the text-world in which Kathy and Tommy hold onto one another.

Whereas ordinary simile excludes any integration of a hypothetical situation into the Rc, this form of epistemically modalised simile has the effect of failing to fully exclude the state of affairs ('being swept away into the night') from the potential reality of the text-world. As such, the text-world ground (i.e. what is literally happening) and the profiled process (what 'seemed' to be happening) are never fully separated. In fact, this literal reality and the profiled process correspond precisely to the target domain and source domain of the conceptual metaphor prompted by the simile. However, the epistemic indeterminacy and vagueness of this literal target domain undermines any firm conceptual mapping readers might make between the two. The simile gives readers a potential source domain, but it is not entirely beyond the realms of possibility that this source domain could not also be the target domain of the metaphor.

3.3   The source domain as literary figure: simile and resonance

So far, I have focused on one key aspect of the simile, which was the modalised marker of similarity, 'it seemed like'. I now broaden the discussion from consideration of this modal mark of comparison to the ways in which the source and target domains of the conceptual metaphor engendered by it are construed. I use the term *construal*, here, in the technical sense: 'as part of its conventional semantic value, every symbolic structure construes its content in a certain fashion' (Langacker 2008a: 55). In CG, construal relates to how we 'view' a scene; with how lexico-grammar encodes a certain perspective which may be more or less focused, or specified. Here is the relevant stretch of text from *Never Let Me Go* again:

> [F]or a moment, it seemed like we were holding on to each other because that was the only way to stop us being swept away into the night.

The first thing to note is the asymmetrical way in which the source and target domains of the simile are construed. I previously suggested that epistemic modals led to the creation of new text-worlds in which the profiled, modalised verb processes took place. I have diagrammed the creation of this new epistemic modal world in *Figure 10.2*. The arrow in the diagram represents the same force dynamic impulse as in the diagram from Langacker (2008a).

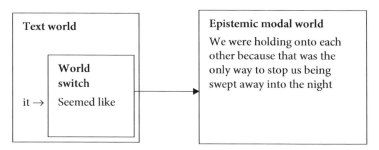

Figure 10.2. The epistemic modal in 'it seemed like…'

In addition to being the ground of the epistemic modal world, the world of 'it', on the left, is also the literal target domain world. Conversely, the epistemic modal world, on the right, is also the source domain world of the figurative comparison. Whereas this modal world is comparatively well defined, its grounded text-world contains only the pronoun, 'it'. 'It', in this context, is acting rather like a dummy subject (as in, 'it is raining', or more precisely, 'it seems to be raining'), and refers more to the general situation; to everything that has come before 'it'. In this respect, the semantic content of 'it' is incredibly dense. 'It' has an incredibly low level of what Langacker (2008a: 55) calls *specificity*, but it also has a very large *dominion*. 'It' could refer to the stretch of previous text:

> And so we stood together like that, at the top of that field, for what seemed like ages, not saying anything, just holding on to each other while the wind kept blowing and blowing at us, tugging our clothes.

Interestingly, in this stretch of text each short adverbial phrase, separated by commas, creates a small attentional frame (see Nuttall, this volume). The force dynamics of these smaller attentional frames emulate the 'tugs' of the wind, until readers hit the final clause of the sentence, 'and, for a moment, it seemed like we were holding on to each other because that was the only way to stop us being swept away into the night', which unleashes a relatively long action chain that iconically mimics the characters actually being swept away. There is a sense, then, in which this iconicity adds further resonances to the metaphor. The grammatical force-dynamics of the sentence echo the schematic force-dynamic relationships involved in the source domain of the metaphor.

Of course, 'it' could even refer to the whole novel. Indeed, in many respects, Tommy and Kathy have been 'swept away' by events in ways they could not begin to control. The novel charts the tragic twists and turns of Tommy and Kathy's lives and their intimate, romantic relationship from their time at Hailsham, a school for clones, to Tommy's slow death by organ 'donation'. The fact that Tommy and Kathy are 'holding onto each other' is easily interpreted as a symbolic expression of this intimate relationship (there is ample linguistic evidence to suggest that the conceptual metaphor PROXIMITY IS INTIMACY is a conventional one – 'close' relationships are intimate relationships). However, both LIFE and RELATIONSHIPS are also conventionally thought of as JOURNEYS. In this JOURNEY metaphor, forward motion is conceived positively. In this instance, then, there is a tension between the static 'holding a relationship together' metaphor and the image-schematic, forward moving properties of being swept away. Being 'swept away' is in this instance antithetical to 'holding together', so there is a sense in which two conventional conceptual metaphors – PROXIMITY IS INTIMACY and RELATIONSHIPS ARE JOURNEYS – are played against one another to tragic effect. Indeed, there is a possibility that this poignant clash of metaphors might even call to mind tragically doomed relationships in which readers have themselves been involved. The pronoun's lack of specificity makes it at once incredibly vague, but also, and because of this, incredibly rich.

In contrast, the epistemic modal world of how things 'seemed' is comparatively well specified and has a relatively fine grained resolution. This contrast between the construed specificity of source and target world further bolsters the feeling of epistemic uncertainty we experience in relation to the source domain of the conceptual metaphor. It is the source domain – the epistemic modal world – which is vivid and foregrounded by this asymmetrical construal, whilst the rich semantic content of the target domain, 'it', is rendered in the most minimal detail possible.

One way of looking at this contrast in the construed vividness of the two text worlds is to see them both as potential attractors of reader attention; as textual figures, or attractors. In Stockwell's (2009a, 2009b) attention-resonance model, textual attractors move up and down a scale of readerly attention, either fading into the background or becoming occluded by other, better attractors. He writes:

> The felt effects of these elements in textual attention are focus, engagement, fading and extinction, which in turn represent a scale of figure and background. Figure/ground in cognitive linguistics and cognitive poetics tends to be regarded as a polar category, whereas from the perspective of scaled readerly attention, it is a cline of prominence, ranging through degrees of foregrounding into vague, undifferentiated but rich background. All together [the scale of readerly attention] represents a cline of resonance, with striking literary intensity at one end, and decay or echo tailing off into a rich sense of textual resonance towards the other.
> (Stockwell 2009a: 22)

Viewed from this perspective, the literal world of 'it' fades into the background, occluded by the newer, more vividly depicted modal world in which Kathy and Tommy hold onto one another for fear of being swept away by the wind. The resonances created by this textual occlusion consist in the fact that this new modal world is also the source domain of a conceptual mapping which loops back onto the 'it' that has been occluded. There is a conceptual oscillation between both domains. At the same time as there is a force-dynamic impulse towards and foregrounding of the epistemic modal world against the rich background of the text-world in which it is grounded, there is also a conceptual mapping being made between the two. However, the combination of epistemic uncertainty thrown over the target world by the modal, 'seemed', and the wide dominion and vague specification of 'it', mean that this mapping cannot be adequately completed. We are left with the vivid and foregrounded possibility that Tommy and Kathy are being 'swept away into the night', but the vague richness of the background onto which this is mapped mean that this is a metaphor with too many (uncertain) targets, all of which 'echo' or 'resonate', as Stockwell (2009a) might put it, on the periphery of readerly attention. I have represented this foregrounding of the source domain against a resonant background in *Figure 10.3*.

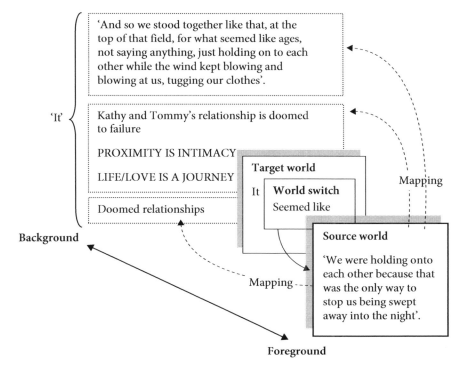

Figure 10.3. The resonant background in Ishiguro

The result of this literary resonance, to me at least, is a feeling of great poignancy. The situation depicted in the extract takes on an emotional significance and, whilst not a centrally important plot point, it does constitute an emotionally climactic moment in the novel.

4.   Conclusion: more than mapping

The aim of this analysis has been to focus discussion not only on the metaphoric conceptual mapping involved in the simile, but on the ways in which the language of the text gives this mapping a particular texture and resonance. Whilst I have made no contrary claim to CMT about the basic cognitive operation underpinning simile, its linguistic difference to metaphor does have an effect on the quality of this cognitive operation. The fact that similes require some linguistic marker of similarity engenders the force-dynamic texturing I described in Section 3.2. Similarly, the resonant quality of the metaphor is a function of the foregrounding and backgrounding of source and target worlds I described in Section 3.3. Simile requires that a linguistically explicit figurative comparison be made between two different areas of human experience. As I argued in Section 3.3, in the case of this simile, the target domain, 'it', was represented with a very low degree of specificity and a very wide dominion. Despite this low level of specificity, however fleetingly, it still functioned as a profiled trajector – a conceived reality with 'evolutionary momentum' (Langacker 2008a: 306) – before action-chaining with a potential reality that came to occlude and background it (in many ways, this 'onstage' modality actually resembles the way in which Langacker (2008a: 304) describes the image-schematic qualities of the early lexical modal verbs). Such an evolutionary, force dynamic momentum would take on a different quality, or be missing altogether, from an alternative metaphorical description of events.

Insights from Cognitive Grammar and Stockwell's (2009a) attention-resonance model provide literary critics and linguists with the terminology to begin to discuss this textured, resonant aspect of metaphor and simile. The cognitive turn in metaphor studies revolutionised the field, but there is more to metaphor than mapping. A return to a discussion of textuality and literary texture can provide the basis for an enriched understanding of the quality of the mappings involved in metaphor and simile. With the help of Cognitive Grammar, stylistics and its sub-discipline, cognitive poetics, are well placed to do this.

CHAPTER 6

Constructing a text world
for *The Handmaid's Tale*

Louise Nuttall

1. World construal

The negotiation of the situations presented by a text through the mental representation of a *world* is a significant aspect of reading, and the focus of a range of worlds-based approaches to literature. The richly detailed and 'text-driven' conceptualisations described by Text World Theory (Werth 1999; Gavins 2007) represent a development of the more generalised phenomena accounted for by Possible Worlds (Ryan 1991) and Mental Space Theory (Fauconnier 1997). As Semino describes in her overview of such accounts: 'the particular way in which a reader imagines the text world projected by a particular text depends on the local and cumulative effects of specific linguistic choices and patterns. This is an area where existing approaches to text worlds are somewhat limited' (Semino 2009:66).

Development at the stylistic level of text world frameworks, even that of Gavins (2007) who goes furthest in this direction, represents a movement towards a psychologically-realistic understanding of this readerly experience, and a specificity in its application to individual literary texts (Semino 2009:65). Langacker's model of Cognitive Grammar (1987, 2008a, 2009), I shall argue, provides an appropriate framework for detailed linguistic analysis of text world construction. In this model the grammatical forms chosen by a speaker or writer are 'meaningful' (2008a:3) in that they constitute a particular *construal*, as a reflection of 'our manifest ability to conceive and portray the same situation in alternate ways' (2008a:43). In an interactive discourse context such as literature, the individual construal chosen in representing a scene (and as I shall argue, a world) can be seen as 'instructions issued by the speaker for the addressee' (Langacker 2008a:460). This interactivity raises to significance the two-layered nature of construal itself as combining the related, but distinct senses of *linguistically portraying* and *conceiving*, applicable in this context to the negotiated construction of a text world between a text and a reader.

In Margaret Atwood's novel *The Handmaid's Tale* (1996 [1985]) the reader is invited to imagine the dystopian world of 'Gilead' through the focalised perspective of its first-person narrator; Offred. This narrator's distinctive voice, and the problematic re-construction of this dystopian reality which Atwood invites in her readers through this means, has received a great deal of attention within literary criticism. Indeed the narrative is often viewed as a critique of the very acts of writing, reading and interpretation involved in our engagement with literature, and representations of reality more broadly (Wisker 2010: 127; Müller 2000; Dvorak 1998). Though recognising the centrality of *language* to this thematic concern (Bouson 1993: 147–9), such accounts rarely feature detailed consideration of the linguistic choices through which our readerly experience of the text comes about. Noteable exceptions are, Staels (1995) and Nischik (1991) who address a similar concern through narratological analysis of the discourse structures which characterise Atwood's novels. In this chapter I shall take a cognitive grammatical approach to the world of *The Handmaid's Tale*. By investigating its particular construal and the reading experience which results, I shall explore Langacker's model as a stylistic tool for increasingly fine-grained analysis of representations of fictional realities, and their re-construction as text worlds by readers.

2.   Structuring reality

In Langacker's account, the processes underlying a grammatical construal are sourced from fundamental cognitive mechanisms. The way in which we make sense of our environment is an 'imposition of structure', effected by a process of *comparison* through mental scanning (Langacker 1987: 105). This scanning mechanism enables the impression of coherence in a scene and also, it is suggested, the recognition of contrast (1987: 121). Such contrast is reflected across all levels of linguistic organisation as a fundamental tenet of Cognitive Grammar. It is manifested through different types of *prominence*: in the *profiling* of part of an expression's conceptual content against a base, and at a lower grammatical level, through the attribution of varying degrees of salience to these profiled participants in a *trajector/landmark alignment* (Langacker 2008a: 66–73). Other kinds of prominence are identified alongside such grammatical forms, reliant upon the 'inherent cognitive salience' of experiential properties such as newness or discreteness within the content profiled by an expression (Langacker 1993: 324). Recognised through comparison operating ubiquitously at multiple levels (1987: 121), these types of asymmetry combine to form a key dimension of the particular structure or construal imposed upon a scene.

This 'imposition of structure' can be applied to the situations represented in a literary text. As in our everyday environment, the 'conceptual space' projected by a text can be said to contain 'more objects vying for attention than can be assimilated in totality, so that one interpretative configuration or another must be imposed to make sense of what is being experienced' (Stockwell 2009a: 20). The 'interpretative configuration' invited at any moment by the linguistic choices of a text in terms of the dimension of construal under discussion here, involves the foregrounding of certain elements against a 'rich background' of others within a 'cline of prominence' (2009a: 22).

In her application of Langacker's model to literary translation, Tabakowska emphasises the choice amongst various 'compositional possibilities' involved in reaching such an overall figure/ground alignment in our conceptualisation of a scene (1993: 53). This aspect of construal is described by Langacker as its *dynamicity*, or the development of a conceptualisation through processing time (2008a: 79). In Langacker's model, such 'compositional possibilities' can be understood in terms of the sequence of mental scanning, and thus comparison invited by the linguistic choices of a speaker/writer. Though describing the same situation, two sentences such as those below are said to be semantically distinct:

a.   An unopened letter lay on the table in the kitchen.
b.   In the kitchen on the table lay an unopened letter.

Here, the different conceptual experience prompted by each stems from a difference in 'the direction of mental scanning', or the path along which a reader is invited to access its final conception by 'zooming out' and 'zooming in' respectively (Langacker 2008a: 81–2). In other words, the two conceptualisations unfold differently through processing time.

This manner of unfolding may differ not only in direction but also in the type of scanning adopted. Langacker differentiates two types of scanning available to us in our conceptualisation of a complex scene. *Sequential scanning* views component states individually and in succession, while *summary scanning* processes components cumulatively, building up to a single gestalt in which all components are conceived as co-existent (2008a: 107–11). Through this latter mechanism, 'a detailed conception is progressively built up, becoming active and available as a simultaneously accessible whole for a certain span of processing time' (2008a: 83). Significantly, these forms of mental access are not mutually exclusive: 'Although two sentences [such as those above] may provide contrasting sequential access to a complex situation, through either path of access we are able to build up a holistic conception of the scene, which may then be available as a single gestalt' (Langacker 2009: 342). The summation of a process' component states is described as one which occurs naturally as a subsequent part of our 'normal observation of events', enabled by traces left in working memory (Langacker 2008a: 111). Though we may attend to only one component state at any moment while watching a film (compared with sequential scanning by Langacker [1987: 145]), our normal ability to recall and combine previously-accessed states into a sense (or in CG terms, a *simulation*) of its overall content at any point during or after viewing, arguably reflects the operation of summation within everyday cognition. Indeed, lacking experimental evidence, it is such everyday introspection upon which Langacker's distinction relies (2008b: 572).

Similarly, both mechanisms can be seen as significant in our dynamic conceptualisation of the situations presented in literary narrative. During reading, individually profiled 'things', 'relationships' and 'processes' are successively attended to through sequential scanning and typically, I would suggest, summed to form a holistic conception or 'rich background' (Stockwell 2009a) which develops as we read. It is perhaps a complex interaction or 'recurring tension' between the two modes (Wójcik-Leese 2000: 175) that is responsible for the 'interpretative configuration' imposed upon this conceptual space and its 'moment-by-moment adjustment' during reading (Stockwell 2009a: 20). As a dimension of construal, the relationship between these two operations might be understood as a continuum. While sequential scanning is arguably fundamental to all experience, the extent to which this dynamicity is manifested is 'a matter of degree' (2008b: 574). The type of mental scanning privileged within a construal can be described therefore as the degree to which the inherent sequentiality of this dynamic experience in 'conceived time' is reflected as part of its conceptualisation during 'processing time' (2008a: 110). Or rather, the extent to which the *temporal profile* of the experience portrayed is made prominent within the corresponding mental simulation invited in the reader.

Applying this model to literary reading, the mental access to situations and events invited as part of a construal and its degree of dynamicity can be seen as a significant aspect of the readerly experience of text world construction. Langacker, it should be noted, does not make any direct claims with regards to the online processing of linguistic structures (2008b: 575). Though viewing our 'mental ability to summarize over temporally distributed occurrences and view them holistically' as 'common and very basic' (2009: 356), Langacker acknowledges the increasingly complex and varied configurations of prominent components observed beyond the clause-level and the difficulties and pitfalls faced by CG in attempting to account for their holistic conception (2009: 327–74). While Langacker's proposals in his discussion of complex sentences, and coordinate structures in particular (2009: 341–74), provide a useful starting point, the need for 'a coherent overall account of grammar, online processing and the directing of attention at multiple levels of organisation' (2008a: 418) represents a key issue in working towards a Cognitive Discourse Grammar.

Langacker also warns against taking the metaphor underlying terms such as 'composition' too literally: 'While component structures serve to evoke a composite structure, and provide a way of apprehending it, the latter should not be thought of- in any strict or literal sense- as being constructed out of them. Stepping stones are not the same as building blocks' (Langacker 2008a: 166). The 'composite structure' evoked by a sequence of words, Langacker points out, often draws our attention away from these components as a meaningful entity in its own right (2009: 11). In the case of conventionalised uses of language 'whose composite forms and meanings are well-known and well-rehearsed', it may not be necessary to separately mentally access these component structures at all (2009: 26). In many instances, often the focus within Construction Grammars, 'viewing a construction in terms of the 'order' in which it is 'built' is rather meaningless' (Evans & Green 2006: 589). However, such constructions can be positioned at the lowest extreme of a scale of 'analyzability' (Langacker 2009: 26). In the majority of language use, Langacker suggests, 'the path followed in reaching the composite structure is a secondary but significant aspect of an expression's form and meaning' (2008a: 167). Furthermore, in novel (or 'fully analyzable') expressions, such as the poetic or unconventional language often employed by literary writers, the conceptualisation invited may necessarily be built up from the meaning of these component elements, and, in particularly anomalous cases, may even provide the primary source of meaning (2008a: 61–2). The relationship between such 'top-down' and 'bottom-up' aspects of processing, or the roles of constructions and composition within language use (Croft & Cruse 2004: Chapter 9) is another area of investigation, significant to the application of Cognitive Grammar to literature.

Though the scaling up of clause-level notions such as compositional paths and composite structures to the discourse level perhaps requires a separate justification not possible within this limited space, as a framework they suggest an insightful approach to textual analysis. The way in which sequentially accessed 'stepping stones' (Languacher 2008a) or individual 'attractors' of attention (Stockwell 2009a: 20) contribute to a holistic conception through summation, and the tension between these mechanisms, may hold the key to a more detailed understanding of the variable experience of text worlds.

3.   Building text worlds

Text World Theory (Werth 1999; Gavins 2007) models the formation of such a holistic conception at a discourse level. Like the 'mental models' described in cognitive psychology (Johnson-Laird 1983) text worlds are essentially 'analogue' and 'holistic' in nature, like maps, and reflect the ability to mentally store perceptual wholes which underpins our memory for faces and complex actions (Gavins 2007: 4). In this framework, world construction is triggered by two types of textual information, distinguished once again through a fundamental recognition of asymmetry or contrast. *World-building* elements furnish a conceptual background with objects and characters situated in time and space, while *function-advancing propositions* move the discourse forward through events and processes within the foreground. Indeed Werth's original model drew upon Cognitive Grammar for the basis of such distinctions (1999: 198–202).

An important aspect of text world construction in Text World Theory is its systematic and 'text-driven' inclusion of readerly background knowledge drawn from the *discourse world* (Werth 1999: 17). Clearly this contextual input is a vital aspect of any cognitive poetic analysis of text worlds. However, as with my earlier discussion of constructions, this top-down schematic dimension must be paired with a bottom-up compositional dimension and the effects of specific linguistic choices should not be overlooked at its expense (see Stockwell 2010). Gavins (2007) makes significant advances in this area, commenting upon the relative prominence and order of world-building elements (2007: 44), and discussing the texture of an evolving text world in terms of processes set out in Systemic Functional Linguistics (Gavins 2007: 43, 56). By (re)incorporating concepts from Langacker's framework, an increasingly cognitively-realistic account of dynamic world construction, or the incremental contribution of components to the holistic conceptual structure referred to by the 'text world', could in my view advance this model further.

The text worlds constructed in this manner during reading interact in large numbers across the breadth of a text. An application of Cognitive Grammar to discourse must therefore also engage with this higher level of conceptual structure. In Text World Theory, successively accessed worlds are represented in a single, diagrammatic configuration or world-structure: 'we connect our multiple representations to form a coherent and meaningful whole in a variety of ways' (Gavins 2007: 9). Comparably, at the discourse level of Langacker's model, the integration of successive conceptions or *mental spaces* (Fauconnier 1994, 1997), each of which 'develops from and builds on the previous one', constructs 'an integrated conceptual structure of progressively greater complexity' (Langacker 2008a: 486). Though much work remains to be done at this level, the possibility of approaching such *structure building*, responsible for our overall mental representation of discourse, in terms of sequential and summary scanning is one which seems justifiable.

In applying Cognitive Grammar in this way, the readerly construction of text worlds can be modelled in terms of an imposition of structure through dynamic processes of conceptualisation, ranging from 'conceptual integration at the lowest levels of grammatical composition to apprehension of the global import of entire texts' (Langacker 2008a: 486). The successful formation of such a coherent, holistic conception has functional significance in a literary context – allowing not only comprehension but often a powerful, immersive experience of the text (Gavins 2007: 10). This mental representation, I would add, is not merely accessible for the duration of reading, but is often imagined by readers for a long time after, as a resonant literary effect (Stockwell 2009b).

4. Reading *The Handmaid's Tale*

Atwood's novel manipulates these cognitive mechanisms in the construal of the fictional world it presents. The extract chosen below is taken from the opening of the novel. It follows a brief flashback which describes the narrator's imprisonment in 'what had once been the gymnasium' alongside numerous other women, guarded by authorities known as 'Aunts' and 'Angels' (Atwood 1996: 13–14). Later in the novel the exact nature of Offred's position becomes clear. A 'Handmaid', it conspires, is a woman whose enforced duty is to be impregnated and bear children for the powerful male leaders of this society. Having established an early sense of this dystopian reality, the following passage introduces the reader to this narrator's immediate surroundings through the first person, present tense narration which characterises the majority of the novel:

> A chair, a table, a lamp. Above, on the white ceiling, a relief ornament in the shape of a wreath, and in the centre of it a blank space, plastered over, like the place in a face where the eye has been taken out. There must have been a chandelier, once. They've removed anything you could tie a rope to.
>
> A window, two white curtains. Under the window, a window seat with a little cushion. When the window is partly open – it only opens partly- the air can come in and make the curtains move. I can sit in the chair, or on the window seat, hands folded, and watch this. Sunlight comes in through the window too, and falls on the floor, which is made of wood, in narrow strips, highly polished. I can smell the polish. There's a rug on the floor, oval, of braided rags. This is the kind of touch they like: folk art, archaic, made by women, in their spare time, from things

that have no further use. A return to traditional values. Waste not want not. I am not being wasted. Why do I want?

On the wall above the chair, a picture, framed but with no glass: a print of flowers, blue irises, watercolour. Flowers are still allowed. Does each of us have the same print, the same chair, the same white curtains, I wonder? Government issue?

Think of it as being in the army, said Aunt Lydia.

A bed. Single, mattress medium-hard, covered with a flocked white spread. Nothing takes place in the bed but sleep; or no sleep. I try not to think too much. Like other things now, thought must be rationed. There's a lot that doesn't bear thinking about. Thinking can hurt your chances, and I intend to last. I know why there is no glass, in front of the watercolour picture of blue irises, and why the window only opens partly and why the glass in it is shatterproof. It isn't running away they're afraid of. We wouldn't get far. It's those other escapes, the ones you can open in yourself, given a cutting edge.   (Atwood 1996: 17–18)

The opening sentence prompts the construction of a text world by evoking pro-totypes of 'a chair, a table, a lamp' from readers' discourse world knowledge. In Cognitive Grammar such contextual knowledge, including that of the dystopian genre evoked by the previous scene, forms part of the *current discourse space* which we bring to bear on the text (Langacker 2008a: 466). Grammatically, readers are invited to apprehend the three nominal profiles of this sentence in separate *atten-tional frames* (2008a: 482) through the use of the comma which forms a pervasive stylistic feature throughout the novel. The relationship amongst these profiles can be seen as a form of asyndetic, or unmarked, coordination. In Langacker's model, coordination prototypically reflects the mental juxtaposition of elements that are 'coequal' in terms of prominence within a sentence (2009: 341–74). As such, these sequentially scanned profiles have no indicated asymmetry other than that sug-gested by their order. These world-building elements are also lacking an indica-tion of deictic orientation in time and space, and further still reality; described in CG as *grounding* (Langacker 2008a: 259). For that reason they may be said to 'float' ambiguously within our conceptualisation. However, the conventional co-occurrence of these objects within a home setting, in a particular spatial arrange-ment paralleled linguistically in their order from lowest to highest, is likely to be activated within readers' contextual knowledge. In my reading, a single gestalt in which 'a lamp' is profiled in relation to the layered background of the other two (as in *on the table above the chair*) is conceptualised as a result. However, the com-plication to summation and the readerly 'imposition of structure' that this gram-matical construal presents, drawing attention to the sequence of activation which underlies it, is a common feature of Atwood's novel.

The inherent directionality in this scanning continues, moving upwardly into the next sentence:

> Above, on the white ceiling, a relief ornament in the shape of a wreath, and in the centre of it a blank space, plastered over, like the place in a face where the eye has been taken out.

The sentence overall profiles a trajector 'a relief ornament in the shape of a wreath' against the landmarks of its global and local setting ('Above, on the white ceiling'), before this trajector then becomes a landmark for 'a black space' within a higher level profile. Once again the breaking up of the sentence into its embedded profiles through commas emphasises the individual salience and sequential recognition of these components in discrete attentional frames. Their decreasing size and increasing granularity is typical of what Langacker terms a 'nested locative'; a type of *reference point relationship* (2008a: 83–5). By representing a natural path of mental access which 'zooms in' on a final target, this construal – continuing from the opening sentence – can be seen to reflect the process of identification through visual perception. For such linguistic iconicity, and the sense of a focalised perspective it invites here even before its explicit indication through 'I', Tabakowska (1993: 55) applies the term 'experiential iconicity' (Enkvist 1981), specifying its iconic order as one motivated by a subjective experience of the world.

In Langacker's model, however, nested locatives are still typically subject to summation, forming a single gestalt with a 'conflated profile' responsible for their 'zooming in' effect (2008a: 195–6). Here, the holistic conception of a single profile with 'a blank space' as overall trajector is problematised by the prominent components of this sentence which compete with it for readerly attention. In the simile which follows, the phonetic parallelism (Short 1996: 63) of 'space', 'place' and 'face' creates a sense of cohesion and equal prominence amongst these profiles which in my reading form a group, emerging into the foreground of the conceptualisation being composed. Similar parallelism, recognised through comparison, might be identified for the half-rhyme of 'relief and wreath' and the grammatical symmetry of 'in the shape of' and 'in the centre of'. In the latter, mental juxtaposition of these profiles invited by the coordinative 'and' contributes to this effect, importing a further sense of equal prominence. Subsequently the definiteness of 'the place' may be recognised as another type of prominence. Finally, the finite relative clause 'where the eye has been taken out' possesses a newness and discreteness with its temporalised process in sentence-final position, which makes its profile unlikely to be subsumed into the background of the main clause. Instead readers are invited to focus upon the strange conception it evokes as the final target of scanning.

Though readers may focus their attention variably according to their personal dispositions (Stockwell 2009a: 53) the succession of prominent components presented by this construal, I would argue, problematises readers' structuring of this scene through comparison. By complicating the recognition of asymmetry, or graded prominence, fundamental to their summation within a single conflated profile, this construal disrupts the sense of depth which could otherwise be experienced through such a 'zooming in' effect. Furthermore, without such structuring, the parallel claims of these separate profiles for attention result, in my reading, in a somewhat cognitively difficult conception of the scene it describes. Emphasis is placed instead upon the independently apprehended meanings of its individual components, and the path, or iconically represented perceptual experience, through which they are construed.

Looking at the extract more broadly, this particular experience of text world construction can also be identified in the characteristic development of world-building elements through description:

1. '...falls on *the floor*, which is made of wood, in narrow strips, highly polished.'
2. 'There is *a rug* on the floor, oval, of braided rags.'
3. 'This is *the kind of touch they like*: folk art, archaic, made by women, in their spare time, from things that have no further use.'
4. '...*a picture*, framed but with no glass: a print of flowers, blue irises, watercolour.'
5. '*A bed*. Single, mattress medium-hard, covered with a flocked white spread.'

In each instance, an object or 'thing' (emphasised here in italics) is modified (or complemented in [3]) through successively apprehended profiles in a list-like form. The use of commas (or full stops/colons) invites us to apprehend these details in separate attentional frames, and in the case of non-restrictive relative clauses (e.g. 'which is made of wood') suggests their coequal prominence, comparable once again with coordinate structures (Langacker 2008a: 429). This compositional path may be seen once again to reflect the focalised sequencing of observations, as another instance of 'experiential iconicity'. As Tabakowska (1993) emphasises in her use of this term, comparable with Leech and Short's (2007: 190) notion of 'psychological sequencing', the order reflected is one 'motivated by the speaker's perspective rather than the state of affairs in the world' (Tabakowska 1993: 54). As before, this particular construal disrupts the reader's holistic conception of this state of affairs through summary scanning. The conceptualisation of a single gestalt for each elaborated 'thing' is complicated by the different kinds of profiles seen, which unlike 'a chair, a table, a lamp' include atemporal relations and processes in past participle form. Rather than automatically imposing a conventional conception of these things, drawn from our discourse world knowledge (perhaps of an archaic worldview or the fairly typical objects described), this construal invites us to follow the subjective thought processes of this narrator through sequential scanning.

These thought processes often draw the reader's attention away from this main text world to a past situation, albeit fleetingly, through the use of the past participle: 'made of wood', 'highly polished', 'framed', 'covered', or to the beliefs and desires such as those which make up 'the kind of touch they like'. The summation of the world-building detail presented in this way can therefore also be discussed in terms of the conceptual integration of successively accessed *mental spaces* or worlds. Though 'mental spaces' and 'worlds' are not quite the same thing (Fauconnier & Sweetser 1996: 12), a detailed comparison is not possible here, and the two notions shall be used interchangeably for the purpose of this analysis. Applying a text world model to *The Handmaid's Tale*, it might be observed that it is in the *modal worlds* and deictic *world switches* triggered by this narrator's beliefs and memories, and richly built up during the narrative (Gavins 2007), that much enrichment of our overall conceptualisation of the text takes place. Such embedded worlds often contain information central to the characterisation of this narrator and to our comprehension of the wider dystopian society in which her immediate circumstances (such as the room described here) are situated. However, this text construes the content of such worlds in a way which complicates their holistic conception as part of an 'integrated conceptual structure' (Langacker 2008a: 486).

Disruption to summation at this level of conceptual structure is seen in the configurations of worlds which readers are invited to access. In the second paragraph 'When the window is partly open' represents any number of real or hypothetical instances of this situation. This epistemic modal world is thus ambiguously grounded in relation to the main text world (or *conceived reality* in Langacker's model – 2008a: 298) in which 'it only opens partly', and alongside which it is mentally juxtaposed through grammatical symmetry. The repetition of 'can' and the breaking up of the description into individual profiles in 'I can sit in the chair, or on the window seat, hands folded, and watch this', invites the reader to conceptualise this modal world through sequentially accessed possibilities in discrete attentional frames. The consistent use of the present tense, and the equal prominence attributed to these parallel conceptions through coordination, complicates their organisation as part of a holistic conceptual structure. Also contributing to this effect, the instance of (free) direct speech: 'Think of it as being in the army, said Aunt Lydia' exemplifies the rapid world switches throughout the text as a whole into memories which are often ambiguously grounded in relation to the main text world in terms of temporal and epistemic distance. This construal, I would argue, disrupts the ease with which readers determine the configurations or relationships between multiple worlds (Gavins 2007: 76) and raises the structuring which takes place at this level, forming an 'integrated conceptual structure' (Langacker 2008a) or 'coherent and meaningful whole' (Gavins 2007), to conscious awareness. With such a holistic conception disrupted at this level, emphasis is placed instead upon the sequential processing of these conceptions as they emerge in the mind of the narrator, foregrounding the movement between memories, direct speech, beliefs and possibilities of which Offred's narrative is composed.

As the novel continues, the problematic integration of mental spaces in this way becomes increasingly marked. In the extract, the use of negation and the mental juxtaposition of mutually exclusive mental spaces invited by 'or' in 'Nothing takes place in the bed but sleep; or no sleep', reflects the construal of a reality which defies comprehension through summation into a unified conception. This distinctive construal is seen in the presentation of alternate versions of events in richly developed modal worlds side by side throughout the novel. One prominent example is the three possible fates of Offred's husband Luke, chased by the authorities known as 'the Eyes' in the narrator's recollected past (Atwood 1996: 114–15). The three possible scenarios, described individually, in which Luke is dead, imprisoned or free, remain unresolved and the reader, like the narrator herself, is invited to attend to all three:

> The things I believe can't all be true, though one of them must be. But I believe in all of them, all three versions of Luke, at one and the same time. This contradictory way of believing seems to me, right now, the only way I can believe anything.
>
> (Atwood 1996: 116)

Similarly, in the concluding section of the novel, Offred lists her available options facing a similarly ambiguous fate, in successive paragraphs beginning 'I could' (1996: 303). Through this representation, these successively accessed modal worlds reflect the failure of an 'imposition of structure' (Langacker 2008a: 105) – the perceived asymmetry or graded prominence which would here enable this narrator to make sense of her situation: 'Each one of them seems the same size as the others. Not one seems preferable' (Atwood 1996: 304). In both cases, the parallel demands upon readerly attention posed by this construal, or the 'contradictory way of believing' it asks us to share with this narrator as another form of 'experiential iconicity', disrupts our formation of a unified holistic conception of the text. It is through sequential access to these alternative worlds within this conceptual structure – and perhaps some *alternating* (Langacker 2009: 342) or *toggling* back and forth (Gavins 2007: 152) – on which we must rely in our comprehension of the reality of Offred's situation. Gavins discusses the experience of 'double-vision' possible through this type of processing in relation to metaphor (2007: 146–64). Indeed the comparison and 'blending' of mental spaces invited by the similes featuring frequently in the narrative could also contribute significantly to this analysis. However, the cognitive processing of simile and metaphor (Browse – this volume) and Atwood's particular manipulation of these devices provokes analysis far beyond the bounds of this chapter.

Finally, in the closing paragraph, the van which has come to take Offred away is described as one which could either represent capture and imminent death at the hands of the 'Eyes', or salvation by an underground resistance movement.

> Whether this is my end or a new beginning I have no way of knowing (...)
> And so I step up, into the darkness within; or else the light.   (Atwood 1996:307)

Here, the reader is invited to undergo a final impossible summation through the mental juxtaposition of two sets of polar opposites: life and death, light and darkness. This closing construal emphasises the reader's unresolved interpretation of the world of the text as a whole, which, by ending in this way, questions the identity of key characters such as 'Nick' (Offred's secret lover) as friend or spy. Through this construal, the conceptualisation of Offred's situation constructed in the minds of readers and the interpretation taken away with them from reading is likely to be unclear and inconclusive.

5.   Simulating experience

This brief analysis reflects the disruption to the structuring of reality underlying the construal of the text world at work throughout the novel as a whole and identifiable across multiple levels of its organisation. In complicating the readerly formation of a coherent holistic conception of this world, Atwood achieves a number of specific, interrelated effects as part of a resonant reading experience.

Firstly, by disrupting the process of summation, the text predominantly invites its readers to conceptualise the fictional world through sequential scanning. This scanning mechanism is associated with our 'real-time viewing' of an event as it progresses through time (Langacker 2008a:111) and therefore a low level of *attenuation* (or high level of vividness) in our mental simulation relative to embodied experience (2008a:536–7). Indeed by foregrounding the inherent sequentiality of the experience of this world as part of its conceptualisation during readerly processing time, this construal was described earlier as a form of 'experiential iconicity' (Tabakowska 1993), producing what Leech and Short (2007:189) term 'an enactment of the fictional reality through the form of the text'. However, drawing attention to the acts of perception and conception in this way, supported by the use of first person pronouns and proximal deixis ('this', 'now'), the fictional world itself becomes subjectified; 'inhering in the subject rather than the object of conception' (Langacker 2008a: 537). Significantly, such a *subjective construal* of this world is associated with a highly attenuated simulation in Langacker's account (2008a: 537). Observed alongside the vivid simulation through sequential scanning, this somewhat contradictory analysis captures a significant aspect of this text's construal. Readers, I propose, are likely to experience a closeness to this narrator's conception but a sense of distance from the 'object of conception' – the text world itself.

The experience shared through this simulation is described by the narrator later in the novel:

> What I need is perspective. The illusion of depth, created by a frame, the arrangement of shapes on a flat surface. Perspective is necessary. Otherwise there are only two dimensions. Otherwise you live with your face squashed against a wall, everything a huge foreground, of details, close-ups, hairs, the weave of a bedsheet, the molecules of the face. Your own skin like a map, a diagram of futility, crisscrossed with tiny roads which lead nowhere. Otherwise you live in the moment. Which is not where I want to be.   (Atwood 1996: 153)

Key to such perspective, or the ability to comprehend any detail or state as part of a wider conception or background with the illusion of depth, I have argued, is the recognition of contrast through comparison, which allows us to view it holistically as a simultaneously accessible whole. By disrupting such an imposition of structure during reading, this construal invites us to share the cognitive experience of a *huge foreground* of details vying for attention and the resulting restriction to *the moment* through sequential scanning.

This iconic experience of the fictional world gains a further level of significance through its association with the individual worldview of this character-narrator, suggested by the text. The disrupted conception of the text world and restricted understanding invited as a result can be identified with the restrictions imposed upon this character's thought processes as a result of her social position as a 'Handmaid'. In the extract discussed, she states 'Like other things now, thought must be rationed. There's a lot that doesn't bear thinking about'. As the novel progresses, this psychological restraint is accompanied by an explicit physical restriction upon her visual perception, through the hood or white 'wings' which she, like all Handmaids, is required to wear around her face. 'Given our wings; our blinkers, it's hard to look up, hard to get the full view, of the sky, anything. But we can do it, a little at a time, a quick move of the head, up and down, to the side and back. We have learned to see the world in gasps' (Atwood 1996: 40). This rationed thought and gasped perception is an experience which readers are invited to simulate through their sequential scanning of the fictional world.

Such a lack of perspective in this character's experience of her immediate environment is reflected in her experience of her context more broadly. The physical restriction of her movements in Gilead ('To the right, if you could walk along, would take you down towards the river' – 1996:40) is paralleled by the limitations of her knowledge of this society beyond her station and of the past events through which these circumstances have come about. This lack of contextual knowledge, denied by the authorities of Gilead, and emphasised in her repeated mantra, 'Context is all' (1996:154, 202), can be identified with the reader's problematic organisation and summation of the multiple world-switches and modal worlds, through the complex configurations described earlier. Furthermore, the intense, repetitive focus upon her immediate surroundings which accompanies this lack of perspective, and the slow pace of text world construction encouraged by the heavy use of comma intonation, produces a reading experience which echoes the 'time to spare' which oppresses this character, much like the 'paintings about boredom' she describes (Atwood 1996:79). Indeed, the fact that the whole narrative is a transcription of an audio recording hidden on cassette tapes, revealed in an epilogue to the novel, makes this paced quality of the narrative, and the vivid simulation of a distinctive *voice*, yet more prominent on subsequent readings. Through such conceived correspondences, the experience of living 'in the moment' captured through this iconic construal can be felt as part of a close and affective engagement with this character.

With the attribution of this distinctive construal to the individual cognitive habits of this character, the specific linguistic patterns observed can be said to reflect more than just 'experiential iconicity' but an individual *mind style*, defined by Fowler (1977:73) as 'the impression of a worldview' created through 'cumulatively, consistent structural options, agreeing in cutting the presented world to one pattern or another'. While a cognitive grammatical account of mind style is a project for future work, the experience of a particular worldview as part of the construction of a text world and its affective impact, provides a significant example of the 'local and cumulative effects' (Semino 2009:66) achieved through the specific linguistic choices made within a text. Indeed Semino outlines the 'potential complexity and variety of the relationships between fictional minds and text worlds' as a further challenge for cognitive poetic accounts (2009:68). Cognitive Grammar, and more specifically the psychological processes which underpin *construal*, offers a means of discussing the relationship between a text world and the minds involved in its negotiated conceptualisation, both inside and outside the text, in systematic and nuanced terms.

Furthermore, the resulting texture of the text world through this simulation, as a 'huge foreground' of components or the 'arrangement of shapes on a flat surface' self-consciously referred to by the text, can be aligned with critical readings of the novel which describe its experience as that of a 'puzzle' (Bouson 1993:137), or 'collage' (Dvorak 1998). The novel's foregrounding of its composition is often observed by literary critics in the fragmented narrative structure which forces readers to 'assemble and construct [Offred's] story' (Bouson 1993:136–7) and the interweaving of cultural and intertextual references which create 'a network of resonances that it is up to the reader to piece together' (Dvorak 1998:456). By attempting to integrate such content, filling in the gaps left by Offred's restricted portrayal using their contextual knowledge and inferential skills, readers are actively and creatively involved in the construction of the text's meaning. The complexity of this information, for example in the novel's scattered biblical and fairytale symbolism (Wilson 1993), once again disrupts this summation, forming what might be viewed as 'a diagram of futility, crisscrossed with tiny roads which lead nowhere' (Atwood 1996:153). Complicating the 'imposition of structure' by readers at this global level of interpretation, alongside the lower levels of linguistic organisation explored here, this text emphasises not only the character's subjective experience of this fictional world through sequential scanning, but also the 'most idiosyncratic form of iconicity' (Tabakowska 1993:55) which results from our own attempts at summation as readers, or puzzle-solvers. 'The artistic work', as Dvorak emphasises in her discussion of the text, 'is not a fixed product that readers consume, but a process, an arrangement, in which they collaborate' (1998:459).

By foregrounding the collaboration involved in this text world 'puzzle' or 'collage', emphasised further by its persistent direct address to an implied reader ('you'), the novel questions our reading and interpretation of the world on a scale far beyond the fictional reality of the text. The narrative through which we are invited to access this reality is merely the narrator's 'reconstruction' (emphasised by her self-reflexive comments throughout – Atwood 1996:144, 275). Furthermore, we discover, the narrative has itself been re-constructed through the transcription and translation carried out centuries later in the year 2195, described in the 'Historical Notes' or epilogue to the novel (Atwood 1996:311). With this subjective and highly questionable construal providing the 'instructions' on which our conceptualisation is based, the world which Atwood challenges us to reconstruct can be viewed as a postmodernist challenge to the processes through which we structure our own reality (Howells 2005:108; Davidson 1988): 'In a blurring reminiscent of the photograph in *Surfacing*, *Handmaid* questions how literary texts and life writing are read and interpreted... problematizing the representations with which we try to make sense of the world' (Dvorak 1998:449).

With such readings in mind, the disrupted experience of text world construction invited through the text's construal at a grammatical level is directly relevant to its critical interpretation. By suggesting an understanding of the complex processes responsible for the experiential effect described here somewhat ambiguously as *a blurring*, cognitive grammatical analysis of *The Handmaid's Tale* has much to offer literary criticism. The enactment of the novel's thematic concerns within our cognitive reading experience through Atwood's use of language, in my view, represents an important contribution to the appreciation of this intricate and evocative novel.

The application of Cognitive Grammar as part of the integrated approach explored here has suggested a means of accounting for the particular impact of *The Handmaid's Tale* as a consequence of the choices made as part of its construal. On a broader scale, the application of Langacker's model I have proposed offers a principled and psychologically plausible approach to the dynamic construction of text worlds and the specific effects of stylistic choices upon this readerly experience. The integration of such a grammatical, bottom-up approach to texts with the top-down schematic input of a reader's background knowledge and experiences represents an ongoing challenge for stylisticians which extends far beyond the analysis demonstrated here. The development of a Cognitive Discourse Grammar capable of bridging this gap, through investigations of the kind presented in this volume, promises a more fine-grained understanding of text world experiences as part of the collaborative process of literary reading.

CHAPTER 7

Point of view in translation

Lewis Carroll's *Alice* in grammatical wonderlands

Elżbieta Tabakowska

Motto: For each type of person interested in language there is a name: 'poet', 'grammarian', 'mathematician', and so on. (Daniel F. Kirk)

1. Preliminaries

Tearing down the wall that had traditionally separated linguistics from literary study seemed hardly possible when autonomous linguistics, and notably the transformational generative theory of grammar, reigned supreme in the Western world. With mainstream linguistics defining its object of study as a 'population of utterances' (Diller 2012:323) rather than individual manifestations of language use, theoretical frameworks did not pay much attention to the unruly 'human factor' that made individual speech events go beyond strict limits of rule-governed linguistic systems. Along with defective products coming from 'non-idealized' language users, creative linguistic vagaries of the human mind were left to psychologists, and their most sophisticated forms, covered by the umbrella term 'literature', to literary scholars.

The advance of an approach to language study now known under the general name of *cognitive linguistics* made possible the wall demolition campaign, as is proved by the growing volume of work done in the past decades within the dynamically developing discipline of *cognitive poetics* (and with the ground laid by *stylistics* before that). No longer a contradiction in terms, the literary linguistics of cognitive persuasion has been providing an increasingly comprehensive theoretical cognitive basis for literary intuitions. Margaret Freeman's (2006) optimism expressed in her seminal position paper on 'the fall of the wall between literary studies and linguistics' proved well-grounded: apart from different foci and deceptive terminological parallels, cooperation between the two disciplines appears mutually beneficial. Cognitive linguistics profits from including literary texts, with all their complexities, among its data, while literary studies find solid support for their insights in theories of linguistic phenomena out of which these insights are shown to stem (Freeman 2006: 404).

The rift between 'the linguistic' and 'the literary' is also being removed from translation studies – the discipline which, although claiming its rights to autonomy, has been naturally drawing heavily from both linguistic and literary discoveries. The 'cognitive turn' which characterises recent developments finds its direct counterpart in the fundamental assumption that underlies modern translation theory: the process of translation is no longer seen as an operation on texts, but as one that involves complicated mental processes (Hejwowski 2007: 47). Cognitive abilities underlying the creation of natural language texts are the same for sources and targets, while pragmatic filters that underlie mechanisms of perception, conceptualisation and expression are culture- and language-specific.

Like cognitive poetics, cognitive translation studies makes use of theories and models offered by cognitive linguistics, but – like cognitive poetics again – it focuses mostly upon such phenomena as metaphor, mental spaces construction or conceptual integration. Theoretical reflection, as well as text and discourse analyses, rarely focus on Cognitive Grammar proper as a means to describe and explain relevant linguistic aspects of translation – both the process and the product. In this respect, Langacker's (1987, 2008a) concept of scene construal and its constitutive dimensions of imagery has been the main source of inspiration (e.g. Tabakowska 1993). This chapter is an attempt to partially restore the balance: its aim is to show how principles of Langacker's Cognitive Grammar can be used to reveal the underpinnings of the process of constructing – and maintaining or shifting – the vantage point, or as literary scholars call it, the point of view, in a literary text.

The problem involved in this enterprise is well known to advocates of the 'above-S-level' grammars, Langacker's model included. While claiming their interest in texts and/or discourse, in their analyses they mostly focus on sub-clause, clause or sentence levels. This seems to be due to practical reasons: it is technically difficult for an author to present and discuss large stretches of discourse, and it is trying for the reader to have to go through exceedingly long analyses. The difficulty doubles in the case of translation studies: texts, or discourses, have to be presented both in the original and in the translation. Compensation strategies work over large stretches of discourse. To minimise the problem, in what follows I will discuss extracts from a literary classic, assuming its knowledge among the general reading public: new editions of Lewis Carroll's *Alice's Adventures in Wonderland* keep appearing, and the number of translations (interlinguistic as well as intersemiotic) has been growing steadily. My own recent translation (Tabakowska/Carroll 2010) has increased the number of Polish translations from eight to eleven, at the same time providing me with data for the analysis presented below. The translators, and the translated editions quoted, are Marianowicz (1955), Stiller (1990), Kozak (1997), Kaniewska (2010) and Dworak (2010).

In what follows, the amount of Polish material will be reduced to a necessary minimum, and the analysis itself will be limited to a single aspect of the text under discussion – a restriction necessary in an essay of limited scope. The focus on *point of view* or POV/vantage point is justified by its crucial role in the macrostructure of the book.

2. POV

Linguistic and literary explorations of their common ground can prove frustrating due to deceptive parallelisms in terminology. The aspect of text/discourse construction to be discussed here is precisely such a case. *Point of view* has been long recognised as one of the main categories in literary studies; it is defined as the position that the narrator assumes when telling about events that make up the plot. It can involve spatial location of the story teller, or 'the perspective of getting to know or understand the world' (Jaworski 2000: 185, my translation). The terms *point of view* and *perspective* are generally used interchangeably. Particular techniques that writers use to convey the POV are investigated by a branch of literary studies called narratology, and the process of their employment goes by the name of *focalisation*. (The literature devoted to focalisation is too voluminous to be quoted at this point. Worth mentioning are Génette's canonical *Discours du Récit* [1972] – which introduces the fundamental opposition between *qui parle?* and *qui voit?* – and the seminal article by Levenston and Sonnenschein [1986]). In many respects, focalisation can be treated as a synonym of POV as a notion developed in Cognitive Grammar.

In Langacker's model of grammar, *viewpoint* is defined as the agglomerate of *vantage point*, which is 'the position from which a scene is viewed', and the 'orientation of the viewer', which is the viewer's positioning in space (Langacker 1987: 123). Vantage point is described as one of the aspects of *perspective*, which Langacker defines as 'the way in which the scene is viewed' (1987: 120), or the *viewing arrangement*, i.e. 'the overall relationship between the "viewers" and the situation being "viewed"' (Langacker 2008a: 73). On the level of grammatical structure, this relationship is characterised as an aspect of particular scene construal, and analysed in terms of the opposition between what Langacker calls *subjectivity* and *objectivity*, or 'the asymmetry between [...] the *subject* and *object* of perception' (Langacker 2008a: 77). It is this opposition that underlies the discussion in Sections 3 and 4 below.

In what follows, *point of view* will be used as the umbrella term to cover relevant aspects of Langacker's viewing arrangement. Consequently, particular POVs will be taken to belong to Langacker's explicit or implicit 'loci of consciousness' (2008a: 77), the psychologists' 'sentient centers' or the philosophers' 'subjects of consciousness'. As the property of an individual 'subject of consciousness', every POV is inherently subjective, with the subjectivity restricted by linguistic conventions. An individual viewer/conceptualiser chooses particular means to express their 'ways of viewing the scene', but the choice is limited by linguistic resources at their disposal. In the diachronic development of a given language, individual POVs petrify, changing into structures sanctioned by linguistic conventions; they become 'common POVs', or the ways of seeing things from the point of view of Langacker's 'generalized observer'. Ultimately, the reality represented in what people say (or write) is always a product of an individual consciousness, which subjectively ascribes properties and values to objectively existing entities in the objectively existing reality. An alternative view, taking those properties and values to be an inalienable possession of the world, would preclude all individuality, which is the gist of literature, or fictional discourse (more in Sienkiewicz 1992: 62). 'Fictional discourse is an invitation to mutual imagining' (Hobbs 1990: 37) – the ability that enables speakers (or writers) and listeners (or readers) to assume fictive POVs: 'We can easily adopt a fictive vantage point and imagine what the scene would look like from there' (Langacker 2008a: 76). It is the convergence of the two statements – from a literary scholar and from a linguist – that establishes the usefulness of CG as a tool that might help to explain at least some of the intricacies of 'making literature'.

At this junction, one more point must be made. Both literary scholars and linguistics of a cognitive persuasion admit that 'fictional discourse' allows for multiple conceptualisers, or mutual 'subjects of consciousness', co-existing in a single discourse. Works discussing and exemplifying possible variants of this multiplicity from the point of view of literary theory are legion; enumerating even the most representative ones would mean going beyond the limits of this chapter. On a general level, their claims can be summarised by Langacker's statement that '[in] principle a proposition – the grounded process expressed by a finite clause – can be apprehended by any number of conceptualizers, each with their own vantage point and epistemic stance regarding it' (Langacker 2008a: 445). And further on, '[d]espite their default identification, C[onceptualizer] has to be distinguished from the speaker, and C[onceptualizer]'s conception of reality from the speaker's, even in single-clause expressions' (2008a: 448). In other words, *qui voit* is not identical to *qui parle*. Now, if it is assumed – in agreement with Langacker's way of thinking – that 'reality' can be taken to mean (also) the 'represented world' of a fictional literary discourse, his claims may provide an interface between 'the literary' and 'the linguistic' approach to the topic dealt with in the following section.

3.   POV in *Alice in Wonderland*

Charles Dodgson's literary output belongs among topics much discussed by literary scholars of all persuasions – from theorists of childrens' literature to semioticians to theorists of translation and practising translators. Quotations from the two *Alice* books belong amongst the best known and most frequently recalled, in all possible contexts – from scientific texts to informal conversations. Biographies of 'the poet logician' abound. And all this nearly one and a half centuries after the first *Alice* book was published! While scholarly analyses focus on psychological and psychoanalytical aspects of Dodgson's-Carroll's (split) personality (for references, see Kirk 1962:2), the popularity of the books among the reading public is explained by what has been called 'double readership': *Alice in Wonderland* can be read and enjoyed both by children and by adult readers.

It will be claimed that the secret lies in the consistent confrontation of two 'worlds': the (familiar) reality of Victorian England and the (unfamiliar) virtual reality of Wonderland. The represented world of Wonderland is presented from several POVs. The POV of a 'well bred little girl of Victorian England' (McLellan 1984) – conveyed either as direct speech or via the narrator's reports (FIS) – is juxtaposed with that of the narrator, who acts in as many as three capacities: as the reporter of Alice's POV, as the teller of the story, and as its author. The two real world personas – Charles Dodgson, an Oxford mathematician with a penchant for little girls a.k.a. Lewis Carroll, and Alice Liddell, a daughter of an Oxford don – are paralleled by two fictitious world characters – Carroll the narrator and Alice the heroine. In addition, the fictional Wonderland is peopled by a host of fabulous characters – each with their own autonomous POV. But it is the opposition between 'the adult' and the 'the children's' POVs that provides the skeleton for the overall structure of the text.

Carroll's adult narrator – the teller of the tale – is in principle construed subjectively, as 'an offstage locus of perceptual experience that is not itself perceived' (Langacker 2008a:77). But quite often he steps on the stage and winks at the readers, revealing his own POV, which is systematically signaled by the author's placing parts of the narration in brackets. Occasionally he also reveals the POV of himself as the author. In the latter case the construal extends the borders of Wonderland, revealing Dodgson's/Carroll's indictment of Victorian manners and his Victorian contemporaries – the satire that has been so much appreciated by his adult readers. The narrator explains and comments upon the fictitious world; the author contrasts it with the real one.

The POV of Alice oscillates between subjective and objective construals. She does not belong to the crazy Wonderland, and watches its bizarre reality from a (conceptual) distance, but whenever she feels forced to look at herself as part of it, for instance when considering the possibility of having changed so as to fit in, the construal becomes more objective: "'I'm sure I'm not Ada", she said...' (*AinW*: 37 – all such quotations from the original are the Gardner (1960) edition). Both aspects of Alice's POV reveal what the commentators call the 'eager simplicity of a child' (Kirk 1962:68): 'she observes as an intelligent child might, and she compares. It is the comparison that makes the book what it is: a fantasy, aptly and succinctly defined by G.K. Chesterton as the genre in which the cosmos goes mad, but the hero does not go mad' (quoted from Kirk in a later edition by Gardner 2000: vi).

If we accept that it is the juxtaposition of different POVs that makes the book what it is, then it becomes obvious that it constitutes its *dominant,* that is an aspect of primary importance for the overall message, whose rendering must become the translator's priority (see Barańczak 2004). Therefore, in the following section, some further claims are made. First, it is grammar that provides building blocks for POV construction. Second, it is grammatical differences between languages that largely account for those constructional problems. Third, grammatical problems need grammatical explanation. And, finally, Cognitive Grammar in its present shape offers the best instruments available to pinpoint the problems and to look for possible solutions.

4.   Grammar

Utterances unmarked for POV shifts are by default taken to represent the speakers' POVs. As far as reported discourse is concerned, both literary scholars and linguists distinguish three ways of establishing POV: *direct speech* (DS, verbatim quotation of utterances made by the actual speaker with POV belonging to the speaker), *indirect speech* (IS, where both the contents of an utterance and its description are constructed by the reporter, with both the voice and the POV belonging to the narrator) and *free indirect speech* (FIS; reporting the original speaker's POV with grammatical adjustments required by giving the voice to the reporter) (see Levenston & Sonnenschein 1986:54–8). Out of the three, it is the last one that has been the subject of the most comprehensive research (see Nikiforidou 2012). Considered as a constitutive aspect of particular literary styles, FIS was also dealt with – albeit only occasionally – by translation theorists

(Ehrlich 1990; Levenston & Sonnerschein 1986; Rivinoja 2004). Apart from FIS, the authors focus on vocabulary items and collocations (e.g. registers, Levenston & Sonnerschein 1986), personal pronouns and articles – a standard challenge for translators working between languages with and without grammatical markers of gender and (in)definiteness (Rivinoja 2004), or grammatical tenses (mainly the perfect: imperfect opposition). Some of the issues will be taken up below, in order to substantiate the claim that an account made with reference to the CG framework might prove more illuminating than analyses carried out with reference to other models of grammar.

4.1 Reference

In English, the opposition between definite and indefinite reference conveyed by the use of articles is a standard means of POV construction. The indefinite article is used when 'the conditions for using *the* fail to be satisfied' (Langacker 2008a: 287), with the definite article being selected when the referent can be identified in the context of the running discourse. The opposition is illustrated by the following example. After Alice engages in an imaginary conversation with somebody referred to as 'Dinah', the narrator explains (in brackets in the original):

   1   a.   (Dinah was <u>the</u> cat.) (*AinW*: 28)

Polish does not have grammatical markers of (in)definiteness. The solutions chosen by the Polish translators differ:

   1   b.   (*Dina była kotką*) (Kozak 1997: 13; 'Dinah was <u>a</u> she-cat')
          c.   (*Dina jest kotem Alicji*) (Kaniewska 2010: 17; 'Dinah is Alice's tom-cat [?]')
          d.   (*Dina to kotka Alicji*) (Tabakowska 2012: 10; 'Dinah – this – Alice's she-cat)

1b categorizes Dinah – subjectively – as a member of the category 'cats'; it is a counterpart of English indefinite reference. 1c achieves identification by using 'Alice' in a reference-point objective construction, but at the clausal level the POV extends the fictive reality of Wonderland. The resulting notional clash explains the critic's or reader's intuitive assessment, typically expressed as 'this does not read well'. Finally, 1d erases clausal grounding (finite verb) and achieves contextual reference by means of a reference-point construction.

   Now consider the following example:

   2   a.   <u>The</u> door led right into a large kitchen, which was full of smoke from one end to the other: <u>the</u> Duchess was sitting on a three-legged stool in the middle, nursing a baby: <u>the</u> cook was leaning over <u>the</u> fire, stirring a large cauldron which seemed to be full of soup. (*AinW*: 82)

2a reveals a different use of the definite article: it is a rendering of Alice's vantage point: it is Alice who enters the kitchen and identifies the Duchess, whom she expects to see there, and then the cook by her action. All Polish translations change this perspective, as in

> 2 b. …*pośrodku, na trójnożnym stołku, siedziała Księżna z niemowlęciem na kolanach; nad paleniskiem pochylała się kucharka, mieszając w sporym kotle pełnym zupy.* (Kozak 1997:54; 'in the middle, on three legged stool, was sitting Duchess with baby on her knees, and over fire was leaning cook, stirring rather large cauldron full of soup')

The word order of the two clauses, that about the Duchess and that about the Cook, implies indefinite reference to the two characters, and the fronting of place adverbials ('in the middle', 'over the fire') turns the passage into a default description made from the vantage point of the narrator, who introduces the reader to a scene viewed – and described – in the canonical order: from the setting to the participants (the literary notion of *medias res*).

Shifts in Alice's POV from a subjective to an objective construal are conveyed by explicit reference to herself, as in

> 3 a. 'Who in the world am I? (…) I'm sure I can't be Mabel, for I know all sorts of things, and she, oh, she knows such a very little!' (*AinW*: 37)

3a profiles the first person singular; the construal of the speaker is objectified by the combination of two markers, which are obligatory in the English construction. In Polish, in which personal reference is canonically marked by the verb ending alone, the analogous effect is achieved by profiling the personal pronoun, which results in a strongly marked construction, as in

> 3 b. …*kimże ja u licha jestem?* (Stiller 1990:49: '…who-INTENSIFYING PART. I in the world am?')

as opposed to, for instance

> 3 c. … *kim* właściwie jestem? (Kozak 1997:30; '…who exactly am?')

Judged by the criterion of POV equivalence, 3b is a 'better' translation than 3c, as it is positioned higher on the scale of objectification.

Personal pronouns point to particular POVs in more ways than personal reference proper. Consider the following two examples:

> 4 a. [Alice] had read several nice little stories about children who had got burnt (…) all because they would not remember the simple rules that their friends had taught them: such as, that a red-hot poker will burn you if you hold it too long… (*AinW*: 31)

    5   a.   To be sure, this is what generally happens when <u>one</u> eats cake. (*AinW*: 33)

In 4a the subject of the clause is construed more subjectively than in 5a, where the 'impersonal *you*' potentially includes also direct reference to the hearer. With the hearer of 'the simple rules' being Alice, 4a is an instance of her POV, while 5a reflects the POV of the distanced narrator. With Polish offering possibilities of this subtle distinction, some of the translators preserve the POV differentiation, as in

    4   b.   *....jeśli za długo <u>będziesz</u> trzymać pogrzebacz rozpalony do czerwoności...* (Kaniewska 2010: 21; '...if too long you-2 P. SG will hold poker red-hot...')

    5   b.   *zazwyczaj tak właśnie się dzieje, kiedy <u>ktoś</u> je ciastko...* (BK 23: 'usually so exactly happens itself when somebody eats a cake')

while others neglect it:

    4   c.   *rozgrzany do czerwoności pogrzebacz oparzy, jeśli <u>się</u> go za długo trzyma* (Dworak 2010: 18; 'red-hot poker will burn if one it too long holds')

    5   c.   *...właśnie to się zwykle dzieje, kiedy <u>się</u> je ciastka* (Dworak 2010: 21; 'exactly this happens when one eats cakes')

Incidentally, the subjective POV construal is strengthened by mass reference to 'cake' – as opposed to the countable '<u>a</u> cake' – in 5a, in contrast to a more objective '<u>a</u> red-hot poker' in 4a. The translators make differing choices: *ciastko* (count sing.) in 5b as compared to 'cakes' (pl count) in 5c; neither renders the subtle distinction observable in the original.

    A natural device to convey POV is lexical choice, or nominal reference – the role which literary and linguistic accounts discuss amply, and with considerable agreement (see Levenston & Sonnenschein 1986 and Langacker 2008a: 263, respectively). In *Alice* there are words that belong to Alice's children's idiolect; although they appear mostly in DS, they can also be found in FIS, as in the description of seaside holidays:

    6   Alice had been to the seaside once in her life, and had come to the general conclusion that, wherever you go to on the English coast, you find a number of bathing machines in the sea, some children digging in the sand with wooden spades, then a row of lodging houses, and behind them a railway station. (*AinW*: 40)

On the other hand, the narration abounds in expressions that 'incorporate [narrator] affect or a limitation to certain social contexts' (Langacker 2008a: 263, Footnote 5): 'poor Alice', 'little wise Alice', or grounding expressions like 'this curious child'. There are also cases when particular expressions echo those plausibly made by other characters – for instance the 'friends' who teach Alice (and other Victorian children) the wisdom of life:

> 4   …she had read several <u>nice stories</u> about children who had got burnt, and eaten up by old beasts, and other unpleasant things, all because they *would* not remember the simple rules that their friends had taught them… (*AinW*: 31)

The Polish translators use a variety of expressions: *milutkie historyjki* (Kaniewska 2010: 19; nice-DIMIN stories-DIMIN), *śliczne opowiastki* (Stiller 1990: 39; lovely tales-DIMIN), *pouczające opowiastki* (Kozak 1997: 15; didactic tales-DIMIN) *urocze opowiastki* (Marianowicz 1955: 17, adorable tales-DIMIN). It is the last one that echoes an educator's ingratiating style, with *didactic little tales* strongly tipping the scale towards the author's (as opposed to the narrator's) voice.

Another category are relative expressions that set up vantage point, as in

> 7   a.   <u>An enormous</u> puppy was looking down at her. (*AinW*: 64)

7a relates to what Alice sees from her actual perspective of a tiny midget. While all the translations use an adjective meaning, roughly, 'of great size', one of them combines two POVs:

> 7   b.   *Olbrzymie szczeniątko wytrzeszczało na nią z góry <u>wielkie</u>, okrągłe <u>ślepia</u> i niepewnie wyciągając <u>łapkę</u> próbowało jej dotknąć* (Stiller 1990: 91; 'Great puppy-DIMIN looked at her from above with large round eyes and uncertainly stretching out paw-DIMIN tried to touch her')

Since the scene is one of visual perception, mixing the sizes, and in consequence the POVs, accounts for a cognitive dissonance, and the fragment 'does not read well'. In other contexts, however, such 'double conceptualization' brings about a humorous effect:

> 8   a.   '… I wonder what Latitude or Longitude I've got to?' ('Alice had not the slightest idea what Latitude was, or Longitude either, but she thought they were nice grand words to say'). (*AinW*: 27)

The first clause conveys the POV of the narrator, and the second one, that of Alice. Some of the translations render the opposition:

> 8   b.   *Alicja nie miała najmniejszego pojęcia, co znaczy Szerokość albo Długość geograficzna, uważała jednak, że są to <u>prześliczne</u> słowa i <u>tak wspaniale</u> się je wymawia* (Stiller 1990: 33–4; 'Alice did not have the slightest idea what Latitude or Longitude mean, but she thought that they are over-beautiful words and so wonderfully itself them pronounces')

8   c.   *Alicja nie miała pojęcia, co to takiego Szerokość czy Długość geograficzna, ale były to <u>bardzo ładne, dorosłe</u> słowa* (Dworak 2010: 13; 'Alice had no idea what to such Latitude or Longitude, but they were very beautiful, grown-up words')

The adjectives *prześliczne* and *dorosłe*, as well as the deictic *tak*, belong to children's speech and so determine the POV as that of Alice.

4.2   Processes

It seems banal to say that English progressive tenses express the 'internal perspective' of a viewer who starts playing his role at the point at which the immediate scope does not focus upon either the beginning or the end of the profiled relationship. Such is the employment of the progressive in the opening passage of Alice:

9   a.   Alice <u>was beginning</u> to get very tired… (*AinW*: 25)

In the absence of parallel construction, the Polish translations choose either the objective POV of the narrator, that is, his interpretation of the scene, as in

9   b.   *Alicja miała dość siedzenia* (Dworak 2010: 12; 'Alice had enough of the sitting')

or a more subjective construal with the imperfective, as in

9   c.   *Alicja była coraz bardziej znudzona* (Tabakowska 2012: 7; 'Alice was more and more bored…')

The complex functions of the perfective:imperfective opposition and grammatical tenses in POV construction is well illustrated by the following fragment:

10   a.   She felt that <u>she was dozing off</u>, and <u>had just begun</u> to dream that <u>she was walking</u> hand in hand with Dinah, and <u>was saying</u> to her, very earnestly, 'Now, Dinah, tell me the truth: did you ever eat a bat?' when suddenly, thump! thump! Down <u>she came</u> upon a heap of sticks and dry leaves, and the fall <u>was over</u>. (*AinW*: 28)

The first four clauses constitute an instance of FIS ('she felt…'), the opening one exemplifies imperfective construal; the second one – the perfective – situates the beginning of the process of dreaming as prior to the two imperfective and simultaneous processes of walking and seeing. The next clause is Alice's DS, and the last two are FIS again, as signalled by the onomatopoeias ('thump! thump!') and the reversed iconic word order ('Down she came…').

The most symptomatic of the Polish translations gives the following rendering of 10a.

10   b.   *Czuła, że usypia, i zdawało się jej, że spaceruje razem z Diną i właśnie zadaje jej bardzo ważne pytanie: – Powiedz mi, Dino (tylko mów prawdę!), czy zjadłaś kiedyś nietoperza? – I w tej samej chwili: łup! chrup! Wylądowała na stercie*

patyczków i suchych liści. Tak oto skończyło się jej spadanie. (Kaniewska 2010:17; '[She] felt she falls asleep-PRES and seemed-IMPERF to her that walks-pres together with Dina and just asks-PRES very important question: – Tell me, Dina (only say truth! if you sometime ate-PAST PERF. bat? – and at the same moment thump! chrump (?).[She] landed on heap of sticks-DIMIN and dry leaves. Thus here ended-PAST PERF. her falling')

In terms of translation quality assessment, 10b merits a more detailed discussion than what can be offered at this point. What is more relevant is the phenomenon traditionally known as *consecutio temporum*: in English it is a feature of conventional construals, while Polish offers the choice between the present and the past tenses, with the present tense in the subordinate clause conveys 'the present time of the viewer', thus shifting the POV in FIS up on the scale of objectivity. In 10b the double deictic grounding expression *tak oto* marks a sharp change of POV to that of the narrator. An element of this particular translator's obvious overall strategy to bring her translation close to a stereotype of childrens' literature, the twist makes the text inconsistent: as shown from further context, it is Alice who realises that 'the fall was over'.

4.3   Epistemic modality

Epistemic modals – obvious grounding elements – account for POV differences, as 'the ground is the vantage point from which the grounded structure is apprehended' (Langacker 2008a:416). As in all standard uses of FIS, it implies the character's evaluation of what things are like, as in

11   a.   …at first she thought it <u>must be</u> a walrus or hippopotamus…
            (*AinW*: 41)

The Polish translations offer a whole gamut of solutions:

11   b.   *pomyślała, że to z pewnością mors albo hipopotam…* (Tabakowska 2012:19; '[she] thought this certainly walrus or hippopotamus ..')

      c.   *pomyślała, że to mors albo hipopotam* (Stiller 1990:19; '[she] thought this walrus or hippopotamus…')

      d.   *ciekawa, czy to mors, czy może hipopotam* (Kozak 1997:23; 'curious whether this walrus or perhaps hippopotamus …')

      e.   *wzięła to zwierzę za morsa albo hipopotama* (Kaniewska 2010:33; '[she] took this animal for walrus or hippopotamus…')

11b removes epistemic grounding, and 11c turns Alice's doubt into certainty. 11d makes her wonder about the animal's identity, and 11e is most explicit in non-ambiguously establishing the POV as that of Alice.

Epistemic adverbs are another means of establishing the POV. A case in point is 2 above, repeated below for convenience:

2 a.   The door led right into a large kitchen, which was full of smoke from one end to the other: the Duchess was sitting on a three-legged stool in the middle, nursing a baby: the cook was leaning over the fire, stirring a large cauldron which <u>seemed</u> to be full of soup. (*AinW*: 82)

The verb *seem* brings in the objectification, which the translations render in differing ways:

2 b.   ... *mieszając w sporym kotle pełnym zupy* (Kozak 1997: 54 '...stirring in big kettle full of soup')

   c.   .... *mieszając warząchwią w ogromnym kotle, <u>prawdopodobnie</u> pełnym zupy* (Dworak 2010: 80; 'stirring with ladle in huge kettle probably full of soup')

   d.   *pełnym <u>jak gdyby</u> gotującej się zupy* (Stiller 1990: 121; 'full as if of boiling soup')

   e.   ... *mieszając w wielkim kotle coś, co <u>wyglądało jak</u> zupa* (Kaniewska 2010: 82; 'stirring in huge kettle something that looked as soup')

   f.   ... *mieszając w wielkim kotle, który <u>chyba</u> był pełen zupy* (Tabakowska 2012: 82; 'stirring in big kettle which probably was full of soup').

Once again, while 2b removes the epistemic element, 2d blurs the POV by adding an element of evidentiality. Although the retranslations of 2c and 2f look the same, they are not. With Polish having a larger variety of epistemic adverbs, *prawdopodobnie* conveys a subjective, and *chyba* an objective construal, which makes the latter a better choice. Finally, once again, 2e strengthens the element of objectification.

4.4   Units and constructions

In their discussion on translation of POV, Levenston and Sonnenshein (1986) mention collocations and clichés as POV constitutive elements, but limit the discussion to a short list of examples. In Langacker's model, they have the status of units, along with idioms (see. Langacker 2008a: 18–19). In *Alice in Wonderland*, Alice's POV is marked by 'de-idiomatization' of English idioms: the ungrounded March Hare and Mad Hatter become specified as particular instantiations. The 'adult' observer – the narrator, the author or the reader – is construed subjectively, having the knowledge of the units, but remaining offstage. The juxtaposition – or collusion? – of 'the subjective' and 'the objective' becomes obvious as the contrast well known to structuralists as the ambiguity of constituent analysis. The case in point is [Mock [Turtle soup]], interpreted by Alice (who presumably lacks culinary expertise) as [Mock Turtle] Soup], with the resulting appearance of one of the inhabitants of Wonderland.

The POV of Alice's author (as different from the narrator, see above) shows in what has probably not been much discussed in terms of vantage point construction or construal characterisation. The famous parodies of Victorian didactic poetry can only be appreciated when they are identified as such. This, in turn, can only be done when the schematic meaning, conveyed by the metre or the rhyme pattern, is recalled. The comparison is, seemingly, inaccessible to 'poor Alice', who can at most 'be sure that those are not the right words' (*AinW*: 38).

While the above aspects of POV construction deserve to be mentioned, they will not be further pursued in the present context of translation. The type of challenge they present is among the standard points taken up by translation critics and theorists of translation.

4.5   Iconicity

As an aspect of POV construction, experiential iconicity (Enkvist 1981) certainly deserves attention. A topic frequently taken up by linguists and literary scholars alike, it is rarely discussed in the context of translation. Yet it is often indicative of the POV in narration. Consider, for instance,

12   a.   'It's – it's a very fine day!' said a timid voice at her side. She was walking by the White Rabbit, who was peeping anxiously into her face. (*AinW*: 110)

The POV is consistently, and iconically, construed as Alice's: she first hears an indefinite 'timid voice', and only then realises (using metonymy as the cognitive mechanism to gain that knowledge) that she 'was walking by the White Rabbit'. All Polish translations change the construal by avoiding both the iconicity and the metonymy, like in

12   b.   – *Co za... co za piękny dzień! – odezwał się z boku nieśmiały głosik. To Biały królik dreptał obok Alicji, popatrując ku niej nerwowo* (Kozak 1997:76; 'What.. what beautiful day! – spoke at side shy voice-DIMIN. This White Rabbit trotted-IMPERF by Alice, looking-ITERATIVE IMPERF to her nervously').

As the result, the POV changes into THAT construed subjectively, from the narrators vantage point. The implication of Alice's surprising discovery is lost.

5.   The grammar of paratext

Typographic conventions have a role to play as well. However, at this point only one paratextual feature will be mentioned: the illustrations. Both the famous original ones, made by John Tenniel and often commented upon (see Gardner 1960; Stiller 1990; Ingpen 2009), and those made by other artists, are just different versions of intersemiotic translation (Chaparro 2000). Their analysis, rewarding as it would certainly prove to be, requires separate investigation. At this point, it is worthwhile to say that the crux of the genre of fantasy, the juxtaposition of 'the mad' with what had not gone mad, is certainly well seen in Tenniel's engravings. His Alice, dressed in her tidy Victorian frock, most of the time looks uncertain and perplexed in her role of the viewer of the subjectively construed world.

6.   Conclusions

What seems pertinent for translation studies is the question whether the issue presented above should be dealt with as a contrastive study, offering some predictions as to how translations should be made, or – alternatively – as an assessment done *ex post* as *sui generis* error analysis (Levenston & Sonnenshein 1986: 56). Although no binding answers can be offered, there are arguments for the latter alternative. It seems clear that linguistic (grammatical) signals serve as guides to interpretation of the narrative in terms of establishing the POVs conveyed. Ultimately, however, POV ascription comes as the logic of reading (Tabakowska 1993, 2007), a complex cognitive process, making use of both linguistic and extralinguistic cues. As seen from the examples discussed above, multiple POVs are a matter of course, and devices used for POV blends extend standard devices, like the much discussed *past + now* construction (Nikiforidou 2012).

   In the absence of overt grammatical clues, POV ascription is difficult, as in

13   a.   The <u>poor</u> little lizard, Bill, was in the middle, being held up by two
            guinea-pigs… (*AinW*: 63–4)

The question of narrator or/and character affect (*poor*) remains unsolved.

   On the other hand, the POV is sometimes unambiguously conveyed by using devices that are traditionally included within the umbrella category of 'rhetoric', as in

14   a.   'I suppose I ought to eat or drink something or other; but the great
            question is "What?"' The great question certainly was 'What?'
            (*AinW*: 66).

The echoing of Alice's ID shows that the POV is that of the narrator. One of the translations makes the point more bluntly:

14   b.   *'Przypuszczam, że powinnam coś zjeść albo wypić, a może zrobić jeszcze co innego... Ale skąd mam wiedzieć CO?' To było rzeczywiście bardzo ważne pytanie: co powinna teraz zrobić?* (Kaniewska 2010:62; 'I suppose I should something eat or drink, and perhaps do yet something different... But how do I have to know WHAT?' This was really very important question: what [she] should now do?')

In 14b the adverb *rzeczywiście* and the repetition of an entire clause of Alice's IS make POV identification more obvious that in the original. The point to be made is that 14b confirms earlier observations on this particular translation – POV construction is one of the devices used within the overall strategy, which aims at making the text 'infantile': addressed to a child reader.

A proper coda is found in Levenston & Sonnenshein (1986:58): '[POV] is a genuine issue for translation theory, and well worth further investigation'. More than a quarter of a century old, the statement has not lost its relevance.

PART II

Studies of poetry

CHAPTER 8

Profiling the flight of 'The Windhover'

Clara Neary

1. Introduction: literature and Cognitive Grammar

Cognitive Grammar offers a principled system for the analysis of literature within the broader field of cognitive linguistics. It chiefly departs from 'traditional' theories of language in its contention that the way in which we produce and process language is determined not by the 'rules' of syntax but by the symbols evoked by linguistic units. These linguistic units include morphemes, words, phrases, clauses, sentences and whole texts, all of which are deemed inherently symbolic in nature. The way in which we join linguistic units together is also symbolic rather than rule-driven because grammar is itself 'meaningful' (Langacker 2008a: 4). In claiming a direct symbolic association between linguistic form (what it terms 'phonological structure') and semantic structure, Cognitive Grammar denies the need for an organisational system to mediate between the phonological and semantic structures (i.e. syntax). Rather, as stated by Langacker, '[t]he basic tenet of CG is that nothing beyond symbolic structures need be invoked for the proper characterization of complex expressions and the patterns they instantiate' (2008a: 5).

The value in adopting a Cognitive Grammar approach to literature is twofold and centres upon its consideration of the interaction between bottom-up and top-down cognitive processing. On the one hand Cognitive Grammar is concerned with how linguistic expressions encode a particular construal of the events represented; on the other it is concerned with how this interacts with the reader's 'elaborate conceptual substrate', that is, the reader's background knowledge and ability to understand an expression's 'physical, social, and linguistic content' (Langacker 2008a: 4). Cognitive Grammar asserts that when we represent something linguistically, we are expressing our conceptualisation of the event/situation/object in question. To linguistically represent something in a 'prototypical' fashion is, then, to mentally construe it in a typical or prosaic manner. In the Jakobsonian tradition from which cognitive stylistics originates, literature is identified on the basis of its ability to do 'extraordinary' things with language. Investigating literature through the lens of Cognitive Grammar, the supposition is that the 'unprototypical' linguistic expression typical of literary texts directly represents an unprototypical or unusual manner of conceptually construing the event/situation/object in question. Of the Victorian poet Gerard Manley Hopkins, the focus of this chapter's CG approach to literature, Gardner remarks: 'his spontaneous, earnest writing is always the utterance of a vigorous and sensitive mind – often humorous or witty, usually searching and stimulating, *never commonplace or pedestrian*' (2008: xiv; emphasis added).

Though largely unread during his lifetime, the deeply religious overtones, innovative formal techniques and enquiry into aesthetic cognition which characterise Gerard Manley Hopkins's (1844–1889) poetic output have secured him posthumous renown and much critical attention. A Roman Catholic convert and Jesuit priest, Hopkins formulated a number of concepts which are integral to the reading of his poetry. The most famous of these are the related theories of *inscape* – essentially the manner by which Hopkins endeavoured to poetically capture the intrinsic uniqueness, the 'particular energy and stress' (Mariani 1970:334) of an entity – and *instress*, the means by which this 'essence' is cognitively conveyed to the reader through its visual appearance. Widely considered 'one of the few strikingly successful innovators in poetic language and rhythm' (Gardner 2008: xiii), Hopkins's work is particularly noteworthy for the phonological and rhythmic effects of what Hopkins termed *sprung rhythm*, his attempt to infuse his poetry with the patterns of Welsh and Old English prosody. In addition, his unique poetic output is notable for its 'adjective pileups, syntactical switcheroos, sentences so grammatically dense they are nearly unparseable, alliteration [and] archaisms', the result being 'gorgeous, complex, tongue-twister poetry (cited without attribution in Tsur 2010:123).

Hopkins considered 'The Windhover' 'the best thing I ever wrote' (Letter to Rupert Bridges, 22 June 1879; cited in Mariani 1970:110). Mariani's description of the sonnet as '"a billion times told" bulkier than its predecessors' (1970:110) provides some insight into why the poem has, as Holloway notes, 'been subjected to as many attempts to release meaning as there are letters in the sonnet' (1993:206). Indeed, as Whiteford remarks, 'it is difficult to think of any English poem of comparable length that has been the subject of as much concerted explication', the result being a body of critical work which is 'as formidable as it is lacking in consensus' (2001:617). This, of course, all raises the question as to why this sonnet has been chosen as the object of a Cognitive Grammar approach. There are a number of reasons for this. Firstly, as Cognitive Grammar posits a direct symbolic relationship between linguistic and semantic structure, the work of a poet known for his 'extreme condensation of thought and language' (as remarked upon by his friend and literary sponsor, Robert Bridges, cited in Gardner 2008:xiv) constitutes an apt object of study. The choice of 'The Windhover' over Hopkins's other poetic output is predicated on the fact that in this sonnet, as Olney notes, 'one sees all of Hopkins's technical resources on fullest display' – including sprung rhythm, end and internal rhyme, assonance and alliteration – all of which are 'handled perfectly, with great skill and to very telling effect' (1993:83). Furthermore, and perhaps most essentially, applying a Cognitive Grammar approach to this sonnet constitutes a means of interrogating the following claim by Tsur that Hopkins's poetry cannot be interpreted without requisite specialist knowledge:

> Hopkins is a difficult poet. It is almost impossible to imagine a spontaneous 'first reading' of any of his poems. It is more reasonable to assume that 'spontaneous' response to a poem by Hopkins becomes possible only after the studious internalization of research done (independently, or by reading footnotes) on his language, imagery and theological conceptions.　　　(Tsur 2010:123)

However, Cognitive Grammar's contention that our conceptual and linguistic systems are inextricably linked challenges this claim on the basis that, if linguistic expression is truly 'intuitive', a basic understanding of all texts must be within our grasp without necessary recourse to contextual information. While cognitive linguistics does not advocate a necessarily one-to-one link between linguistic form and the conceptual domains it evokes, with background knowledge always playing a part in readerly interpretation, by positing the 'naturalness' of linguistic expression it presupposes that there are 'systematic connections between conceptualizations and observable phenomena like sounds and gestures' so that 'all valid grammatical constructs' are 'reducible to form-meaning pairings' (Langacker 2008a:6). Finally, given that cognitive stylistic approaches on the whole endeavour to make overt the cognitive processes underlying the reading of literary texts, it seems particularly shrewd to apply them to a text such as 'The Windhover' which, as Olney remarks, 'is one of those poems that seem almost miraculous in coming so far from the beginning of the poem that *one cannot see how it has been done*' (Olney 1993:84; emphasis added).

Cognitive Grammar as an approach is centred upon the distinction in linguistic expression between figure and ground. Drawn from the field of cognitive linguistics, when applied to the visual field, this distinction endeavours to encapsulate the way in which certain elements stand out as *figures* against a background: for example, a winter landscape might act as the visual backdrop against which a bird in flight stands out or, in CG terms, is *profiled*. A bird in flight would stand out against a static background because it is in motion. If the bird was stationary but bright pink in colour, it would be the contrast between its colour and the muted almost monochromatic shades of a winter landscape which makes it stand out. On the other hand, if the bird was small, grey and stationary, it might very well fade into the background. It should be obvious in any case that certain features of an object in the visual field will make it more likely to stand out against its background. To relate this to CG, 'the prevalence of figure/ground organization in conceptual structure entails its importance for semantic and grammatical structure as well' (Langacker 1987: 120); that is, just as figures can be cognitively distinguished from their ground in the visual field, they can also stand out in the linguistic field. As Stockwell (2002a: 14) notes, the recognition of figures and ground in reading is a 'dynamic' process which is constantly updated as one reads a text and different figures are thrown into relief against various grounds. Certain features will contribute to the 'naturalness and likelihood' (Langacker 1987: 120) of a particular linguistic entity being recognised or chosen by the reader as the figure which stands out against the ground. These features are those which grab the reader's attention, typically through deviance from a background linguistic norm as evidenced in unprototypical grammatical or semantic construction. (See Stockwell 2003: 15–20 for a discussion of potential *attractors* of cognitive attention in the textual field).

In CG, the figure/ground distinction is discussed in terms of how a figure stands out or is *profiled* against the ground. Profiling refers to the perceived relationship between two entities. In CG, this relationship operates at a number of different levels. As noted above, at the conceptual level, profiling denotes the relationship between a *figure*, an entity which attracts your cognitive attention because it stands out in some way, and the *ground* or background against which it stands out. This reflects the way in which we cognitively interact with the world around us: in paying attention to figures in the visual, spatial and conceptual fields we take cognitive shortcuts which allow us to more effectively process and prioritise the constant stream of incoming data with which we are constantly bombarded. At the linguistic level, the figure is termed the *trajector* while the ground is called the *landmark*. At the grammatical level, within CG all of the major word classes – nouns, verbs, prepositions, adjectives and adverbials – are perceived as profiling or designating different concepts. A noun, for example, 'profiles a thing' while a verb 'profiles a process' (Langacker 2008a: 151); in both cases they do so by participating in an unprofiled relation to another entity. For example, *mother* is obviously a noun as it profiles a thing, but the 'definition' of *mother* is based upon and activates an additional entity which is understood but not profiled. To be a mother entails being the mother of someone; therefore, the term *mother* 'activates' not only a *relationship* between two conceptual entities (mother and offspring) but also the entity which it is the mother of. Neither the relationship nor the offspring are mentioned in the word *mother*, as such they are unprofiled; but in order to understand the term we must have an awareness of these unprofiled entities. All expressions (other than referring noun phrases) are comprised of these two layers: the *profile* is the term itself (which stands out as a trajector) but it invokes an unprofiled *base* against which it is understood (which acts as the landmark). Relational profiles can be sub-categorised according to what is referred to in 'traditional' accounts of grammar as tense and aspect. Verbs designate temporal relations, that is, encoded within a verb's profile is a temporal element which denotes a specified span of time (akin to the traditional grammatical notion of tense). There are two kinds of temporal relations. The first is stative, that is, the temporal relation profiled is presented as unchanging; this is called a simple temporal relation. The second is dynamic, that is, the temporal relation profiled is presented as changing, as denoting a change in the relation between trajector and landmark; this is a complex temporal relation.

Finally, it is important that a clear distinction is drawn between the many labels that have been introduced thus far. Conceptually, we profile entities as *figures* (against an unprofiled *ground*) while linguistically we profile entities as *trajectors* (against an unprofiled *landmark*). In profiling entities as trajectors, we must identify their semantic roles in the utterance in question; CG does so by conceptualising the events depicted at the level of the clause in terms of an *action chain* which centres on the way in which entities participate in the process being profiled. In endeavouring to describe the prototypical process of a prediction or 'dynamic situation', Langacker employs a metaphor of energy transfer (1991b: 283). Each of the various participants (usually designated by a noun phrase) in a clause performs different roles as designated by the predication or relational profile of the clause; these roles are based upon *cognitive archetypes*. Prototypically, at least one participant in a clause will act as *agent*, that is, the 'doer' of an action. The participant which is the recipient of this action (the 'done unto') – and is altered in some way as a result of the action – is called the *patient*. If a participant in the clause is utilised in any way by the agent, this participant is labelled the *instrument*. A prototypical 'dynamic situation' would hence be represented as follows:

Jo closed the door with her foot

Jo is the agent, *the door* is the patient and *her foot* constitutes the instrument. Prototypically then, the predicative 'energy' is transferred from agent to patient through an instrument. The agent is hence highest on this dynamic chain which Langacker calls an *action chain*, the patient is second highest and the instrument comes last, as in the above example. If the dynamic process encoded in the clause represents a cognitive process, the participant which is the locus of this cognitive or perceptual operation – that is, an entity in which processes such as thinking, feeling or seeing occur – is termed an *experiencer*. Finally, a *mover* is the term accorded to a participant who relocates to another physical space. In English, the agent, experiencer and mover roles are prototypically represented by the grammatical subject and as such are conceptualised as having control over the represented predication. Clausal elements do not always participate in the predication process. For example, in *the cat is on the table* the cat constitutes a *zero participant* as it simply exists without 'doing' anything while the table does not participate in any way and hence constitutes part of the background *setting*. The zero position is also, as Stockwell notes, the default role for all participants in a clause as 'all participants begin fundamentally with existence and attributes' (2002a: 64).

2.   Profiling Hopkins's 'The Windhover'

For the purposes of the current analysis, I will focus on the sonnet's relational profiles and associated participants. Despite the huge volume of critical writing on 'The Windhover' – which focuses on many prominent features of the sonnet including its phonological patterning (see Scott 1974; Rudanko 1982), its use of religious allegories and motifs (see Cosgrove 2004; Gallet 1991; Rehder 1992; Cervo 1981), and its lexical 'ambiguities' – little has been done on its use of verbs, or, as Tsur (2010: 129) notes, its 'lack of verbs used as verbs'. Indeed, in the whole sonnet, there are only 11 verbs which actually function as verbs, the remainder predominantly functioning as nouns. Given Hopkins' conviction that the *inscape* or essential essence of all entities was dynamic in nature, that 'all is in act, all is in flux' (Holloway 1993: 207), this is surprising, particularly as dynamism is often encoded in verb use.

Consideration of the relational profiles in 'The Windhover' reveals interesting patterns in terms of the ways in which processes and their associated participants are profiled and thereby elucidates the cognitive processes by which the reader arrives at poetic interpretation. This is not to suggest that there is one definitive interpretation of 'The Windhover': this fact is evident from the number of published critiques of the sonnet which grapple with its metaphoric constructions, its innovative phonological patterning and its idiosyncratic use of syntax. Whilst the allegorical nature of the poem renders it impossible to fully unravel the 'literal' meaning from the 'figurative', this analysis will focus on what would be perceived as the 'literal' meaning, for two reasons. Firstly, it does so in the belief that, and following Hopkins's critic Paul Mariani, 'a literal reading [of this sonnet] must come first' (1970: 111). Mariani goes on to remark: 'The religious significance in this sonnet is so continually bursting through the natural scene that many commentators have spent most of their time on the secondary meaning without grounding it in the perceptual world' (1970: 111). Secondly, it does so in the current context as CG does not make a distinction between literal and figurative language; rather, it treats figurative language as 'a natural, expected phenomenon rather than a special, problematic one' (Langacker 1987:1) and therefore 'accommodates' it 'as an integral facet of linguistic organization, one that can be expected to interact with grammatical processes' (Langacker 1987:38). In short, given that CG focuses on the 'surface form' (Langacker 1987:4) of language in the belief that all linguistic units are 'inherently symbolic and hence meaningful' (Langacker 1987:12), such a distinction is rendered void. This analysis in no way constitutes an exhaustive account of the sonnet; such a feat, as the voluminous nature of previous critical commentary on 'The Windhover' attests, seems impossible in any case! Rather, this analysis constitutes an attempt to view this sonnet, the subject of much critical reflection and contention, through new, 'Cognitive Grammarian' eyes. The aim is not to add yet another interpretation to the dozens that have gone before, but rather to trace the cognitive pathways by which these interpretations have been arrived at.

> ### The Windhover
> I caught this morning morning's minion, king-
> > dom of daylight's dauphin, dapple-dawn-drawn Falcon, in
> > > his riding
> > Of the rolling level underneath him steady air, and striding
> High there, how he rung upon the rein of a wimpling wing
> In his ecstasy! then off, off forth on swing,
> > As a skate's heel sweeps smooth on a bow-bend: the hurl
> > > and gliding
> > Rebuffed the big wind. My heart in hiding
> Stirred for a bird, – the achieve of; the mastery of the thing!
>
> Brute beauty and valour and act, oh, air, pride, plume, here
> > Buckle! AND the fire that breaks from thee then, a billion
> Times told lovelier, more dangerous, O my chevalier!
>
> > No wonder of it: shéer plód makes plough down sillion
> Shine, and blue-bleak embers, ah my dear,
> > Fall, gall themselves, and gash gold-vermilion.   (Hopkins 1918:4)

Downes summarises 'The Windhover' as 'a redescription of the reality of total Christian love through the interpretive mediation of a richly composited sequence of metaphorical figures of Christ: cross-falcon-poet-disciple; the slicing plow and the falling ember' (Downes 1993:128). The fourteen lines of this sonnet are comprised of seven sentences which run over an octet and a two-part sestet. The first sentence consists of a main and complement clause, runs across six and a half lines (from 'I caught this morning' to 'In his ecstasy!') and is centred upon the main verb 'caught'. It is interesting to consider here the grammatical profiling of the poet-speaker as subject and the falcon as object which takes place in the opening line of the sonnet. 'Caught' in this instance means 'caught sight of' and is hence intransitive. (In a journal entry on the poem, Hopkins explains that 'caught' here means 'inscaped', that is, in seeing the bird Hopkins divined its essential essence: see House & Storey 1959:230, also cited in Whiteford 2001:618. While this certainly adds an additional layer of meaning, it does not preclude the more prosaic understanding of the term, especially given that the sonnet's octet is devoted to Hopkins' description of seeing the falcon in flight). It profiles a stative process with a bounded temporal span making it a simple temporal relation. It also profiles two participants: the 'see-er' ('I') and the 'seen'. The 'see-er' is the poet-speaker, and the 'seen' is the bird. The prototypical grammatical profiling of the main clause of this first sentence – in which the subject is in topic or sentence-initial position – aligns with its semantic profiling; as such, 'I' may also be labelled the *experiencer* as it is the entity which has 'caught sight of' the *stimulus* (the falcon). The positioning of the subject in this instance is also prototypical in terms of the empathy scale, as 'the speaker is usually expected to be the subject of an utterance' (Stockwell 2002a:61), as is the case here. Conceptually then, 'I' is the *figure* in this utterance and the falcon constitutes the *ground*.

However, as the first sentence progresses, the reader's attention becomes drawn away from the 'see-er' to the 'seen'. The poet-speaker occupies the subject and experiencer participant roles, but this grammatical profiling is soon superseded by its semantic structure which sees the falcon take over the role of trajector. This is achieved in two ways. Firstly, it may be noted that there are actually two constituents to the 'seen'. The first is the bird itself, which is referred to, variously, as the servant or favoured one (interpretations differ) of the morning ('morning's minion'), the prince of the kingdom of daylight ('king- /dom of daylight's dauphin'), and the falcon 'dappled' and 'drawn' upon by the emerging rays of the sun ('dapple-dawn-drawn Falcon'). The very use of apposition cognitively foregrounds the bird: while the grammatical subject and linguistic trajector ('I') is only mentioned once, the object/landmark (the falcon) is referred to thrice through apposition. Secondly, the unprototypical nature of the grammatical profiling of each of these apposite phrases draws further attention to them. The first and second nominals – 'morning's minion' and 'kingdom of daylight's dauphin – are not prototypically profiled, with the subjects ('minion' and 'dauphin') relegated to the end of the phrase in each case. The third reference ('dapple-dawn-drawn Falcon'), a noun phrase comprised of a series of three hyphenated words that premodify the noun, is grammatically profiled in a prototypical fashion in that modification is occurring before the noun; the noun acts as trajector and the premodifier acts as landmark. However, it is the premodifier which is semantically profiled through the unusual elliptical manner in which the three words have been conjoined. The whole noun phrase has been interpreted in a number of ways. Some readings conceptualise 'drawn' as a relational profile meaning 'to attract', with two participants profiled – the attractor and the attracted; hence the dawn is perceived as attracting the falcon with its dappled light. Another potential interpretation is that the dawn acts as an agent which 'draws' upon the falcon with its dappled light thereby rendering it more visible to the watcher. However, its syntactical ambiguity allows for both interpretations to co-exist simultaneously. The second stimulus 'seen' by the poet-speaker in the first sentence is, more specifically, the *flight* of the bird as depicted in the sentence's complement clause ('in his riding/Of the rolling level underneath him steady air, and striding/High there'). The relational profile of 'seeing' therefore has two direct objects; the first – the bird itself – is the *primary* stimulus and the second – the bird's flight – is the *secondary* stimulus. Indeed, the bird's flight is itself linguistically profiled through the use of two separate but interrelated gerunds: 'riding' and 'striding'. While 'riding' and 'striding' are technically functioning as nouns, the dynamism of their related verb forms mean they still profile a relational process of sorts. The overall consequence of this presence of nominal apposition and co-stimuli is that the reader's attention shifts from the experiencer to the stimulus.

The complement clause in the first sentence ('how he rung upon the rein of a wimpling wing/In his ecstasy!') is centred upon the verb 'rung'. Grammatically, 'rung' operates here in a transitive sense and profiles two participants: the ringer and what is rung. Consideration of the interaction between grammatical and semantic profiling continues to be of interest here. Grammatically, the subject of this complement clause is the falcon: it is the agent while the patient is the falcon's 'wimpling wing'. However, the fact that this clause is a complement clause and hence relative to the main clause is highlighted through the use of the conjunction 'how'. Semantically, the presence of this conjunction functions to reinstate the participant role of the falcon to that of an object 'seen' by the poet (despite its 'upgrade' to the agent role in the relative clause). The participants profiled by the use of the verb 'rung' are the falcon and the falcon's 'wimpling wing'; the former acts as agent while the latter is the patient in what is a metonymic representation. The image evoked by this construction is of the falcon's 'spiralling upward movement' (Holloway 1993: 207). The nominal profile of the word 'rein' draws upon a base domain with equestrian schematic links; hence, this image of the falcon also evokes the manner in which a horse is 'reined' or exercised in a ring. Here it is the falcon who acts as agent participant, that is, it is the falcon that is 'ringing' upon the reins, effectively acting as 'rider'. This image constitutes the first in a series of linguistic expressions which symbolically link the falcon to Christ, the 'chevalier'. (This is latently profiled earlier in the poem in the reference to 'riding' but it is probably not until the reader encounters the words 'rein' and 'chevalier' that the semantic links are activated).

The next sentence ('then off, off forth on swing/As a skate's heel sweeps smooth on a bow-bend: the hurl and gliding/Rebuffed the big wind') commences with a main clause conspicuously lacking in a relational profile. It is only in the relative clause that a verb is employed; the verb 'sweeps' profiles a complex temporal relation as it denotes a dynamic action which is on-going. The relational profile is intransitive in this instance and has one participant, the 'skate's heel', which acts as agent. Effectively the heel of the skate is sweeping on a trajectory round a bend. Here the grammatical and semantic profiling accord with the conceptual image evoked: the skate's heel is the linguistic trajector on a metaphorically evoked trajectory. Following a colon, the line recommences with 'the hurl and gliding/Rebuffed the big wind'. 'Rebuffed' is used here transitively and profiles two participants: the 'rebuffer' and the 'rebuffed'. The 'rebuffer', that is, the agent of the process of 'rebuffing', is the falcon, metonymically represented here as 'the hurl and gliding', two linguistic elements constructed from the nominalisation of their respective verb forms. The patient profiled by this relation is 'the big wind'; the relation itself is a complex temporal relation as it profiles a dynamic process which takes place over a certain span of time. This is the second instance in which the falcon acts as agent, but on this occasion its agency is not tethered in any way to the poet-speaker. Grammatically and semantically, the falcon is becoming 'freer'. The increasing dynamism of the relational profiles of which the bird is agent further reinforces the sense of its growing freedom: it has progressed from 'ringing' or 'riding' upon its own wings to 'rebuffing' the very elements.

In the third sentence – the last in the octet – the poet-speaker exclaims the significance of the event witnessed ('My heart in hiding/Stirred for a bird, – the achieve of; the mastery of the thing!'). Again, there is the elision of a verb; in this case a form of the verb 'to be' is absent from the phrase 'My heart [which is] in hiding'. This absence does not affect the reader's ability to conceptualise the utterance but rather pushes the reader on to the relational process which is at the literal and metaphorical heart of the exclamation. 'Stirred' is used intransitively and only profiles one participant: the 'stirred', that is, the poet's 'heart', while the cause of the 'stirring' is 'the bird'. Any potential confusion as to the cause of the 'stirring' profiled by the use of the preposition 'for [the bird]' rather than 'by' is soon cleared up as the line progresses to specify that it is 'the achieve of; the mastery of the thing' which acts as agent. The use of apposition here ('the achieve of; the mastery of the thing') serves to highlight exactly what it was that caused the poet's emotional reaction.

If this circumstance was syntactically represented in a prototypical manner, it would be represented as 'the bird stirred my heart', with the agent acting as subject and topic in sentence-initial position. In Hopkins's poem, use of the preposition 'for' partially disguises what is effectively a passive construction: as such, 'my heart' denotes the object which has been 'stirred' and 'the bird' denotes the entity which has done the 'stirring'. However, Cognitive Grammar is, as Langacker notes (1987:46–7) concerned with 'surface grammatical form', that is, it is solely concerned with the surface linguistic representations of an utterance. He asserts that 'Surface grammatical form does not conceal a 'truer', deeper level of grammatical organization; rather, it itself embodies the conventional means a language employs for the structuring and symbolization of semantic content' (Langacker 1987:46–7).

As such, in CG terms, this line in the sonnet is cognitively processed on the basis of its current linguistic construction: 'My heart in hiding/Stirred for a bird, – the achieve of; the mastery of the thing!'. This is because, in CG, the way in which an event is linguistically represented is symbolic of the way in which that event has been construed. What would be the patient in a prototypical (active) construction of this utterance ('my heart') is here linguistically represented as the *figure*, while the agent (the bird) is the *ground*. This accords with the role of the poet-speaker in the sonnet thus far: the poet has been grammatically profiled as agent throughout the octet and maintains that position through this figure/ground reversal. Yet, the poet-speaker is referred to metonymically in terms of his 'heart'; this results in a metaphorical 'shrinking' of the poetic persona which is further reinforced by the fact that his heart is barely present, is actually 'in hiding'. While the poet-speaker's participant role of experiencer is again semantically profiled, on this occasion however, passive 'seeing' is displaced by the active 'stirring' of his heart when faced with the 'achieve of; the mastery of the thing!'.

As Edgecombe notes, while 'the octave of the sonnet has proved much less difficult to construe', 'the ambiguities in the sestet … have elicited screeds of commentary and debate' (1994:357). This is partially because of the heavily ellipted nature of the syntax, with so many linguistic elements absent that it is difficult to recover meaning from what remains. But it is also the result of the ambiguities in the meaning of certain words. The first tercet commences with what is probably the most heavily scrutinised and debated sentence in the whole sonnet ('Brute beauty and valour and act, oh, air, pride, plume, here/Buckle!'). It pivots upon the single verb 'buckle', 'the word that has become a famous crux in the poem' (Olney 1993:83) and one which has generated 'a variety of interpretations' (Whiteford 2001:617). If interpreted to mean 'submit', it could be issued as an imperative (an interpretation reinforced by its status as an exclamatory or what is known in CG as an *expressive*), in which case it acts transitively, profiling all of the preceding nominals ('Brute beauty and valour and act, oh, air, pride, plume') as participants cumulatively acting as patient of the relation profiled. This is at odds with the grammatical profiling which pushes the nominals to the fore as co-subjects placed before the verb. The same meaning of the verb may also be used as indicative and intransitive, in the sense that all of the nominals profiled '*do* buckle' (see Easthope 1985:328). Other interpretations of 'buckle' include 'prepare for action', 'fasten together' and 'crumple up' (see Gardner & Mackenzie 1967) and all can similarly function as imperatives or indicatives. In any case, its use profiles a complex temporal relation as the various interpretations of 'buckle' are all dynamic. Despite the continuing lack of consensus surrounding the term's meaning, cognitively, however, there is little doubt that 'Buckle!' is the trajector in this linguistic expression, standing out, not only as an expressive pushed through enjambment to the start of a new line, but also on the basis of its ambiguity. The reader's inability to easily process the meaning of 'buckle' in its context ensures that it captures and maintains attention; effectively it stands out as a figure against the ground of both its immediate syntactical environment and of the sonnet as a whole. The entire meaning of the sonnet appears to hinge upon this word; indeed the *volta* or 'turn' which typically occurs at the end of the octet of a Petrarchan sonnet – usually signified by a note of 'contrariness' – is here centred upon this single word which marks the poet's epiphany. Essentially then, the precise nature of Hopkins' epiphany does not necessarily matter; the ambiguity ensures that each reader will experience their own version.

The sixth sentence makes up the second half of the tercet. The verb 'breaks' – used here in the sense of 'breaking out' – is embedded in another relative clause ('that breaks from thee then') which acts as subject complement. Two participants are relationally profiled: the 'fire' which acts as agent of the process of 'breaking out' and 'thee' – that is, Christ who is directly addressed at the end of the line through the vocative 'O my chevalier!' – is the object from which the fire has broken out. The fire is profiled by the verb use as linguistic trajector and its image dominates the remainder of the poem. The profiling of Christ as the patient is interesting here and conveys the intensely personal tone of the poem. The use of both the formal second person singular accusative pronoun ('thee') and the vocative suggests that Christ has been the addressee throughout.

The final tercet contains four relational profiles: 'make (shine)', 'fall', 'gall' and 'gash' ('No wonder of it: shéer plód makes plough down sillion/Shine, and blue-bleak embers, ah my dear,/Fall, gall themselves, and gash gold-vermilion'). 'Make shine' as a relational profile is transitive and profiles the 'maker' and the 'made': the 'maker' here is 'shéer plód' but the varying interpretations of the line hinge upon how one construes the second participant, that is, the 'made'. The suggestion is that the plodding activity of ploughing ('shéer plód') either makes the plough itself shine as it cuts through the soil and comes up clean, or, that it makes the 'sillion' – the thick slice of soil turned over by the plough – 'shine'. In either case, 'shéer plód' is the agent of the action, a semantic role which is similarly profiled grammatically. The structure of this first clause is paralleled by the second one which is joined to it by co-ordination. In the second clause 'blue-bleak embers' are grammatically profiled as the subject of three different relational profiles: 'falling', 'galling' and 'gashing' ('and blue-bleak embers, ah my dear,/Fall, gall themselves, and gash gold-vermilion'). 'Fall' is used intransitively, with the sole participant being that which falls, that is, the 'blue-bleak embers', which act as mover in this process. 'Gall' means to 'hurt'; it is transitive and used reflexively ('gall themselves') so the 'blue-bleak embers' are simultaneously profiled as both agent and patient of the process. The use of 'gash' is interesting as grammatically it could be acting as either a verb or a noun; however, I think *conceptually* a relational process is being profiled. The whole sense of the final tercet is both predicated upon and echoes that laid down in the preceding tercet: that appearances can be deceptive. Just as the plough can be 'made to shine' by the dirty soil or the dirty soil can be made to shine by the plough, so too the 'bleak' embers in a fireplace can break apart to reveal the beautiful 'golden-red' sparks within.

Overall, a pattern can be discerned in the ways in which processes are profiled throughout 'The Windhover'; this is predominantly achieved through verb use but the dynamism suggested by the three gerunds ('riding' 'striding', and 'gliding') also cognitively encodes the related processes. Of the eleven verbs which actually function as verbs in the sonnet, only the very first – 'caught' – profiles a cognitive process, with the poet acting as experiencer and the falcon as stimulus. As Taylor notes (2002:422), cognitive processes do not lend themselves as well to the energy-transfer metaphor encoded in action chains, which profile dynamic processes. Nevertheless, degrees of agency can be detected: for example, to 'see' an entity is rather less agentive that to 'watch' it. As such, the poet-speaker is profiled as a passive agent-experiencer; the poetic persona, though grammatically profiled throughout much of the octet, is nevertheless conceptually overshadowed by the dynamism accorded to the other participants in the relational processes profiled in the sonnet. In the octet, while the poet-speaker merely 'sees', the falcon 'rides', 'strides', 'glides', 'rings', 'sweeps' and 'rebuffs'. And, though the poet is not grammatically profiled in the sestet, the conversational register invoked by the use of 'thee' and the vocatives 'O my chevalier' and 'ah my dear' foreground his presence. Yet once again, the poetic persona is inactive while abstract nouns 'buckle' and even inanimate embers 'fall', 'gall' and 'gash' themselves. The whole octet may be said to effectively encode an action chain in which the falcon's dynamism results in a metaphysical transfer of energy from the bird to the poet whose heart 'stirs' for 'the achieve of; the mastery of the thing!'. Energy continues to be expended in the sestet: once again, it comes not from the poet but from the now profiled figure of Christ. The depiction in the octet of the falcon as 'riding' and being 'rung' activated a conceptual blending of the bird with Christ which is now fully realised through Christ being addressed in the sestet as a 'chevalier' – a blend which Downes recognises as a 'semantic tension between bird and knight' (1993: 128). The result is a pervasive image of the falcon-Christ *moving* across the *whole* sonnet. Langacker notes that '[m]otion is a highly influential factor' in determining which entity is likely to stand out against a ground: 'If it is possible to construe one entity in a scene as changing position vis-à-vis the rest (which have constant relationships to one another), that entity is normally chosen as the figure and interpreted as moving against the backdrop provided by the others' (Langacker 1987: 120).

Throughout the sonnet, then, the nature of the relational profiling coupled with the associated participant roles secure for the falcon-Christ the role of trajector profiled against landmark. This accords with the striking visual image profiled throughout the sonnet: that of the *figure* of the falcon in motion profiled against the back*ground* sky.

As this analysis's approach to the ambiguities in 'The Windhover' has demonstrated, there is nothing to be gained by being grammatically or semantically prescriptive with this poem. Fortunately, in emphasising the direct symbolic association between linguistic and semantic structure, Cognitive Grammar offers a means of investigating the origins of the sonnet's heavily 'imagistic' style without the necessity of first endeavouring to unravel its syntactical complexities, a feat as yet unaccomplished by critics. To seek singular definitive interpretations of 'The Windhover' is to ignore not only its polysemy but its personality. As Noel Lees notes, interpretations of this sonnet are 'obtained by inference, not directly from the words' (1950: 36); this 'inference' is often multi-faceted, with varying interpretations existing simultaneously. Gardner remarks upon Hopkins's ability to 'give to a living, developing language its peculiar tang, colour, range, and expressiveness' (2008: xiv). The purpose of this CG approach to 'The Windhover' has not been to generate new or alternate interpretations but to trace the cognitive pathways by which such linguistic 'tang, colour, range, and expressiveness' evokes existing interpretations. It is the poem's very ability to generate multiple meanings and activate manifold cognitive domains through its innovative linguistic expression that makes it such an interesting object of study. To pin the poem down is to capture the bird in full flight.

CHAPTER 9

Foregrounding the foregrounded

The literariness of Dylan Thomas's 'After the funeral'

Anne Päivärinta

Let me begin with a quotation that sums up the literariness of Dylan Thomas's 1936 poem 'After the funeral' in a rather polemical way and also sets the mood for a cognitive poetic interpretation of the text. In his book *How to Read a Poem*, Terry Eagleton argues the following about a line that occurs near the end of the poem, 'Her fist of a face died clenched on a round pain':

> [...] pains are plainly not round. The image only works if we subscribe to a version of the way the world is which we know to be false. As a result, the line is more grotesque than illuminating. Though it is meant to be abrasively physical, it is conceived in the head rather than the guts. It is the kind of conceit that might occur to you after a hard night on the town, one you might even scribble down excitedly at two o'clock in the morning; but to commit it to paper in the sober light of day and release it to the general public betrays an alarming lack of judgement. This is not to say that while reading literary works we do not sometimes provisionally accept assumptions or hypotheses which we would not readily sign up to in real life. This is known as the suspension of disbelief. But there are limits to our disbelief, just as there are to our faith. (Eagleton 2007: 30)

In Eagleton's opinion, the parameters of the 'real world' (that is, our schematic knowledge of it) are violated too bluntly by this particular line. Even though Eagleton bases his argument on the old and widely accepted idea of literature enabling us to perceive of things that are not in keeping with our experience of the world, he wants to draw a line for how defamiliarising literature in all its literariness can be. However, the dismissal of this line's communicative value is rather hasty in my view, though granted, the line is cryptic indeed – and I will return to it later on – as Eagleton does not try to place it in the context of the whole poem, or even approach it with any specific analytical tools at all. In fact, I would say it is telling that he labels the line a 'conceit' in a rather evaluative tone, bringing to mind a much older derogatory use of the term by Samuel Johnson when criticising the style of the metaphysical poets (see Johnson 1990), who, I might add, are among Thomas's most important influences when it comes to figurative language.

That said, of course it is fair to ask what kind of relevance this overwhelmingly 'poetic' poem might have to a reader seeking to appropriate its view of the world to their own. The poem deals with the death of Thomas's aunt Ann, but it evades the emotional core of what it means to lose a loved one, and to me it seems as if on purpose. We could then ask: is there a cognitive pay-off to be had at all – along the lines of Pinker's (2007) notion of a rhetorical pay-off? I shall argue that there is, and I begin from the idea that Cognitive Grammar as a comprehensive conceptual apparatus (Langacker 2008a: 4) will serve as a relevant aid in thinking about how exactly one should read this poem. Stockwell (2009a: 171) has emphasised the role of construal when applying Cognitive Grammar to literature – and, as constructed a text as 'After the funeral' is, its linguistic make-up is still the starting point for any experiential sense-making (on experientality, see Fludernik 1996). In fact, I hope to show that the poem's experiential core is not artificial at all, and that it can be reached precisely through analysing how the verbal complexities are constructed.

It is obvious that 'After the funeral' is a particularly literary text, but my argument is that we need to ask why the very resonant subject matter of the poem has been presented to us in this manner. To take this idea a bit further, I suggest that *figuration* becomes the figure in this poem *in order to* highlight the experiential nature of the subject matter at hand: the difficulty of coping with the death of a loved one. This could be summarised in the form of a cliché familiar to all of us, that sometimes there are no appropriate words – in my view, the poem thematises, rather paradoxically of course, the fact that it is impossible to compress human life into a memorial speech, and that words are of no real consolation in the depths of despair.

In order to dig into how exactly the detached treatment of grief in 'After the funeral' is built, I shall analyse the distribution of prominence in the poem on three different levels. First of all, I will discuss the *figure/ground* organisation of the poem in a very broad sense. In Langacker's Cognitive Grammar, this is a type of prominence profiling that is 'almost wholly subjective' as it is 'not inherent in a situation but a matter of construal' (Langacker 1991b: 308). In fact, if we understand figure/ground alignment simply as the process of conceiving of one situation against the background of another (Langacker 1999: 208), the constellation is inevitably rather metaphorical in nature. Moreover, it even resembles the process of metaphorical mapping in which the source domain serves as a background for structuring and understanding the target domain (see Langacker 2008a: 58). These 'structural' similarities have thematic significance as well in the analysis of 'After the funeral', as we shall later see.

Secondly, I shall look at prominence on the clause level, with reference to the concepts of *trajector* and *landmark*. The former is defined as a participant with primary focal prominence in an expression, whereas the latter carries a secondary degree of focal prominence (Langacker 2008a: 70). More specifically, I will sketch out trajector/landmark alignments that profile relationships as opposed to those that profile things, since the poem puts forth a striking on-going contrast between isolation and belonging on the one hand, and the static and the dynamic on the other. According to Langacker, 'things represent a "contractive" force, the capacity for pulling entities together', and relationships, by contrast, 'an "expansive" force, the capacity for "reaching out" so that an entity is not conceived in isolation, but as part of a configuration involving others as well' (2005: 125–6). Such relationships can be manifested instantaneously, as with prepositions (Langacker 2005: 127), but I am especially interested in their temporal manifestation by means of verbs, as the poem seems to portray a process of coming to terms with loss. As regards the role of conceptualisation, this typically involves *sequential scanning* as opposed to *summary scanning* (Langacker 2008a: 111; see also Langacker 1987: 244). I shall be referring to prototypical event conceptualisations in my analysis though they are not present in Thomas's poem as such; this is of course a typical way in which literature works in that it makes us aware of the way it communicates *against* the background of conventional language use.

The third type of prominence analysed, then, is literary specific traits influencing the two previously mentioned kinds, namely ways in which the rhetoric of the poem foregrounds isolated expressions. It should be taken into account that 'After the funeral' is not a typical elegy formally or content-wise: its use of metaphor and hyperbole in particular make the point that the aim is neither to idealise the deceased nor to present a romanticised image of what dealing with grief is like. This reversal of conventional generic traits is reflected in the shifts in prominence on the level of linguistic expression as well, I shall argue. Since all of these levels interact throughout the poem, they will be analysed side by side instead of in a hierarchical treatment. Therefore I will proceed in accordance with the linear progression of the poem: the focus is on the presentation of grieving as a process.

There are three particular stand-out places in the poem that relate to the speaker's emotional distance to the loss. They are clearly signalled with the explicit use of the pronoun 'I' in conjunction with predicates – the bulk of the poem consists of (metaphorical) nominal phrases that describe the memorial as well as the deceased. However, there are also subtle markers that anticipate the turning points, and I suggest that the analysis of this progression takes us right to the thematic core of the poem.

For a start, looking at the first twelve lines of the poem, the number of novel metaphors is striking:

> After the funeral, mule praises, brays,
> Windshake of sailshaped ears, muffle-toed tap
> Tap happily of one peg in the thick
> Grave's foot, blinds down the lids, the teeth in black,
> The spittled eyes, the salt ponds in the sleeves,
> Morning smack of the spade that wakes up sleep,
> Shakes a desolate boy who slits his throat
> In the dark of the coffin and sheds dry leaves,
> That breaks one bone to light with a judgment clout'
> After the feast of tear-stuffed time and thistles
> In a room with a stuffed fox and a stale fern,
> I stand, for this memorial's sake, alone [...]   (Thomas 2000: 87)

What is more, the metaphors form a flow that seems to lack coherent sentence structure. Now I shall not go into any specifics of defining metaphor as a linguistic unit in contrast to the idea of metaphor as a conceptual entity (see Langacker 2008a: 51), but it is curious how we can trace many basic metaphors in the poem while their delivery is very defamiliarising indeed. I will refer to a few basic metaphors shortly. The main thing to note here, though, is that it is difficult to map out trajector/landmark alignments due to the way the setting is presented, and since the opening of a text is supposed to get us appropriated into the text world, I would say this results in an awareness that the poem resists such patterns of easy immersion. This is something a reader wanting to bear with the poem will take with them when reading on.

How is the resistance structured, then, and how does it link to the portrayal of grief? First of all, a key thing to note is the rather macabre nature of the metaphors. The mourners are compared to mules to begin with, and the setting is also personified in a less than flattering manner, for example in the punning metaphor 'blinds down the lids'. The mocking tone set by 'mule praises' and continued in expressions like 'teeth in black' suggests the people present are acting according to certain behavioural patterns that the speaker disapproves of. All this, of course, is rather alienating for the reader: no sympathetic identification is evoked. From a grammatical point of view, the succession of nominal phrases, all implied to be set in the past, only comes to its completion in the final line excerpted above, but before that there is a noteworthy point that slows down the reading. This is where the hyperbolic depiction of the situation intensifies: the sound of a 'morning smack of the spade' makes a 'desolate boy' snap out of his despair and into a drastic act of sadness, the metaphorical slitting of his throat in 'the dark of the coffin'.

Now trying to make sense of what is going on here, it seems especially significant that the sentence structure of these first twelve lines is not easily abstracted. If one does not read very carefully, the seventh line, '[s]hakes a desolate boy', might seem like a finite construction; however the comma at the end of the previous line refutes this and puts this 'event' in its place as an apposition: 'Morning smack of the spade that wakes up sleep, [that] Shakes a desolate boy [...].' The potential of 'misreading' is so prominent here that I would argue it makes the reader process the 'event' as an active element even though it is an abstract post-modifying construction set in the past, 'After the funeral, [...] [after the] Morning smack of the spade [...].' Of course the mode of speaking makes it evident that the event described is metaphorical as well, but there is more to it than that: in my view, the structural complexity of the 'event' captures what is at stake in the situation more broadly speaking. Let us take a look at it in more detail.

Examining the lines as an event reveals an interesting dynamics of topicality. The *agent* here, the sound of the spade 'that wakes up sleep', is an abstract, metaphorical entity, while the human in the equation, the 'desolate boy', is a *patient*. The former, then, does not rank high in Langacker's (1991b: 307) *empathy hierarchy*, a scale that reflects a conceptualiser's egocentric evaluation of the different kinds of entities known to inhabit the world:

speaker > hearer > human > animal > physical object > abstract entity

Furthermore, the patient is indefinite, though in the broader context of the poem it would be relevant to ask whether this is the speaker seen from outside. All this contributes to a sneaking sense of detachment: it is as if the person in question is at the mercy of a greater 'force', an entity that is rather obscure at this point.

In addition, the relationship between the participants is interesting from the point of view of causation as well. In terms of the operation of conceptual integration in contrast to dissociation, that is establishing the identity of entities as being distinct or unified (see Langacker 2008a: 527–8), grammatically speaking there is partial conceptual overlap here, as illustrated by the rough sketch in *Figure 6.1*.

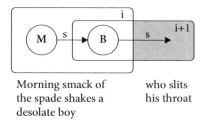

Figure 6.1. Apparent causation in 'After the funeral'

The shading in the window marks new content that was not covered in the previous window. However the later event is in no obvious sense a semantic follow-up of the first, apart from them both sharing the more or less implied domain of death – something that would not show in an illustration of this kind, which, of course, is metaphorical in itself.

A likely objection to this kind of conceptual mapping would be that there is little point in talking about causation with metaphorical constellations like this one: the events evoked are not 'concrete' physical events taking place (or events that have taken place) in the fictional world of the poem. However, a sense of directional dynamicity is nevertheless present and seems to require further elaboration. Langacker (2010:166) makes a distinction between *effective* and *epistemic causation*: the former involves physical activity and actual events, while the latter involves mental activity, or knowledge of events. Although it is difficult to describe the particular mental activity going on in these lines in any detail, clearly a sense of artificial dynamism is built here: a *fictive motion* (Langacker 2008a:529) that underlines its own fictive nature. On the basis of our cognition being embodied (Langacker 2008a:58; Fauconnier & Turner 2002), a lot of metaphorical expressions need not be 'isolated' as artificial in terms of their conceptualisation, even if their linguistic expression is defamiliarising enough. As Langacker points out, even though metaphorical expressions present us with things that do not exist in reality, we are still perfectly able to think and talk about them, and what is more, this kind of processing is not restricted to metaphors: 'Even for the kinds of entities that do exist, what we refer to linguistically is often a *virtual* (or *fictive*) instance, i.e. an imaginary instance "conjured up" for some purpose' (Langacker 2008a:36, original emphasis). Now, if we are dealing with some kind of epistemic causation that is expressed in the guise of novel metaphor, in other words an expression that 'induces the construction of mental spaces representing a belief and an attitude' (Langacker 2008a:41), why such an elaborate guise?

It is obvious that in this case the reader will set up mental spaces *only* as 'imagined potential occurrences' (Langacker 2008a:41), but the kind of prominence these imaginative potentials gain seems important as well. So far I have argued that aligning the boy as the patient in the constellation creates a sense of detachment, and that this sense of detachment is further strengthened by the character's indefiniteness in contrast with the reading that he is most likely the lyric 'I' himself, seen from outside. To take this idea further, I suggest that the dynamics created by the projection of a metaphorical event give rise to the subjective point of view of the speaker, a point of view the reader will ultimately try to identify with. Thus the lines could be characterised as a stylised instance of epistemic causation, that is, a state of mind brought on by a particular situation. Langacker writes: 'Through subjectification, the dynamicity inherent in the apprehension of events is transferred to the conception of static scenes' (2008a: 529). We are at the core of the numerous arguments that have labelled Thomas's poetry as overly abstract, Eagleton being just one example of such a critic: metaphor is used here to create a very artificial kind of dynamicity in order to make a point, but it is easy to see how it can come across as merely complicating the situation for the sake of artistic self-indulgence.

However as unconventional as the constellation is, it could still be called an instantiation of the basic *Event Structure Metaphor* in which things like states or processes are expressed metaphorically in terms of space, motion, and force (see Lakoff 1993). It has become evident that nothing is *actually* happening here: the hypocritical speeches and acts of mourning have taken place earlier. Instead something abstract is given agency, and this entity is supposedly causing things to happen. 'The morning smack of the spade' is a metonymical reference to digging a grave, which means that an act relating to death – something that can be said to represent the finality of death in people's conceptualisations – brings about metaphorical death: the boy slitting his throat 'in the dark of the coffin'. However, this is communicated through an ambiguous punning metaphor, since morning as the metaphorical dawning of life is also a homonym of 'mourning', as in grieving. The same kind of ambivalence is present in the post-modifying clause 'that wakes up sleep': the sound that buries a loved one *reverses* death by simultaneously being something that possesses the power of waking up a person, insofar as sleep can be read as referring to the basic DEATH IS SLEEP metaphor. What we have here, then, are two contrasting consequences of realising the finality of a loved one's death: waking up to the reality of someone being gone, and intense grief as a result, but also to the reality of life's finiteness and thus to the value of one's own life (a sort of 'wake up call').

This ambivalence, combined with the fact that such banal metaphors for life and death are used in the first place, suggests that the mourners are in a way trapped in hyperbole, imprisoned by their own personal dramas. The use of the PEOPLE ARE PLANTS metaphor adds to this: the boy can only shed 'dry leaves' in that his tears are fake as well. That said, the boy is still compared to a living thing as opposed to a machine for instance, thus not eradicating the naturalness of such feelings and such a situation. In fact, I would say this construction in all its complexity is something that encourages identification from the reader's part, provided one does not get frustrated with the complexity of expression, of course: mixed feelings and the inability to put things into a larger context when experiencing a personal crisis are very human tendencies indeed.

Turning to the first instance of the pronounced 'I' now, the metaphorical nominal phrases that form the opening of the poem in a way postpone and obscure the actual present of the poem: only in line 12 do we fully realise that this is simply the speaker alone in Ann's presence after the funeral. That is, in terms of sentence structure, the completion of the very beginning comes now: 'After the funeral [...] I stand, alone'. Although I argued earlier that there is metaphorical dynamicity before this, it is not until now that we encounter a finite verb construction. Furthermore, the line is also very simple in expression compared to the earlier flow of detailed metaphorical description. This is a clear reversal of background and foreground: something clearly outlined, (presumably) non-figurative and non-static emerges almost as a relief to a reader trying make sense of the poem's situational details.

The speaker is of course elevated above the circumstances described earlier as a result of this reversal. In addition, the fact that 'alone' gains emphasis due to being placed at the end of the line (even though the sentence goes on) marks a clear contrast to the observations made about the other mourners, the speaker possibly being the desolate boy seen as if from outside. Indeed the tone of speaking changes overall and from now on the others and the very outward way of looking at the situation is left behind: the poem focuses on the speaker's conception of the deceased instead. In short, a shift from an external portrayal of experiential material to inner experience takes place here. This shift is further manifested the second time the speaker says 'I': he later actively claims his position as 'Ann's bard'.

However, the poem does not quite adopt an elegiac mode of speaking at this point still. Ann is described as 'humped' and her body 'broken', hardly an idealised portrayal of someone dear:

> [...]
> I stand, for this memorial's sake, alone
> In the snivelling hours with dead, humped Ann
> Whose hooded, fountain heart once fell in puddles
> Round the parched worlds of Wales and drowned each sun
> (Though this for her is a monstrous image blindly
> Magnified out of praise; her death was a still drop;
> She would not have me sinking in the holy
> Flood of her heart's fame; she would lie dumb and deep
> And need no druid of her broken body).   (Thomas 2000:87)

In fact, it could be argued that the conventional idea of an elegy bringing the person lost close to the speaker once more is *literalised* here: realistic, physical descriptions of the deceased bring in the human scale rather concretely (see again Langacker's empathy hierarchy above). Furthermore, since the speaker's reference to himself as the 'druid of her broken body' is negated locally but of course entertained in the very existence of the poem, the artificiality of the idealising traditions of elegy is emphasised.

More specifically, these physical expressions form both a link and a contrast to the earlier part: while the mourners had 'blinds down their lids', it is only Ann's physical stature that is described as impaired, not her perception of the world. In fact, the basic human body as a container metaphor is used in this contrasting way as well. The mourners are stuffing themselves with food ('the feast of tear-stuffed time'), and the desolate boy is stuck inside a coffin, whereas Ann's heart – the locus of emotions according to a conventional metaphor – is overflowing in an almost holy-sounding way, communicating that she was a very loving person. The former is a static state of affairs, whereas the latter involves (metaphorical) motion. The contrast between such inward and outward profiles is summarised in *Figure 6.2*:

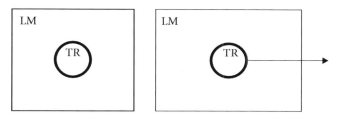

Figure 6.2. BODY IS A CONTAINER profiling in 'After the funeral'

In my reading, this links to the way the poem comments on conventional modes of remembrance: while it is easy and very human to get trapped in banal and selfish modes of mourning, in the end it is the actual shape and doings of a person that is relevant, not the magnified praises.

The mentioned contrasting exploitations of the human body as a container schema also link to the earlier reversal of foreground and background with the first occurrence of the lyric 'I'. Moreover, this kind of building on the difference in the conceptualisation of 'inside' and 'outside' occurs throughout the poem. To simplify, the contrasting trajector/landmark alignments in these cases create a similar sense of contradictory 'overlapping' as the sound of the spade waking up sleep. The two sides of the same coin are being introverted and self-centred when struck by sorrow on the one hand, and struggling to really appreciate the relationship one had with the person that is being so acutely missed on the other. More broadly speaking, the metaphors in this poem seem to be interconnected *metonymically*, in that they form a network based on part/whole relationships. As has already been implied, a vast majority of the metaphors are physically grounded, building on the human body as a container schema, and after the prominence of metaphors of this kind has been established, they become a background for a metonymical narrowing down of embodiment, focusing on significant detail. This pattern is also the main means of offering a sense of consolation for the reader.

Consequently, at this point I shall return to the line Eagleton was so critical of, since hands become a clearly defined figure towards the end of the poem, and they feature implicitly in the criticised line. The line occurs near the end of the poem:

> I know her scrubbed and sour humble hands
> Lie with religion in their cramp, her threadbare
> Whisper in a damp word, her wits drilled hollow,
> Her fist of a face died clenched on a round pain;
> And sculptured Ann is seventy years of stone.   (Thomas 2000: 88)

To go back to the specific objections Eagleton makes, the claim that pains cannot be round is a bit odd to begin with: pains can certainly be the opposite of round, sharp, and therefore also dull. Thus the first part of the line exemplifies one of the basic patterns of metaphor creation mentioned by Lakoff and Turner (1989), negation: the speaker makes the point that the pain in question *cannot* be characterised as sharp or strong. In order to decipher the whole line, we need to look at the details of how hands gain prominence in the first place and end up in a clenched fist in this line. The previous lines describe Ann's hands as 'sour', 'humble' and 'cramped' due to religion. Transferring the image of hands being cramped as a result of praying, and humble and sour possibly due to hard labour as well as due to Christian humility, onto the 'fist of a face' that is 'clenched on a round pain' combines multiple senses of being 'cramped': a life of working hard and simply accepting one's share. This then suggests that only a round pain is left, instead of something stronger that will leave a mark; 'her wits dried hollow' hints at a similar insignificance in that there are no thoughts of one's own to share. Ann's life is then characterised by a not-so-ideal realisation of the ideal of *ora et labora*, but this is suggested in a sympathetic rather than an evaluative tone. Noteworthy is also the framing of this whole succession: the speaker *knows* this to be true, in other words he wants to emphasise the experiential basis for his argument. Significantly, this is one of the places where the explicit use of 'I' draws the reader's attention.

With all of this in mind it is hard to agree with Eagleton that the line fails to create an emotional response in a reader. Surely for this reading to emerge some interpretive efforts need to be put in, but in my view the cognitive pay-off is strengthened by the sense of accomplishment created by being able to construe metaphorical networks of this kind. The network of metaphors also provides the potential for a kind of catharsis, as was already suggested. This is because hands form a link between Ann and the speaker, and the embodiment in the poem evolves once more as a result. At the same time, the meta-level of the poem being aware of its own function as an elegy becomes more explicit. The speaker's hands are made of marble, which refers back to 'sculptured Ann' being 'seventy years of stone', but this is also aligned with the poem's own communicative efforts:

> These cloud-sopped, marble hands, this monumental
> Argument of the hewn voice, gesture and psalm
> Storm me forever over her grave until
> The stuffed lung of the fox twitch and cry Love
> And the strutting fern lay seeds on the black sill.   (Thomas 2000:88)

Writing a poem in someone's honour is then compared to setting something in stone, a concrete and permanent reminder of that person's life. While Ann worked with her hands, resulting in the cramp analysed above, the speaker's craft is in his words, illustrated in the subtle linkage of hands, words, and stone. In addition, the speaker's singing in Ann's praise – though the praise is unconventional – is described as a natural phenomenon that is not momentary but ongoing ('storm me forever over her grave'). It is significant that here the poem is temporally speaking reaching into the future, a clear marker of progression in contrast to the beginning and middle of the poem. In addition, the poem gains a rather biblical tone at the end, also undermining death's dominion, to quote another poem by Thomas.

In summary I would say that the progression in the treatment of embodied metaphors as well as of the traditional traits for elegy – or expectations for such – serves to thematise the inevitable distance between an experience and its expression in words. The distance will always be negotiated in linguistic expression in one way or another. This is something we as humans, as conceptualising beings, have to live with, though a poet might do slightly better coping verbally.

CHAPTER 10

Conceptual proximity and the experience of war in Siegfried Sassoon's 'A Working Party'

Marcello Giovanelli

1. Introduction

Twenty-six years after the end of the First World War, Siegfried Sassoon published the final book in his second autobiographical trilogy. Like its predecessors *The Old Century and Seven More Years* and *The Weald of Youth*, *Siegfried's Journey* was a more reflective account of Sassoon's life and poetry, with none of the name changes and other elements of the fictional autobiography genre that had marked the earlier George Sherston trilogy. On its opening page, Sassoon remembering his arrival as a soldier in France wrote:

> At the front I had managed to keep my mind alive under difficulties, and had done some writing when we were away from the line. But it wasn't easy to be a poet and a platoon commander at the same time, and I was overflowing with stored-up impressions and emotional reactions to the extraordinary things I had observed and undergone. (Sassoon 1946: 1)

In these lines, Sassoon reflects on what for him had been key issues regarding his role as both a soldier and a poet in the early days of the war. He emphasises the acts of observing and experiencing, and questions the relationship of poetic composition to the trauma of extreme experience. Sassoon's concern is not just with the reality of trying to write under such conditions, but with how the poet-soldier can capture these observations and experiences into a form that faithfully preserves their intensity and immediacy for future readers. In essence then, Sassoon is concerned with how the poet's responses to his experiences can be shaped into a form where the feeling of proximity to conceptual content remains central. In this chapter, I use one of Sassoon's early war poems, 'A Working Party' to account for this concern. The poem is reproduced in full below.

A Working Party
Three hours ago he blundered up the trench,
Sliding and poising, groping with his boots;
Sometimes he tripped and lurched against the walls
With hands that pawed the sodden bags of chalk.
He couldn't see the man who walked in front;   5
Only he heard the drum and rattle of feet
Stepping along barred trench boards, often splashing
Wretchedly where the sludge was ankle-deep.

Voices would grunt 'Keep to your right—make way!'
When squeezing past some men from the front-line: 10
White faces peered, puffing a point of red;
Candles and braziers glinted through the chinks
And curtain-flaps of dug-outs; then the gloom
Swallowed his sense of sight; he stooped and swore
Because a sagging wire had caught his neck.   15

A flare went up; the shining whiteness spread
And flickered upward, showing nimble rats
And mounds of glimmering sand-bags, bleached with rain;
Then the slow silver moment died in dark.
The wind came posting by with chilly gusts   20
And buffeting at corners, piping thin.
And dreary through the crannies; rifle-shots
Would split and crack and sing along the night,
And shells came calmly through the drizzling air
To burst with hollow bang below the hill.   25

Three hours ago he stumbled up the trench;
Now he will never walk that road again:
He must be carried back, a jolting lump
Beyond all need of tenderness and care.
He was a young man with a meagre wife   30
And two small children in a Midland town;
He showed their photographs to all his mates,
And they considered him a decent chap
Who did his work and hadn't much to say,
And always laughed at other people's jokes   35
Because he hadn't any of his own.

That night when he was busy at his job
Of piling bags along the parapet,
He thought how slow time went, stamping his feet

And blowing on his fingers, pinched with cold.   40
He thought of getting back by half-past twelve,
And tot of rum to send him warm to sleep
In draughty dug-out frowsty with the fumes
Of coke, and full of snoring weary men.

He pushed another bag along the top,   45
Craning his body outward; then a flare
Gave one white glimpse of No Man's Land and wire;
And as he dropped his head the instant split
His startled life with lead, and all went out.

2.   'A Working Party' and the importance of 1916

'A Working Party' is an important poem in the development of Sassoon's war verse. As Campbell (1999) notes, although the poem was not Sassoon's first to focus on the trenches themselves, it did draw extensively on the impact of the trenches on soldiers' lives in a way that his other writing pre-1916 had not done. The poem details the experience of a single soldier who is a member of a working party, a group of men sent out above ground either to repair parts of a trench that had been damaged by shells, or to consolidate reinforcements preventing enemy penetration. This work was an integral part of ensuring that the trenches remained operational (see Fussell 1975: 47); Sassoon himself writes extensively of being part of these in numerous diary entries (see for example Sassoon 1983: 46, 51, 67, 73).

Sassoon wrote 'A Working Party' in March 1916, four months after he had arrived as an officer on the front line. In addition to the death of his brother Hamo at Gallipolli in 1915, he suffered a further personal loss when his close friend David Thomas was killed in March 1916. The impact of these events on Sassoon place the early months of 1916 as an important period in the context of his attitude towards the war. It is during this time that Sassoon's verse moves from early patriotism and support to a more precise and keenly felt understanding of the war's implications and its effect on the common man. 1916 also marks the beginning of a remarkable eighteen months in which Sassoon was involved in the Mametz Wood offensive, became a patient at Craiglockhart Hospital, and had his statement against the continuation of war both read out in the House of Commons and published in *The Times*. The poems in Sassoon's first non-privately published collection *The Old Huntsman and Other Poems*, published in 1917, were largely written in 1916 and were fuelled by his experiences in these turbulent months.

In his study of how soldiers' experiences in the trenches impacted on writing during and about the First World War, Das (2005: 35) argues that in such dark and claustrophobic spaces, touch replaced vision as the dominant sensory mode, as soldiers were subjected to a life in the trenches that was primarily an engagement with mud. Das suggests that first hand accounts and experiences of what would have been a distinctly foreign landscape provided the motivation for a poetic revolution for poets to distance themselves from early Georgian war poetry with its emphases on chivalric heroism and the virtue of sacrifice for a noble cause. Instead they turned to a style of writing that concentrated on the physicality of the trench, the interaction of human form within confined spaces, and a sharp focus on the male body in the form of 'muddy narratives'. So called 'trench poetry' had an intensity of experience and an inherent focus on the human body, allowing the reader privileged access and proximity to the 'immensity and chaos' (Das 2005: 37) of the muddy trench, and relaying in all its horror the reality of the common soldier's encounters on the battlefield (Silkin 1979: 51).

Caesar (1993) argues that this desire to write poetry that remained as close as possible to trench experiences manifested itself in a relentless focus on the working class male that preoccupied Sassoon throughout his 1916 poems. In 'The Redeemer', which is regarded as his first trench poem and was written in November 1915 shortly after he arrived at the front line, an anonymous soldier offers his body, Christ-like, as a sacrifice for his country. 'A Working Party' fits neatly into a group of poems that follows and explores the individual male body's interaction with his physical environment. It was written very shortly following David Thomas's death, and as Dollar (2004) has argued is a prime example of Sassoon's reconfiguration of the heroic, glorious battlefield into a banal, mundane landscape that is imbued with horror and tragedy. Hugh Moore (1969) suggests that the experiences that influenced the poem must be significant in the context of Sassoon's attitude towards the war and his increasing pity for the exploitation of the many by the privileged few. Read as a poem that is exclusively centred on one individual and the impact felt by his death, 'A Working Party' can also be viewed as the beginning of a journey that marks Sassoon's own pre-occupations with the haunting resonance of closely observed trauma, worked out for example in 'Sick Leave' and the nightmare experience in *Memoirs of an Infantry Officer* (Sassoon 2000: 179–80).

Das (2007: 77) suggests that trench poetry above all used the destruction of the individual human body to challenge previous literary representations of war as noble and heroic, arguing that in the writing of trench verse 'poetry is refashioned as missives from the trenches'. In other words, such poetry is the poetry of *close experience* and *close observation*. It is this definition I shall use as the basis for my following analysis of the poem using Cognitive Grammar.

3. The distribution of -ing forms

> Three hours ago he blundered up the trench,
> Sliding and poising, groping with his boots   (lines 1–2)

'A Working Party' is split into three verse paragraphs. In the first, the opening lines set up the temporal and spatial parameters within which the narrative action takes place. In this instance, the temporal adverbial 'three hours ago' acts to set up a *viewing frame* (Langacker 1995: 196) as the setting within which the profiled relationship between the participants, the soldier and the trench is situated. Initially the soldier, anonymous and referred to simply through the use of the third person pronoun 'he', has his movement conceptualised and tracked as he makes his way in darkness along the walls of the trench.

One immediate observation in these opening lines is a clustered pattern of three post-modifying participle clauses in line 2 in contrast to the finite verb form 'blundered' that is used to describe the first action event of the poem. A distinction can be made between finite and non-finite forms on the basis of the *mental scanning*. *Sequential scanning* (Langacker 2008a: 111) involves a conceptualiser following an event state by state as it occurs through conceived time, so that these states are viewed as unfolding in a sequence as part of an ongoing and dynamic process. In this respect, sequential scanning operates in the same way as a motion picture does, simulating real-time viewing. In Cognitive Grammar, finite verb forms such as the past tense 'blundered' are *processes* that both construe an event as extending temporally, and offer mental accessibility through conceptualising events as though they are occurring in real-time.

Alternatively, events can be construed and mentally accessed through *summary scanning* (Langacker 2008a: 83). Here, successive stages of an event are accumulated holistically and projected into a single 'snapshot' in a manner that is analogous to the viewing of a still photograph (Langacker 2008a: 109). In contrast to finite forms, non-finite infinitives and participle -ed and -ing forms suspend sequential scanning and instead impose a summary view on the verb process. So, in the opening lines of the poem, 'sliding', 'poising', and 'groping' despite all having the same conceptual content as their finite-form counterparts, are construed holistically in single gestalt-form rather than a successive sequence of states occurring through time.

It is significant that this type of scanning and mental access afforded to the reader is given prominence in the opening lines of the poem. In the absence of the visual (the poem's events take place at night and the opening verse paragraph's action takes place exclusively in darkness), the emphasis is very much on what can be felt and heard, and it is these sensory modes that construct the world of the trench for the reader, in the same way as the poem represents the experience of the trench for the soldiers. These lines both emphasise physical interaction and reflect chaotic body movements that oppose a conventionally balanced and vertically oriented notion of a body. They are responsible for the construction of what Rodaway (1994: 41) terms a 'haptic geography', the establishing both of a sense of place, and of an individual's relationship within that place through the 'tactile receptivity of the body'.

As well as suspending sequential scanning and imposing a summary view on conceptual content, -ing participle forms also crucially alter the vantage point from which the profiled content is viewed. In the instance of 'sliding', 'poising', and 'groping', the shift from sequential to summary scanning imposes a limited *immediate scope* (Langacker 2008a: 63), which places a constraint on the range of attention and observation that can be possibly afforded to the verb process. As Langacker explains: 'Since the limited scope is the 'onstage' region, the locus of the viewing attention, those portions of the processual base that fall outside its confines are excluded from the profile' (Langacker 2008a: 120).

Consequently, the start and end points of the summarily scanned event are not present, and instead remain part of the unfocused and unavailable off-stage *maximum scope*. Since an -ing participle excludes the start and end points of the verb process, indicating simply that the event itself has begun, the form acts as a type of self-limiting 'zoom in' (Langacker 2008a: 65). In *Figure 7.1*, the on-stage immediate scope (IS) that is foregrounded through the use of such a form is shaded, with its excluded points X and Y remaining in the expression's maximal scope (MS).

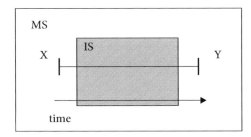

Figure 7.1. Maximal and immediate scope in -ing forms (adapted from Langacker 1990: 92)

Using Langacker's distinction, Verspoor (1996: 438) argues that -ing forms necessarily construe an event as being 'very close by'. Here, as well as suspending the verb's sequential scanning, the -ing form becomes meaningful in its own right as a point of access for viewing the semantic content denoted by the verb. The use of the -ing form is a kind of syntactic iconicity that reflects a sense of proximity; the effect on conceptualisation is to promote the sense of taking an 'internal perspective' on the conceptual content and view those actions as up close. In the context of Sassoon's concerns about his integrated roles of soldier and poet, and his remit to present the realities of war in striking and emotional intensity, the poem's grammar presents the observed as the proximal; the suspension of sequential scanning and the atemporality afforded by the participial clause patterning offer the reader, as conceptualiser, the opportunity to pause and afford attention to the soldier's actions. In simple terms, it can be viewed as not just being close to an event but simulating the experience of that event.

However, there is variation in the type of mental scanning across the verse paragraph as a whole. Although the chaotic and dehumanised actions remain, the suspension of sequential scanning is discontinued from lines 3–7, at which point two further participle forms 'stepping' and 'splashing' mark a return to summarily accessed content. Since these again allow access through imposing an internal perspective, these too are viewed as 'close by' in contrast to the finite forms that precede them. In addition, the description of the trench is made to appear familiar rather than distant, with the emphasis on creating a landscape that relies on what appears to be easily understood. The sustained use of the definite article 'the' in the noun phrases 'the trench', 'the walls', 'the sodden bags of chalk', 'the drum and rattle', and 'the sludge' suggests that the poem's speaker places all of these as readily accessible, since definite referencing is generally used when specific referents are understood by the reader. Here again, this promotes a kind of conceptual proximity.

This shift in scanning is also apparent at the end of the poem. In verse paragraph four, 'piling', 'stamping' and 'blowing', temporarily suspend sequential scanning whilst the sole participial clause in the final verse paragraph affords attention to the action of craning itself, and positions the conceptualiser-reader as occupying an internal perspective. Similarly, the iconicity inherent in this verb form is in imitation of a conception of reality. Read in conjunction with this textual detail, the overall effect of these shifts in the type of scanning that is undertaken would appear to be analogous to the experience of moving from a broader to a more finely tuned detail; the poem's grammar offers an invitation to move from following action events at distance to observing them at close hand. Viewed as a matter of deliberate poetic choice, these shifts in scanning mirror the process of the closely observing eye that attends momentarily to discrete aspects of movement in the immediate landscape, and registers those movements as both salient and as conceptually close. In fact, they reflect the process of observation itself and distillation of that observation into poetic form that becomes available for processing by readers. This, of course, is the consequence of a series of authorial decisions. As Langacker (2008a: 111–12) explains, it is not the case that sequential and summary scanning are mutually exclusive but rather offer different ways of conceptualising the same event; the mode chosen for that conceptualisation will foreground either the intention to replicate the real-time viewing of an event or impose a summative print where the conceptualiser – here poet, speaker and reader – construes a highly schematised version of the event in progress. Or rather, the way in which the contents of the trench in this poem are shown is motivated by how and what the poet wants us to see.

4.   The third person pronoun 'he'

The second way in which I suggest that the poem's grammar evokes a sense of closeness is in the exclusive use of the third person pronoun 'he'. Pronouns can be used to refer to a potentially opened-ended number of candidates, with only some obvious limitations, such as those that are specific to person and gender. So, for example, the third person pronoun 'he' can have as its referent any individual male human entity. The type of open-endedness that is a feature of pronouns is in contrast to a definite article + lexical noun construction, which allows either the selection of a unique referent or, at the very least, a narrowing down of potential candidacy. In the case of third person pronouns, it is usually the surrounding extra-linguistic detail that provides the context for enabling the singling-out of the referent. As Langacker explains: 'as an inherent aspect of its meaning, a third person pronoun presupposes that a referent can be identified with a *particular entity* sufficiently salient in the linguistic or extralinguistic context to offer itself as the *only obvious candidate*' (Langacker 2007b: 177, added emphasis).

However, there is no 'particular entity' or 'obvious candidate' here. Despite some added descriptive detail in the second verse paragraph, the poem identifies its central protagonist at a very generalised level, although even here we get minimal modification and the use of the indefinite 'a young man' rather than 'the young man'. At one level, and with such a large number of potential candidates as the referent of 'he', this might mean reading the poem schematically. In this instance, there is the possibility that any of the candidates available as potential referents might be understood as being identified, and consequently the use of the pronoun refers to what Langacker (2009: 115) terms a *generalized participant*. This is the type of position that is emphasised in those readings where the soldier is viewed as the archetypal 'everyman' that Sassoon wanted to portray as being affected by the war (see for example Moeyes 1997). However, there is an alternative way of explaining a motivating factor for the use of the third person pronoun in the poem over an alternative lexical choice, and for this we can turn to *accessibility theory* (Ariel 1990). Accessibility theory offers a way of looking at speakers' contextual motivation for referencing by proposing that a speaker will use one of a number of *markers of accessibility* to allow for the retrieval of a mental representation, depending on its potential for identification in a given context.

At one extreme, the use of a proper noun with some modifying description such as 'Siegfried Sassoon, the war poet' has *maximum specificity* (there is – as far as I know – only one potential referent), but marks *low accessibility*. In this case, it would be assumed that the discourse context, either linguistic, extra-linguistic or both, would fail to provide straightforward access through any other choice of marker and that this level of specificity would be required. This might be the case if, say, there were several 'siegfried sassoons' that were known, which would mean that greater specificity would be required to nominate the specific entity as the referent. Alternatively, markers such as 'Siegfried Sassoon', 'Sassoon', 'that soldier who fought in the First World War', and 'that soldier' decrease in specificity but indicate increasing accessibility. A pronoun such as 'he' represents the least specificity but the greatest accessibility of all since its use assumes that a reader/listener is able to identify its referent easily. In the case of 'A Working Party', the sustained use of the third person pronoun as the least specific marker therefore implies high accessibility; the pronoun is used not to anonymise or provide a universal archetype but because there is a clear and easily accessible mental representation of that entity. In these terms, 'he' refers to an individual of whom we sense that we are *aware*.

This notion of awareness can be explained using Langacker's stage model (Langacker 2008a: 356). The use of a third person pronoun implies conceptual proximity by placing in the on-stage region a conception of a person who is also clearly known to the off-stage discourse participants and in this instance is also off-stage. The use of the third person pronoun thus results in a kind of *split referent* (van Hoek 2003: 174), which is shown in *Figure 7.2*. As van Hoek explains: 'because a third person pronoun indicates that the person is part of the off-stage region, part of the intimate conceptual world shared between the speaker and addressee, it indicates *a subtle sense of closeness or intimacy*' (van Hoek 2003: 175 added emphasis).

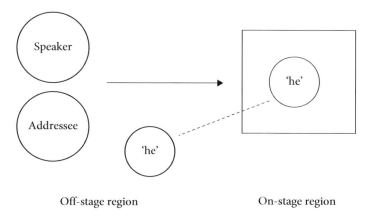

Off-stage region   On-stage region

Figure 7.2. The third person pronoun 'he' and the split referent

Read in this way, the use of the third person indicates a particular kind of proximity since the soldier, being configured as part of the same off stage region as the speaker and addressee, is positioned as either physically or mentally close. Thinking about degrees of awareness in this way might of course also legislate for how readers identify the referent in this poem and similarly stylised war poems based on their own background knowledge, and in the context of the loss of friends or relatives during either the First World War or other conflicts (see Grayson 2010: 84). Of equal interest here is the fact that this type of referencing appears to be an important feature of Sassoon's style across his other war poems composed during or after 1916. A review of his *Collected Poems* shows that of the fifteen poems in the 'war poems 1915–1917' section of his 1917 collection *The Old Huntsman and Other Poems* that explicitly describe the trench-life of a soldier, twelve rely solely on the use of 'he', with no signalling of a clear referent through an alternative accessibility marker. There is a similar pattern in Sassoon's more famous collection *Counter Attack and Other Poems* (1918), where nine out of thirteen such poems exclusively use the high accessibility marker 'he'. Indeed, Moeyes (1997: 38–9) distinguishes 'A Working Party' and other poems from 1916 onwards from the 'first phase of his war poetry' on the basis that the use of first person pronouns is replaced by the poet adopting an alternative vantage point from which the individual soldier, identified simply through 'he', is now the centre of focused attention.

5.   Reference point relationships and action chains

In this final section, I draw on Cognitive Grammar's notion of *reference point relationships* (Langacker 2008a: 83, 504), another type of mental scanning, to consider how the tight textual cohesiveness around the represented soldier and environment of the poem is a marker of conceptual proximity.

In Cognitive Grammar, reference point relationships form a cohesive chain that allow for mental access across a specified path, providing progression from an initial entity, the *reference point* (R), to a series of potential *targets* (T) that form part of the reference point's *dominion*. Moving along this path is a dynamic process of movement that involves selecting an initial reference point on the basis of its textual prominence, and then using that as a platform for further progression within its dominion. These links are made across a series of reference points, targets within that reference point's dominion, and further pathways as those targets subsequently become reference points themselves. Together they form important markers of textual and thematic coherence and can be traced through the text in what Langacker (1995) terms a *line of sight*. This kind of tracing within a dominion as well as being path-directing, necessarily involves the exclusion of potential targets that will have been available for selection. Consequently authorial choices in allowing and restricting access along mental paths are important.

Looking back at the first verse paragraph of 'A Working Party', we can identify two obvious starting points that extend out and are scanned along a mental path. Since reference points are selected initially on the basis of their prominence (van Hoek 2003: 182) in Cognitive Grammar, a simple figure/ground distinction within the clause can be used. 'He' and 'trench' stand out for selection on the basis that together with the verb process 'blundered', they are primary clausal participants that act as figures against the more peripheral adverbial 'three hours ago' that is viewed as the ground. Following this initial identification, it becomes possible to follow the respective lines of sight as we move through the poem. In the first verse paragraph, the potential targets in the dominion for 'he' are reduced to single out parts of the soldier's body, 'boots', and hands. When another soldier, simply referred to as 'a man', is targeted within the dominion, and subsequently becomes a reference point with its own dominion, the targeted entity still remains a body part 'feet' and its associated movements, 'stepping', 'splashing wretchedly', and 'ankle-deep'. The emphasis – and line of sight – here then is on embodiment, the experience of the trench through a range of sensory modes, and the extremes of the working class soldier's body that are accessed on a mental path, and consequently rendered close and immediate.

A similar pattern emerges towards the end of the poem. In the final two verse paragraphs, the selected targets within the dominion activated through the consistent third person pronoun 'he', remain those related to either the body or its constituent parts. The line of sight here extends to extremes, 'feet', 'fingers', 'body', and finally the 'head'. These emphases on the body, on its primary capacity for locomotion, and on its dominant non-visual sensory modes of touch, hearing, taste and smell are viewed, in the context of the poem, as tools with which the experience of the trench is captured to be re-read by later readers. Consequently, the line of sight through activated dominions around the primary reference point 'he' not only provides a tight textual coherence, but a thematic one as well.

The second initial reference point set up in the first verse paragraph is 'trench', which broadly sets up the spatial deictic parameters from which the main world of the poem is fleshed out. Despite the fact that a typical First World War trench would have been densely populated with soldiers and their associated possessions and objects, and would have been busy with activity (Fussell 1975: 36–51), the 'fleshing out' is very specific and again, access is provided along a very selective mental path. So, in the first verse paragraph, the line of sight extends across three targets within the activated dominion. Put simply, the only access afforded to the trench is that of the 'walls' and then the carefully modified -and consequently explicitly detailed – 'sodden bags of chalk', and 'barred trench boards'. This narrowly defined space, which profiles the relationship between what touches and what is touched, emphasises the physical aspect of experience, the coming together of soldier and landscape, and the observational proximity that these construals allow. Although the poem opens out in its middle section to provide a wider ranging description of the surrounding environment in which the action takes place, the strict emphasis on a restricted mental path is a distinct feature of the final two verse paragraphs. Here, the selected path contains only the 'parapet' and the 'bags' that the soldier uses to reinforce it. Strikingly, an alternative desired state of future affairs is set up in the mind of the soldier as he comforts himself by thinking of 'a tot of rum to send him warm to sleep', and exists as part of a more richly defined mental path through a series of reference points and their subsequent targets with the 'draughty dugout', its 'fumes of coke' and its 'snoring weary men'. However, this only represents a fleeting departure from the main event of the poem; in this instance, the unrealised potential of the denied desired path is understood as tragically ironic in the sudden death of the soldier that follows five lines later.

In the discussion above, I have emphasised the restricted nature of access that the reader has in undertaking paths from the initial reference point. Since a reference point's dominion consists of the entire range of its associated knowledge, the way access is controlled, here in the deliberate choices made by the poet-author Sassoon, would appear in itself to be worthy of attention and comment. Of course, the soldier and the trench could have been described in any number of ways drawing on the various possibilities afforded by readers' schematic and encyclopaedic knowledge; indeed this kind of restricted and minimalist description of a trench is not necessarily representative of the poetry of either Sassoon or his peers. This kind of dominion *control* then might not only be considered an integral part of authorial style, but in the context of this poem, be viewed as fundamentally important in explaining how Sassoon captures the minute and focused details of close observation, rather than the broader all-encompassing panoramic sweep of the trench, its human subjects and their actions within it.

The discussion of reference points naturally leads to a discussion of another kind of relationship, this time how the setting of the trench and its participants are organised into various action chains that portray events and the participants involved in them across the poem. Action chains represent interactions between participants that involve the transfer of energy from one to another in a *force-dynamic event* (Talmy 1988), within which participants can be designated as fulfilling *archetypal roles* (Langacker 2008a: 356). Of these roles, two are important in the discussion of event processes. In a *canonical event model* (Langacker 2008a: 357), an *agent* is responsible for carrying out actions as a source of energy output, whilst a *patient* typically is the participant affected by the source of energy through undergoing some internal change of state.

In the first verse paragraph, the soldier is profiled at the head of an action chain, and given focal prominence as the primary participant or *trajector* moving against the trench, which has secondary focus and stands as the *landmark*. This pattern continues through to the end of the verse paragraph, with a series of explicit movements that convey the transmission of energy from an agentive source that is absorbed by the various parts of the trench. Here the trench is profiled as more than just a setting since its 'walls', 'sodden bags of chalk', and 'barred trench boards' are the end points of the various action chains; in Langacker's terms they represent an *energy sink* (2008a: 356). However, this configuration of action chains and participants moves towards reversal by the end of the second verse paragraph, where the soldier assumes a different participant role as patient when the focus moves to the energy that stems from the trench itself, evident in the agency implied in the processes 'swallowed' and 'caught his neck'. In the third verse paragraph, this shift is complete. Here the energy emanates not from the soldier but from alternative sources: the flare that spreads its 'shining whiteness' but then fades out 'in the dark'; the wind that exerts 'chilly gusts'; and 'rifle shots' and 'shells' stand as subjects at the head of profiled action chains that semantically carry a high amount of energy, all of which is absorbed into the environment that surrounds the trench. At this stage the soldier's initial role as prominent agent is downplayed to the extent that he is not mentioned at all. Although he forms part of the surrounding area that is now the landmark to the various trajectory movements, he also verges on adopting a *zero role* (Langacker 2008a: 356) in that he is understood as simply being in a particular setting, and arguably undertakes no role as part of any energy chain. This is maintained throughout the section of the poem that merely describes and provides information about his background.

The last verse paragraph is structured in a similar way to the beginning of the poem, consisting of a temporal process that is scanned sequentially followed by the participle 'craning' as part of a clausal adverb that suspends that mode of scanning temporarily. In the initial clause of this final verse paragraph, the soldier is the agent in the action chain 'he pushed another bag along the top', but there is a significant reversal in participant roles and a shift in energy that are marked grammatically by the way in which the soldier's death is construed. A single flare halts the soldier's mundane and repetitive actions, before he is shot and dies instantly. Subsequently, the soldier undertakes the patient role in this final action chain as the very obvious recipient of and final resting place for energy, although crucially the agent of the chain is not specified. We can explain and explore the effect of this particular construal using Langacker's (2008a: 389–90) notion of a *setting-subject construction*, which is shown in *Figure 7.3*.

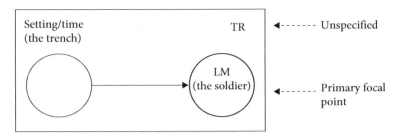

Figure 7.3. The setting-subject construction at the climax of 'A Working Party'

Here, 'the instant' refers to the immediate spatial and temporal parameters of the trench, which hosts the occurrence and indicates that anyone in that bounded area could have carried this out. In this way, the status of trajector shifts from a particular participant and instead is conferred on the setting itself. Since agency subsequently is stated in a general and non-specific fashion rather than being attached explicitly, its prominence is downplayed. This way of construing the climatic event of the poem ensures that the soldier remains the primary focal participant, before the final summary of action 'and all went out'. This final focus on the soldier, and on his death as a result of being the 'energy sink', diverts attention to stasis rather than action, to the loss of life, and to the sense of absence that follows. Consequently, this primary focal point, just like the observed experience of the soldier's death, is a force that resonates once the poem ends.

6.   Conclusion

In his diary entry of 30th March 1916, Sassoon wrote the following descriptions of life in the trenches.

> Bullets are deft and flick your life out with a quick smack. Shells rend and bury, and vibrate and scatter, hurling fragments and lumps and jagged splinters at you; they lift you off your legs and leave you huddled and bleeding and torn and scorched with a blast straight from the pit.
>
> …There are still pools in the craters; they reflect the stars like any lovely water, but nothing grows near them; snags of iron just from their banks, tin cans and coils of wire and other trench-refuse. If you search carefully you may find a skull, eyeless, grotesquely matted with what once was hair, eyes once looked from those detestable holes.   Sassoon (1983:48)

These lines appear just before an early and slightly different version of 'A Working Party' to that which was published in 1917. From these observations, it seems that in his everyday writing Sassoon was reflecting on his experiences in the trenches and shaping these around those very ideas that permeate 'A Working Party': models of energy and inverted forms of agency; the relationship between the soldier and his immediate surroundings in the trench; and the striking prominence of the isolated individual in the trench. All of these are captured in a strategy of observation that becomes an emerging poetics of conceptual proximity. In writing about the First World War, Fussell (1975: 90–2) argues that Sassoon was above all a poet of 'binary vision', who in all of his writing recalled, selected and expressed 'most directly from the polarities which the war pressed into the recesses of his mind'. These polarities might be read as those that are played out over the space of 'A Working Party': the conflicting roles of soldier and poet, broadly experienced phenomena and the finer detail of observation, and the perilous line between safety and danger, and between life and death. These then become synthesised into a poetic representation that mirrors the significant change that occurred in both Sassoon the soldier and Sassoon the poet during 1916. Furthermore, if we accept that one of the defining features of First World War poetry is its movement away from epic forms to refashion verse as the reflection of, and comment on, life in the trench at close-hand, then we ought to have some method of describing how that movement is played out in the language of the poems themselves. In this chapter, I have shown that paying close attention to the language and structure of 'A Working Party' using Langacker's Cognitive Grammar can explain a poem that relies on close observation to evoke a sense of proximity, and to illuminate the horrific intimacy of the trench.

CHAPTER 11

Most and now

Tense and aspect in Bálint Balassi's 'Áldott szép pünkösdnek'

Mike Pincombe

'Áldott szép pünkösdnek' is one of the most appealing lyrics by the great Hungarian Renaissance poet Bálint Balassi (1554–94). It does not have a title, only a series number (11), the name of the tune to which it is to be sung, and two generic headings. These are 'Borivóknak' ('For wine-drinkers') and 'In laudem verno temporis'. It is a poem in praise of the time of spring, directly addressed by the singer as *te* ('thou'), and, more specifically, as *pünkösd* ('Whitsun' or 'Pente-cost'). Seven three-line stanzas are taken up with this *laus*. The poem is rounded off by a one-stanza coda, in which the singer turns melodiously to his fellow-soldiers all about him, and urges them to praise God and to eat, drink, and be merry. The poem is a pleasure in its own right, then, but it is also a very interest-ing instance of a particular type of poetry, and an example of the kind of text which poses all sorts of problem for any language-based analysis. The poem is a *laudatio*: a composition based in the *laus* of its subject; but Balassi's praise of spring-time is also delivered in the form of a *descriptio*. Ancient rhetoric reserves a special place for 'description' in the *laus* of persons and things in a panegyric (Lausberg 1998: § 243). But events can also be the subject of a *descriptio* – and Greek and Latin epic are full of examples. 'Áldott szép pünkösdnek' is interest-ing in that spring-time is praised by an enumeration of the various activities engaged in by various persons and things: soldiers, yes, but also trees, night-ingales, streams, indeed *minden teremtett állat* ('all creatures great and small'). All of these activities are expressed in the present tense, but it is more difficult, perhaps, to be sure of their aspect.

In this chapter I will discuss this problem in the light of the way tense and aspect are treated in Cognitive Grammar. Ronald W. Langacker has written quite extensively on these topics, of course, but, for various reasons – including the layman's natural timorousness before the *maestro* – I shall not presume to discuss his arguments here. Instead, I shall focus on a passage from John Taylor's (2002) textbook on *Cognitive Linguistics*, which is particularly useful for my own discussion of Hungarian tense and aspect. Fortunately, this book has also been described by Langacker as covering the basics 'quite well' (2008a: viii). That is good enough for me. I shall also draw on the semiotic theory of Algirdas-Julien Greimas and Joseph Courtés, partly as a point of comparison with Taylor, but also as a means to elucidate CG as well as Balassi's poem. As a clue to what follows, I shall give some consideration to the etymology of the word *aspect*. It comes from the Latin *aspicere* ('to look at'). The Hungarian term is *igeszemlélet*. This eloquent word is a compound of *ige*, which means 'verb', and *szemlélet*, which is the noun derived from *szemlél*, a verb meaning 'to look at carefully' (ultimately derived from the word for 'eye': *szem*, as are the related words *szemlélődni*, 'contemplate' and *végigszemlél*, 'survey').

We begin with Balassi's poem, together with my own translation. Then I will make a few very brief comments on tense and aspect in Hungarian. Like other linguistic theories which have achieved global status, CG tends to rely on English for its examples; but Hungarian grammar is very different from English grammar, so some detailed discussion will be needed before we can move on to Taylor, Greimas and Courtés, and to what they have to say about aspect. Finally, I want to discuss one of these details at greater length. This is the one flagged up in the title of this chapter. The Hungarian word *most* means 'now', or in Latin *nunc* – one of the three canonical elements in the deictic triad of proximals along with *hic* and *ego*. The word *most* clearly has important implications in terms of aspectualisation, and I shall be treating these as problems for the translator of Hungarian poetry into English.

1. The poem

I	*Áldott szép pünkösdnek gyönyörű ideje,*	1
	Mindent egészséggel látogató ege,	2
	Hosszú úton járókat könnyebbítő szele!	3

Delightful season of blessed fair Whitsun! With the sky bringing the gift of health to everything, and the breeze easing travellers on their long road!

II	*Te nyitod rózsákat meg illatozásra,*	4
	Néma fülemile torkát kiáltásra,	5
	Fákot is te öltöztetsz sokszínű ruhákba.	6

You let the roses open up to their perfume, and the voiceless nightingale to its song, and you also make the trees dress in many-coloured garments.

III   *Neked virágoznak bokrok, szép violák,*   7
        Folyó vizek, kutak csak neked tisztulnak,   8
        A jó hamar lovak is csak benned vigadnak.   9

For you the bushes and the fair violets bloom; for you alone the streams and the
springs clean their water, and the fine swift horses also enjoy themselves only during
your time.

IV   *Mert fáradság után füremedt tagjokat,*   10
        Szép harmatos fűvel hízlalod azokat,   11
        Új erővel építvén űzéshez inokat.   12

For you fatten them up with sweet dewy grass, their limbs refreshed after tiredness,
building up their muscles with new strength for the chase.

V   *Sőt még a végbeli jó vitéz katonák,*   13
        A szép szagú mezőt kik széllyel bejárják,   14
        Most azok is vigadnak, az időt múlatják.   15

Even the fine brave soldiers of the frontier charge all over the sweet-smelling plain;
now they, too, enjoy themselves, and pass away the time.

VI   *Ki szép füvön lévén bánik jó lovával,*   16
        Ki vígan lakozik vitéz barátjával,   17
        Ki penig véres fegyvert tisztíttat csiszárral.   18

One attends to his horse out on the pasture; one feasts merrily with his brave friend;
and another has the blacksmith clean his bloody weapon.

VII   *Újul még a föld is mindenütt tetőled,*   19
        Tisztul homályából az ég is teveled,   20
        Minden teremtett állat megindul tebenned.   21

By your power, also, the earth renews itself everywhere, and the sky, too, clears away
the darkness with your help; every creature gains vital strength from you.

VIII   *Ily jó időt érvén Isten kegyelméből,*   22
        Dicsérjük szent nevét fejenkint jó szívből,   23
        Igyunk, lakjunk egymással vígan, szeretetből.   24

Since we have received this fine season by the grace of God, let us praise his holy
name each one with a glad heart. Let us eat and drink and be merry together,
lovingly.

A much better translation by Keith Bosley and Peter Sherwood may be found
in Klaniczay (1985: 159–60). Modernised versions of the Hungarian text of Balassi's poems vary from edition to edition. Here I have used Kőszeghy & Szabó
(1986: 34–5), where it is headed by the melody. If you want to listen to it, there are
several renditions available online. The best interpretation, in my view, is by Ádám
Buda and László Csergő-Herczeg, which may be accessed via the *New Musical
Express* YouTube site. The various early versions of the poem can be consulted

via the site constructed by István Horváth and Tünde Tóth at the Eötvös Lóránd Tudományos Egyetem in Budapest.

2. The song-situation

We do not know when Balassi wrote 'Áldott szép pünkösdnek'. But it is usually agreed that the poem dates – or at least refers – to the period of his service on the *vég*: the military frontier between the Habsburg and Ottoman empires which divided Renaissance Hungary into two unequal parts. Round about Whitsun-tide, or a little earlier, the two sides would call a truce so that their horses could graze on the new pasture (Szentmártoni Szabó 2004: 46; cf. Kőszeghy 2008: 287). Some time during the 1580s seems the most likely, since this is when, on and off, Balassi was stationed at the front. The evidence for all this is internal. In Stanza VIII, the singer seems to include himself amongst the company of feasters as an equal, and his injunction that they should feast merrily – *lakjunk egymással vígan* – is so similar to the detail of the feasting soldier in Stanza VI – *vígan lakozik vitéz barátjával* – that we may assume the company is made up of the same front-line soldiers that the singer includes in his description of the spring-time landscape.

So the song-situation in 'Áldott szép pünkösdnek' is a coherent composite of two related parts. Stanzas I–VII are addressed by the singer to Whitsun as a *te*; then, in Stanza VIII, he 'turns', as it were, to his comrades and addresses them as a *mi* ('we'). He himself is included in this *mi*. The relation between these parts is perhaps complicated by the description of the song as a *laudatio*. The only time the theme of praise is specifically mentioned in the song is in the final stanza; but it is not the *vernum tempus* which is praised here, but God's holy name: *dicsérjük szent nevét*. Moreover, the song is also defined in its head-line in terms of its intended audience: *Boriνόknak* ('To wine-drinkers'). So 'Áldott szép pünkösdnek' is also a drinking-song. Once again, the only specific allusion to drinking (presumably wine) is in the final stanza: *igyunk* ('let us drink').

There is a slight disjunction between the two parts, then. It is probably quite significant, since the effect of the repeated use of the pronoun *te* and its postpositional forms (*neked, tebenned,* and so on) suggests a hymn to God, rather than a song merely in praise of spring. But what matters for our present purpose is the temporal relationship between the two parts. They are successive: one follows the other in singing-time – and thus listening-time or reading-time as well. The point seems to be that the members of the soldier-audience recognise themselves in the *laus* part of the song, *and then* are moved by its beauty to praise God for giving them *ily jó időt*. The *idő* ('time, season') in question is, of course, the same *idő* that is praised as *gyönyörű* ('delightful') in the very first line of the poem. And so we come to the question of the tense and aspect of the poem.

3. Tense and aspect in Hungarian

Like English, Hungarian has only two tenses (*idők*): past and present. Only present tenses are used in the *laus*, and there are three imperatives in the coda. The situation here is thus relatively straightforward. But English and Hungarian have different ways of grammaticalising aspect. There is obviously a good deal of overlap. For example, in English, the progressive aspect is marked on the verb by the use of the construction *be V-ing*. Words like *just* can be used as well, and the same is true of the Hungarian word *éppen* (Kenesei et al. 1998: 302–3). Hungarian also uses syntactic and accentual means to express progressivity. But it does not use anything like the *be V-ing* construction. The nearest it comes to a morphological marker on the base verb is to add the flexional suffix which produces the *durative* aspect, especially *-gat/get/ogat/eget/öget*. (The different forms are used to satisfy rules of vowel-harmony and cluster-breaking.)

However, there is a problem here. Kenesei et al. (1998: 306) give the following examples of the durative suffix:

> *hall* 'hear' – *hallgat* 'listen',
> *beszél* 'speak' – *beszélget* 'talk',
> *köt* 'knit' – *kötöget* 'be knitting',
> *töröl* 'wipe' – *törölget* 'be wiping',
> *söpör* 'sweep', *söpröget* 'be sweeping'.

The three durative verbs denoting domestic activities are all translated here with the *be V-ing* construction – but *hall* and *beszél* seem to produce duratives which have a different meaning to the base verb. Indeed, Bánhidi et al. (1965: 343) use these very examples to illustrate the non-standard function of the *-gat* suffix. They use a different technical description as well: 'In Hungarian we find Frequentative Verbs which denote that the action is continued for an extended period of time, with or without interruption'. Only the second of these – uninterrupted action – is included by Kenesei et al. as *durative*. The other they call *iterative* – and again we find among the examples a verb with stem vowel *ö* denoting a domestic activity: *ölt* 'stitch' – *öltöget* 'stitch repeatedly, sew' (1998: 303). The needle goes in and out and in and out. But is this not exactly what happens when we talk? We speak and then stop and then speak again. Here, too, there are verbs which change their meaning when the suffix is added. One example given by both grammars is *lát* and *látogat*. This, as it happens, is the only *-gat* verb that occurs in 'Áldott szép pünkösdnek', so let us examine it in more detail.

In the second line, the singer describes the spring-time sky as *mindent egész-séggel látogató ege*, which I have translated rather loosely: 'With the sky bringing the gift of health to everything'. In this case, the base verb is *lát* ('see') and its frequentative form (to stay with the older term for a moment) is *látogat*. The suffix *-ó/-ő* produces its present participle. Thus, the Hungarian word-pair *lát-látogat* is the same as the Latin *videre-visitare*; and, though I have had to translate it differently here, the word *látogat* does indeed mean 'visit' in the Hungarian of Balassi's day and that of our own. Here, Balassi is using the word in the same sense that Jerome uses the word *visitare* on several occasions in the Vulgate, as, indeed, in the first verse in which it appears: 'visitavit autem Dominus Sarram sicut promiserat et implevit quae locutus est | concepitque et peperit filium in senectute sua tempore quo praedixerat ei Deus' (Genesis 21.1–2). In the King James Version: 'And the Lord visited Sarah as he had said, and the Lord did unto Sarah as he had spoken. | For Sarah conceived, and bare Abraham a son in his old age, at the set time of which God had spoken to him'. Here, *visitare* means 'bring fertility' (Sarah, we recall, was barren). In the Hungarian Károli version, composed in the late 1580s (so at just the same time that Balassi wrote 'Áldott szép pünkösdnek') the first verse reads: '*Az Úr pedig meglátogatá Sárát*'. Here is our word, then, with the *meg-* prefix, which is a marker of perfective aspect (Kenesei et al. 1998: 300). Balassi's Whitsuntide sky, then, brings health to the earth below by making it fertile (though *visitare* and *meglátogat* can also mean 'bring tribulation').

But let us leave philology and return to grammar! Gábor Zaicz (2006: 477) suggests that *látogat* is probably a calque of the Vulgate's *visitare*, in which case we may have an example of an 'inorganic' frequentative verb. But even here the frequentative is not completely fossilised. When the sky 'visits' everything on the earth below with its blessings, it does not do so only once, but frequently. Kenesei et al. (1998) split the function of the *-gat* suffix into durative and iterative aspects (one is tempted to say: 'aspects of the frequentative aspect'). Here it is the iterative that counts. Surely, Balassi intended his audience to hear the word *lát* in *látogat* and to make the connection with the 'eye' of the heavens: the sun. It is the warmth of the sun that brings health and vitality to the natural world in spring – and each and every spring. (Rain is also necessary, of course, and there is a Hungarian proverb which makes rain in May as welcome as gold.) Even if we limit the temporal frame of reference to this particular spring that the singer and his comrades are enjoying at the time of the song's performance, the sky gives its blessings every day as the sun comes up in the morning.

4.   Taylor on tense and aspect

CG follows traditional grammar (TradG) in basing its discussion of aspect on the distinction between the binary categories of *perfective* and *imperfective*. TradG defines this distinction by arguing that perfective expressions draw attention to the fact that an act has a beginning and an end, whereas imperfective expressions do not do this. Some examples from English:

1   (a) The soldier feasts merrily with his friend all day long.
    (b) The soldier is feasting merrily with his friend.
    (c) The soldier feasts merrily with his friend.

In 1(a), the phrase 'all day long' supplies a beginning and an end to the act of feasting; the expression is thus perfective. In 1(b), however, there is no reference to the beginning and end of the act, so the expression is imperfective. In 1(c), too, we have to do with an imperfective expression, but of a different kind to 1(b). In the latter, our attention is drawn to something which is happening at the same moment in time in which the expression is itself located. Balassi says to his audience: 'Look over there, under the sumac-tree! The soldier is feasting merrily with his friend'. But in 1(c), as we have already explained, the expression is imperfective because the act of feasting happens not just once, and not just at this moment in time, but repeatedly.

Ki vígan lakozik vitéz barátjával. As it happens, *lakozik* is the frequentative form of *lakik* in line 24. Kenesei et al. (1998: 306) list *-oz(ik)/ez(ik)/özik* as a durative suffix. We might be inclined to interpret this line in terms of the progressive, then, as in 1(b). But still there are problems. Stanza VI uses an anaphoric *ki* to indicate that all the activities it describes are happening simultaneously. We might well 'see' the soldier in the middle of a protracted act of feasting. The soldier who is attending to his horse might take some time over what he is doing, too. But the final act is more difficult to see in these terms: *Ki penig véres fegyvert tisztíttat csiszárral*. The base verb here is *tisztít*, formed from the word *tiszt* ('bright, clean') and the transitivising verbal suffix *-ít*. The complementary intransitiving suffix is *-ul/ül*; and we find the verb *tisztul* in connection with streams and springs (line 8) and the sky (line 20). But *tisztít* is here extended by the causative suffix *-at/et/tat/tet* (Kenesei et al. 1998: 287). We could say that the third soldier in the scene 'is having the blacksmith clean his bloody weapon'? But somehow I cannot 'see' this as a visual image in the way I can with the verbs *bánik* and *lakozik*. One is grooming his horse; the other is lifting a goblet; but the third? He could be standing by and giving instructions, but we have to do a lot more imaginative work with the verb *tisztíttat* than with the other two. But this is a problem for cognitive poetics. Let us return to CG.

CG uses the terms *bound* and *unbound* to designate verbal expressions with perfective and imperfective aspect, and uses the same terms to designate count and mass nouns, too. This is one of the most pleasingly 'neat' parts of CG's classification of different kinds of word. In the case of verbal aspect, then, the perfective 'binds' the act between its beginning and its end, as a book binds all its pages between its front and back covers. But Taylor produces some interesting complications of this basic division between bound and unbound categories of the *process*, which corresponds (broadly) to the TradG notion of *verb*, as can be seen in the tree-diagram (*Figure 8.1*) he uses to illustrate the 'taxonomy of process types'.

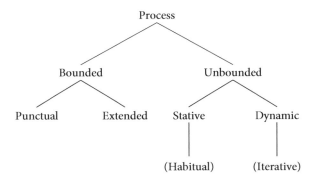

Figure 8.1. Process types (after Taylor 2002: 401)

Bounded processes can be *extended* or *punctual*. The first is the default, it seems, where the beginning and the end of the action are indicated, and the middle is assumed. In the latter, there is no middle: the action begins and ends in a single moment.

Will you be surprised to learn that Bánhidi et al. (1965: 343) explain that Hungarian has a set of 'Momentaneous Verbs'? And perhaps you will also have guessed that Kenesei et al. (1998: 305) offer a slightly different account, referring to such verbs in terms of the *semelfactive*. They give a very satisfying demonstration of the relationship between semelfactives and iteratives: *bólogat* means 'nod repeatedly', but *bólint* means 'nod once'; and *horkol* means 'snore', whereas *horkant* means 'snore once'. Furthermore, they note that duratives can also express semelfactivity by adding the perfectivising prefix *meg-*, so that *csókol* means 'kiss' and *megcsókol* means 'kiss once'.

The Hungarian system provides an interesting perspective on Taylor's extension of the canonical stative-dynamic binary into a distinction between *habitual* and *iterative* verbal expressions. Let us follow him by starting with the iterative, which designates 'an extended dynamic activity, which comprises an unspecified number of instances of the simple punctual event' (Taylor 2002: 402). As an example he gives: 'The child coughed all night'. In Hungarian, as Kenesei et al. (1998: 305) remind us, the word *köhög* means 'cough', and *köhint* means 'cough once'. (There is also a verb *köhécsel*: 'give a little cough several times'!). But *köhög* also displays the frequentative-durative marker *-og/eg/ög* (306). In such complementary pairs, it is hard to tell whether the durative is an extension of the semelfactive or the semelfactive a contraction of the durative. Kenesei et al. (1998: 305) also inform us that 'punctual aspect is not expressed by any formal or derivational means'; but the semelfactive is clearly quite similar if not exactly the same.

Now for the habitual: 'Certain processes can easily be construed as habitual, as when a process occurs at more or less regular intervals over an unspecified period of time' (Taylor 2002: 403). He gives as an example: 'I have breakfast at 8'. That is: 'I have breakfast at 8 every morning'. (Hungarian has an iterative case as well as an iterative aspect: 'Steve goes for a swim every morning' is in Hungarian: '*Pista reggelente/enként úszni jár*', where the word *reggel* is in the iterative: Kenesei et al. 1998: 251). The example provides a convenient alimentary connection with Balassi's soldiers once more: *Ki vígan lakozik vitéz barátjával.* We might translate this as: 'one is feasting merrily with his brave friend'. But I have actually translated it as 'one feasts' not 'one is feasting'. I have thus opted for Taylor's habitual, because I construe this feasting as 'a process [which] occurs at more or less regular intervals over an unspecified period of time'. It is perhaps not a 'habit' in the sense of the routines used as examples by Taylor: 'have breakfast at 8', 'drive to work', and 'smoke a packet a day'. It is rather a *seasonal activity*. It is what soldiers do at Whitsuntide.

Moreover, though Taylor only gives examples of human habits, it is obvious that animals also have habits: our cat Barney has breakfast at 8 and 9.30 and 11.15. Balassi's horses feast as well, eating the fresh grass and drinking the dew upon it – every spring-time. And it is not just animates that can have this sort of seasonal habit. The merest glance at Balassi's 'Áldott szép pünkösdnek' reveals a tendency towards personification. Its most obvious expression is in line 6: *Fákat is te öltöztetsz sokszínű ruhákba.* The notion that trees are dressed in new clothes (*ruhák*) when they put out leaves and flowers in spring is a very ancient poetic conceit. Otherwise, Balassi is more discreet; but it is still hard to resist the impression that roses and the streams are somehow just as animate as the nightingale and the horses. In line 21, the phrase *minden teremtett állat* literally means 'every created animal', where *állat* is derived, not from a root meaning 'spirit', but the word *áll*, meaning 'stand' (Zaicz 2006: 21). An *állat* stands up on its own two feet – or four feet. In any case, the point to make here is that Balassi depicts a scene in which all the objects of created nature – the undifferentiated *minden* of line 2 (*mindent* is the accusative) – are actively engaged in the great transformation motivated by the advent of spring.

All of the verbs in the *laus* part of the poem, then, could be regarded as examples of Taylor's category of the *habitual*. In five of the seven stanzas, the singer is definitely addressing a personified Whitsun as *te* ('thou'). Only in Stanzas V and VI must this address be assumed to be continuously operative between Stanza IV (*hízlalod*: second-person singular of *hízlal*, meaning 'to fatten up') and Stanza VII (*tetőled*, meaning 'from you', and also *tevéled* and *tebenned*). There is a reason why we should perhaps not jump to conclusions on this point. Human beings – the soldiers – appear only in the two stanzas where there is no evidence of direct address to Whitsun. But even though there does seem to be a significant difference between these two groups of stanzas, nevertheless, the verbs in all of them may still be construed in terms of Taylor's habitual. The violets and the springs are simply repeating the sort of things they habitually do at Whitsuntide – just as the soldiers do. The *laus* part has all the air of a hymn to Nature, in fact, which has to be modified and brought in line with Christian orthodoxy in the final stanza. The depiction of the spring landscape with soldiers, then, is perhaps not presented by the singer to his audience as a description of what they can actually see all around them, which would require them to be feasting out of doors and in daylight. Rather, it is meant to conjure up in their minds a picture of a spring landscape which is ideal-typical in its reiteration of details already established as conventions of yet another genre to which this poem may be allocated: the *tavaszi-ének*, or 'spring-song'.

In my conclusion, I shall ruminate on some of the problems which face the project of marrying CG and literary analysis; but here let me suggest a possibility for future research. We have just alluded to the genre of the *tavaszi-ének*, and earlier on we mentioned other genres such as *laudatio* and *hymn* and *drinking-song*. But the idea of *genre* remains a difficult concept (as anyone who has tried to teach it to British undergraduates will readily confirm). I incline towards the position of Tzvetan Todorov et al. (1983) that, as an object of study, genre belongs to the history of literary criticism rather than to the study of literature, where we should be looking instead for a theory of *types*. For Todorov, types are determined 'on the basis of a theory of literary discourse' (1983: 149). These words are from the *Encyclopedic Dictionary of the Sciences of Language* he prepared (in French) with Oswald Ducrot in 1972. The same idea appears more hesitantly in his famous book on *The Fantastic*, written (in French) slightly earlier in 1970. Here the distinction is between 'historical genres' and 'theoretical genres' (1975: 3–24). But the theory of types might well be enhanced by the theory of grammar. Perhaps we could devise a typology of lyric poetry based on the way poems manipulate tense and aspect. In this case, 'Áldott szép pünkösdnek' might be categorised – and analysed – as a literary *habitual*. Todorov himself tried out such an approach in his *Grammaire du Décaméron* in 1969. Sadly, tense and aspect are not topics he deals with in this work.

5. Greimas and Courtés on aspectualisation

With Todorov we have already moved into the Golden Age of Parisian structuralism. In this final section, we will briefly consider the account of *aspectualisation* in the first volume of *Sémiotique* by Greimas & Courtés (1993). It is a pity that there seems to be so little conversation between the grammatical theory developed by Langacker and the semiotic theory of Greimas and Courtés (and their respective followers). For example, Greimas, in particular, is committed to the foundational semiotic importance of the Four Elements, and there is a moment in Langacker (1991b: 283) where he wonders (in a footnote) if it is 'fanciful to see a connection [between] the four elements posited by the Greek philosophers' and the four elements of space, time, material substance and energy in the famous billiard-ball model. Is it beyond hope that a *rapprochement* might root in this fertile soil? In the meantime, we shall merely make a few remarks on the entry on aspectualisation in Greimas and Courtés in its full complex glory.

First, we may note that they highlight the visual metaphor encoded in the word *aspect* by virtue of its etymology. It is '*le point de vue sur l'action*' (Greimas & Courtés 1993: 22). They then explain that in order to connect the various kinds of aspect with 'the underlying actantial structure' of any given utterance, 'we are led to introduce into this discursive configuration an actant-observer for whom the action realised by a subject installed in the discourse appears as a process, that is, a "forward motion", an "unfolding"'. This underlying actantial structure is part of the logical grounding of discourse, according to Greimas & Courtés. At a deep structural level, shadowy actants participate in equally shadowy acts, and it is only through a process of *actorialisation* that their correspondent discursive forms – the *actors* – can come into being.

But note the way Greimas & Courtés reintroduce the visual metaphor encoded in the word *aspect* in their *actant observateur*. They explain that aspectualisation occurs when the enunciator 'delegates' one part of its discursive duties to an '*actant-sujet du faire*' and another to a '*sujet cognitif*', who 'observes and decomposes this *faire* by transforming it into a process'. In this case, the *faire* is the act which produces discourse, by means of procedures such as actorialisation, but also spatialisation and temporalisation. The temporalisation of the discourse is achieved, for example, by the grammatical resources of the language with regard to tense. This is the business of the *sujet du faire*. But he (*sujet* is masculine) can produce a sequence of sentences, say, in which the actions still require more explanation for their relation to each other and to the enunciatee. This is where the *sujet cognitif* steps in. He 'observes' the *sujet du faire* at work, and de- and recomposes his ordering of events so that they make sense, using the range of aspectualisers involving, for example, 'the semes of durativity or of punctuality'. We see at once the similarity – and dissimilarity – with Taylor's (2002) categories of the *extended* and the *punctual*. In Taylor, *punctuality* is a convenient expression which describes a grammatical feature, but in the semiotic theory of Greimas and Courtés it is the name of a seme, a semantic component of certain words and phrases such as *just at that moment* – or *now*.

The Greimas-Courtés model of aspectualisation needs to be treated with care. At first glance, it may look as if the *sujet du faire* is an apprentice discourse-maker, whose work has to be corrected by the master identified as the *sujet cognitif*. But really they mean that temporalisation and actualisation are complementary operations which occur simultaneously during the process of discourse-generation. It is their realisation of the etymological potential of the word *aspect* that produces the idea of the *observateur*, I think. But the notion of a sort of dialectic between tense and aspect is useful, and here we might turn at last to the word *most* in line 15 of 'Áldott szép pünkösdnek'.

Here is Stanza V in full:

Sőt még a végbeli jó vitéz katonák,	13
A szép szagú mezőt kik széllyel <u>bejárják</u>,	14
Most azok is <u>vigadnak</u>, az időt <u>mulatják</u>.	15

I have translated these verbs (underlined) into the simple present tense, but, as we have noted above, I might equally well have used the progressive form: *the soldiers are charging around, enjoying themselves, and passing the time away*. Indeed, the word *most* seems to invite such a translation. At the very moment that the singer sings his song, there are soldiers amusing themselves out there on the fields full of flowers. On the other hand, when we consider that the singer has an audience of soldiers, who are also looking at this scene with pleasure and delight as they listen to his song, the fact that they are supposed to be watching other soldiers having fun with their horses whilst they eat and drink may incline us to think twice about using the progressive. In this case, the simple form of the present, which I have actually used, will probably give the impression that the singer is rather making general statements about what soldiers do when they are released into the green world at Whitsuntide. This is my preferred option – but what of that word *most*?

It need not present a problem. *Most* may refer not to the present moment at which these soldiers are playing in the sun, but to the *idő* – the time or season – of Whitsun when it is their habit to do such things. 'Now, in the delightful time of Whitsun …' The first half of this line reads: *most azok is vigadnak*. Two of the words here act as aspectualisers: *most* and *is*. The word *most* means 'now', and *is* is an enclitic meaning 'also'. The *is* serves to insert the soldiers and their enjoying-themselves into a series of other noun-predicates, most notably the one which refers to the soldiers' horses and their enjoying-themselves in line 9: *a jó hamar lovak is csak benned vigadnak.* All of these events are presented as occurring simultaneously.

But *most* is more complicated. Clearly, it refers to the verb *vigadnak*, and thus to the time at which the event of the soldiers' enjoying-themselves takes place. This time (*idő*) is marked by the suffix *-nak* which indicates present tense (also *idő*). We might regard *most* as a temporaliser in that it confirms the simultaneity of this event with all the others that have been mentioned. But it is also an aspectualiser, in the sense intended by Greimas & Courtés (1993), in that it establishes the non-sequential relationship of the events produced through temporalisation. If we take the contradictory opposition *sequential* vs. *non-sequential,* we can invest the negative pole with a positive meaning by construing it as *simultaneous.* On the other hand, however, we have also seen that *most* could be interpreted as referring to the moment at which the singer is singing this line to his comrades. In this case, the temporalisation remains the same, but the aspectualisation serves to establish the simultaneity of some soldiers' enjoying-themselves out in the fields and of some other soldiers' enjoying-themselves at the table.

I have already given my reasons for preferring the first reading, but a final remark may also be useful. To revert to English, the word 'now' is a canonical item in the system of deictic markers establishing 'point of view' (and the same is true of *most* in Hungarian). It is part of the 'here-and-now' pole of the deictic axis: *proximal* vs. *distal.* But it can be used in a quasi-distal context as well. Here we turn back to *descriptio.* Ancient rhetoric has a special name for the detailed descripion of a place: *topographia.* A particularly well-stocked example would be the set-piece description of the *locus amoenus.* Mediaeval and Renaissance rhetoricians added a temporal equivalent: *chronographia* – the detailed description of a time. The two are often combined in the description of a scene, especially as an *exordium* to longer poems of various kinds. 'Áldott szép pünkösdnek' is an example of a *chronographia* as well as of a *laus* because it is a *laus temporis.*

As a *chronographia,* the poem employs *descriptio* as a rhetorical figure which is also called *evidentia.* The idea is that descriptions should be so vivid that the speaker can put his audience into the position of an 'eye-witness' of the scene he is describing (Lausberg 1998: § 810). As Quintilian (2001: 9.2.40) observes: 'Cicero calls [*evidentia*] "putting something before our eyes"'. You can 'see' the scene in your mind's eye, then – and *evidentia* is obviously derived from the verb *videre* ('to see'). One of the tricks orators use is *translatio temporum:* 'The use of the present tense [...] even for objects which do not belong to the present time' (Lausberg 1998: § 813). (Quintilian notes that the correct term for *translatio temporum* was the Greek *Metastasis* – which, incidentally, was also the name of Quintilian's cat).

Is not this what Balassi's singer does in 'Áldott szép pünkösdnek'? The present tenses of the *laus temporis* are used for objects which do not belong to the present time of enunciation. And we recall that the stanza in which the word *most* occurs is one which is not specifically marked as belonging either to the 'singer-Whitsun' song-situation nor to the 'singer-soldiers' song-situation. The word *most* is used here because it is a detail in the *translatio temporum* which makes a non-proximal situation seem more vivid by using words normally associated with the proximal pole of the deictic axis. It is a little detail added by the *sujet cognitif* in the Greimas-Courtés model – prompted, perhaps, by the *actant observateur*. Perhaps this is not a move which is contemplated in grammar – but it happens all the time in poetry.

6.   Conclusion

This brings me to my main point. There are limits to what CG can offer students of literature. These are fixed mainly by the material constraints of time and space. One reason why grammarians – of any school – tend not to stray beyond the sentence, surely, is that close grammatical analysis takes up so much time to complete and so much space on the page. Langacker has recently announced that the first phase of his personal development of CG is now at an end, and that he is ready to embark on a new adventure, which will include a more detailed exploration of topics such as 'Discourse' and 'Engaging the World' (2008a: viii). But future problems are already visible in his own analysis of a short snatch of (invented) discourse: *I just ran into Jill. // She's upset. // She really thinks // her daughter might move, // so she won't see her any more* (Langacker 2008a: 488–9). The characteristic diagrams that illustrate his discussion of these three sentences (to stay with the TradG term) are real works of art, I think, which would not have been out of place in some of the publications of the Situationist International in the 1960s. It would be wonderful to have a whole short-story diagrammed in this way. But who would do it? And who would read it?

Yet such feats have been achieved by analysts working with other equally (or almost equally) complex methods of investigation. A famous – indeed notorious – example of such an achievement in Barthes's dazzling 'essay': *S/Z* (1970; trans. 1974). Balzac's short novella *Sarrazine* occupies 34 pages of the book, as opposed to 220 pages of analysis. The ratio of analysis-to-text is even higher in Greimas's *Maupassant* (1976). 'Les deux amis' takes up 6 pages of text – and the other 260 are devoted to its analysis. These projects were immensely time-consuming. *S/Z* is what Barthes calls the 'trace' of the work he led over two revolutionary years (1968–9) at the École Pratique des Hautes Études in Paris (Barthes 1974: vii). It took Greimas, patiently labouring in solitude, three years (1972–5) to complete the 'practical exercises' which make up *Maupassant* (1976: 267). Perhaps a team of scientists and computers could produce a CG account of, say, a Sherlock Holmes story in a shorter period – and, surely, the prospect of tackling longer texts is only imaginable with the aid of some kind of CG-analytical programme to be developed in the future. The analysis I have in mind will only be 'readable' by means of some sort of hypertextual database accessible via the internet. The vast potential of this new means of production has yet to be grasped, but it will be necessary to harness it before Cognitive Grammar – or cognitive poetics – can produce detailed analyses of relatively large-scale texts. In the meantime, work on short texts is likely to bring the best returns, but we may still dream.

CHAPTER 12

Fictive motion in Wordsworthian nature

Wenjuan Yuan

1. Wordsworth and the picturesque

The picturesque originates in the art of tourism, when travel within Europe by upper-class Europeans (the Grand Tour) became popular in the eighteenth century. Gilpin (1802) defines the picturesque as '[…] a term expressive of that peculiar kind of beauty, which is agreeable in a picture' (xii). This peculiarity, according to Gilpin, is most closely associated with roughness, as opposed to the smoothness of the beautiful. For Price (1810), in his 1794 book *Essays on the picturesque, as compared with the sublime and the beautiful*, the picturesque is distinguished by three characteristics: roughness, sudden variation, and irregularity. A calm, clear lake, for example, would appear to Price as beautiful, whereas a rapid, raging stream would count as picturesque (more examples are a smooth young beech and a rugged old oak). The picturesque later extends to visual arts, landscape gardening and poetry.

In other words, scenes and objects with certain features tend to become the subject matter in a piece of art characterised as the picturesque. When it comes to the manner of representing this tradition, Levy (1966: 391) points out that the peculiar value of the picturesque tradition may lie with its 'power to organise the visual experience of nature in a relatively static pattern'. This is echoed by Miall (1998: 98), who suggests that the picturesque is 'essentially an aesthetic of the static, the freeze-dried image'.

As the heirs of the picturesque movement in their approach to nature (Watson 1970), Romantic poets are frequently examined to see how much they have been influenced by this tradition. Among them, Wordsworth is one of the first inheritors and also most frequently studied regarding this aspect of nature description (Lucas 1988; Nabholtz 1964; Noyes 1968; Salvesen 1965; Spector 1977; Watson 1970). Wordsworth's attitude towards the picturesque is more complicated and ambivalent than his attitude towards the beautiful and the sublime. On the one hand, his work is more or less influenced by his picturesque predecessors; on the other hand, he despises the excesses of the picturesque and attempted to revolutionise this tradition. For example, Nabholtz (1964) points out that Wordsworth (2004) makes regular positive reference to the picturesque tradition in his 1810 book *Guide to the Lakes*, which is intended to be a corrective to picturesque writers like Gilpin; Watson further argues that Wordsworth's initial ambivalent attitude towards the picturesque is transformed to a 'precarious balance between the descriptive poetry of earlier writers and the visions of a poet like Shelley' (1970: 103).

This chapter aims to look at Wordsworth's manner of representing nature from the perspective of fictive motion, which is widely studied in cognitive linguistics (Matlock 2004a, 2004b, 2010; Matsumoto 1996; Rojo & Valenzuela 2003; Talmy 2000). Particularly, I attempt to examine how the representation of fictive motion in Wordsworth's works reveals his attitude towards the picturesque.

2. Fictive motion

Talmy identifies various types of fictive motion: *emanation, pattern paths, frame-relative motion, advent path, access paths* and *coextension paths*, as illustrated in the following examples.

a.	The sun is shining <u>into</u> the cave.	[emanation path]
b.	As I painted the ceiling, a line of paint spots slowly <u>progressed across</u> the floor.	[pattern path]
c.	I sat in the car and watched the scenery <u>rush past</u> me.	[frame-relative path]
d.	Termite mounds are <u>scattered all over</u> the plain	[advent path]
e.	The bakery is <u>across</u> the street from the bank.	[access path]
f.	The fence <u>zigzags from</u> the plateau <u>to</u> the valley.	[coextension path]

(Talmy 2000, emphases added)

The underlined words in these sentences, be it the motion verbs or directional locative modifiers, seem to characterise the relevant entity as moving. However, it is not difficult to infer that all these entities (the 'sun', the 'paint', the 'scenery', the '[t]ermite mounds', the 'bakery' and the 'fence') are actually static in the referred situations. For the sake of brevity, I will only expand on those types that are applied for my upcoming analysis, presenting them in the same order as they will be used in the following section.

Fictive emanation refers to the fictive motion of something intangible or imagined issuing from a source, travelling along a path and finally terminating upon some object in a similar way as the emanation does. This pseudo-emanation entity can be radiation (e.g. 'The sun is shining into the cave'), shadow ('The tree threw its shadow into the valley'), eye light (e.g. 'I looked into the valley'), or a mere sense of orientation (e.g. 'The cliff wall faces toward the valley'). Talmy further asks why it should be that one entity (e.g. 'the sun') rather than another (e.g. 'the cave') is the source of emanation. He attributes this to what he terms an 'active-determinative principle' (2000: 117), according to which the entity that is considered to be more active and/or more determinative will be construed as the source of emanation. 'The sun', for instance, is both more active and deterministic than 'the cave', given that the sun is movable as opposed to the static cave, and the shining (such as its magnitude, colour and time of presence) totally depends upon the sun.

According to Talmy (2000: 135), an advent path is 'a depiction of a stationary object's location in terms of its *arrival* or *manifestation* at the site it occupies' (emphases added). Site arrival involves a fictive *motion* of the object before reaching its site (e.g. 'Termite mounds are scattered all over the plain'; see Talmy 2000: 136), whereas site manifestation involves a fictive *appearing* of the object at its site ('This rock formation occurs/appears/shows up near volcanoes').

A coextension path fictively represents a spatially extended object as dynamic. Take this sentence for example, *'The fence zigzags from the plateau down into the valley'*. Literally, the motion verb 'zigzag' and path prepositions 'down'/'into' characterise this sentence as describing a motion event, whereas the real moving entity is most probably one's focus of attention.

A general overview reveals that there are some imbalances in the research on fictive motion. Firstly, most of the research focuses on only one subtype of fictive motion, namely, coextension paths (see Matlock 2004a, 2004b, 2010; Matsumoto 1996; Rojo & Valenzuela 2003 and many others). Secondly, there are few studies about the representation of fictive motion in literary language. Let us look more closely at the second imbalance and examine some exceptions that have explored the representation of fictive motion in literary language. Lakoff & Turner (1989) essentially treat fictive motion as a metaphorical use of language. They identify a common metaphor – FORM IS MOTION – underlying everyday expressions such as 'The road runs on for a bit and then splits' and 'The path rises along the shore of the lake' (142), which belong to the coextension path under Talmy's taxonomy. They further point out that some poetic images are rendered natural and understandable by extending this conventional metaphor. However, they do not deal much with the literary significance of fictive motion. The same can be said about Bruhn (2008), who is not concerned with the appreciation of fictive motion in literary language *per se*, but rather with the potential theoretical and experimental insights from these examples. Rice (2012) goes further by illustrating how fictive motion activates mental simulation and thus creates a felt sense of self in literary reading. In short, to explore fictive motion *from* a literary context for linguistic purposes and to investigate fictive motion *within* a literary context for its literary significance is not exactly the same thing. For the current study, I will adopt the latter approach and aim to demonstrate what the representation of fictive motion tells us about Wordsworth's poems.

3. Fictive motion in Wordsworthian nature

3.1 Light and shadow travels

As introduced earlier, fictive emanation, if distinguishing the nature of what is virtually travelling, can be instantiated by radiation, shadow, eye light or a sense of orientation. Wordsworth makes extensive use of emanation paths in describing different varieties of light (be it 'twilight', 'beam', 'splendour', or 'glare') and shadows. See the following examples:

1. Thus, while the Sun sinks down to rest
    Far in the regions of the west,
    Through to the vale no parting beam
    Be given, not one memorial gleam,
    A lingering light he fondly throws
    On the dear hills where first he rose.   ('Extract', p.1)

2. There's nothing to be seen but woods,
    And rocks that spread a hoary gleam.   ('Peter Bell', p.192)

3. Almost at the root
    Of that tall pine, the shadow of whose bare
    And slender stem, while here I sit at eve,
    Oft stretches toward me, like a long straight path
                        ('The churchyard among the mountains', p.673)

Light, as a frequent and widely examined poetic image, can be exploited in its many meaning potentials in literature, one of which, as Tsur (2003, Chapter 12) and many others point out, is its metaphysical significance: light both originates from and may travel to the place we cannot physically reach. In Kaufman's terms, light helps to put us in contact with experiences that are beyond the 'absolute limit' of our experience (1972: 54). This is echoed in Davis (1984), who points out that the representation of light and shadow in Wordsworth's poems represents Nature's metaphysical communication to the poet.

Light and shadow are pervasive images across Wordsworth's whole works. The above extracts exemplify the manner in which Wordsworth presents light and shadow as a fictive movement, profiling the very act of emanating ('throw', 'spread') or travelling ('stretch toward'). In these extracts as elsewhere which I will show below, Wordsworth focuses on what is going on in nature. We can also see that these examples of light or shadow can originate from various entities in nature. Of course, we know the original source is still the sun, but the attribution of light and shadow to 'woods', 'rocks' or the 'pine' extends the metaphysical experience to everywhere in nature. We may further recall Wölfflin's (1950: 19–20) comment on the painterly exploitation of light and shade, who suggests that 'the emancipation of the masses of light and shade' helps to fill the space between concrete objects with an 'immaterial' and 'incorporeal' atmosphere. This observation, I suggest, also applies to Wordsworth's representation of light and shadow. The movement of light and shadow in his works helps to instil the atmosphere with an animate, mysterious and spiritual dimension.

Having discussed the fictive representation of natural light and shadow, I will proceed to the fictive motion of a special light: eye light. As introduced earlier, the very act of looking is sometimes encoded as a fictive motion event, as if there is some sort of light coming from the eye, travelling along the visual path and landing upon certain objects (see the afore-mentioned example 'I looked into the valley'). There are also many fictive representations of eye sight in Wordsworth's poems. Here, we shall see a particular instance of this type of fictive motion:

4.   SHE had a tall man's height or more;
      Her face from summer's noontide heat
      No bonnet shaded, but she wore
      A mantle, to her very feet
      Descending with a graceful flow,   5
      And on her head a cap as white as new-fallen snow.

      Her skin was of Egyptian brown:
      Haughty, as if her eye had seen
      Its own light to a distance thrown,
      She towered, fit person for a Queen   10
      To lead those ancient Amazonian files;   ('Beggars', 1–11, p.151)

This extract is from the poem 'Beggars', in which the persona recounts his encounter with a beautiful beggar woman, to whom he gives a 'boon' despite the implausibility of her tale of woe ('Such woes, I know, could never be', l.16). Later on his way, he meets two boys and judging from their looks, he infers that they are the beggar woman's sons. The two boys, however, tell the persona a lie that their mother is dead, in order to beg from him. After a few failed attempts to deny that they are lying, the two boys run off to play.

In the first stanza, the beggar woman's 'mantle' is described as 'to her very feet/Descending with a graceful flow' (ll.4–5). 'Descending' and 'flow' suggest a smooth and graceful movement. The mantle itself, however, is not moving. What is descending, one may argue, is the eye light of the persona when visually scanning the mantle from top to bottom.

The felt quality of the second stanza, particularly the way her haughtiness is depicted, can perhaps be described as vivid, mocking and original. First, imagine a typical image of someone with a haughty manner: he probably would raise his head (and perhaps cross his arms). One consequence of lifting up one's head is to increase the scope of visibility. In other words, his eye light is cast to a farther distance and still in Wordsworth's words, 'as if her eye had seen/Its own light to a distance thrown'. In this way, this sentence, similarly to the first stanza, unveils a common but unconscious manner of perceiving the act of 'seeing' as involving a fictive motion of eye light. The haughtiness of her manner is also reflected in the choice of the verb: *throw* ('thrown', l.9). I would suggest that understood in this context, the word 'throw' implies a careless and casual manner of looking, which epitomises a corresponding way of perceiving people around and this best captures an arrogant attitude. One may also note that the pronunciation of the word 'thrown' also imitates that of the noun 'throne', which corresponds with the theme of comparing 'she' to a 'Queen'. As such, it does not only depict a vivid image of her but also generates an exaggerated and comic effect. One can also see a teasing persona who speaks with affectionate and fantastic good humour. I will also briefly refer to the 'active-determinative principle' which, according to Talmy (2000), operates underlying the fictive emanation paths. The fact that the beggar acts as the source of emanation signals her activeness and this is in harmony with her haughtiness.

The originality of the image is attributable to a defamiliarised objective construal of seeing. A brief illustration may help clarify the point at issue. Illuminating here is Langacker's (1994, 2008a) eyeglasses example in exemplifying the notions of *subjective* and *objective construal*, which pertains to the asymmetry between the perceiver and the perceived. In the act of seeing, eyeglasses are conceived as part of the perceptual apparatus and they are not put onstage for perception. Therefore, they are normally subjectively construed. In a similar vein, one's eye light is normally subjectively construed in the act of seeing and we tend not to be aware of it. Contrary to this is the objective construal of eyeglasses when one takes them off and puts them at the focus of attention in the perceptual field. In other words, eyeglasses are normally used as a tool to look, but they can also be regarded as the target to look at. In the episode, the eye light is represented as the object of perception. This is an even more defamiliarised case than taking one's eyeglasses as the object of perception, given that eye light is itself invisible and only exists as an imaginary construct. The fictive motion of eye light here may also recall the pre-Newtonian view of optics, which holds the view that there is light emitting from eye and dropping somewhere. Despite the discrepancy between this view and the modern scientific account, we have noted that this way of encoding the act of looking is rather common but only subtly encoded in language (e.g. 'I looked into the valley'). Here in this extract, the explicit mention of the eye light as something that can be thrown renders the fictive motion all the more obvious. The intentional representation of the eye light in terms of fictive motion in this extract adds an archaic flavour to the text, which is in line with the fact that the women beggar is compared to an ancient Queen.

3.2   Mountains rise

Recall that Talmy has identified two types of advent paths: either a fictive move-ment or a fictive appearing before the arrival of an entity at its existing location. There is a particular type of fictive motion interesting to note, fictive upward motion, which is characterised by a fictive movement of an entity departing from its current location. Critics have commented upon many facets of how Word-sworth presents the world around him, such as objects of great height and great depth (Thomas & Ober 1989), and the great distance, both spatially and tempo-rally between the poetic object and the observing poet (Ogden 1973; Salvesen 1965), but there is hardly any comment on Wordsworth's frequent representation of static entities as ascending. Here are some examples:

5.   In my mind's eye a <u>Temple</u>, like a cloud
     Slowly surmounting some invidious hill,
     <u>Rose out of darkness:</u> the bright Work stood still;
     And might of its own beauty have been proud,
     But it was fashioned and to God was vowed
     By Virtues that diffused, in every part,
     Spirit divine through forms of human art:
                                         ('Miscellaneous sonnets', ll.1–7, p.224)

6.   Forth from a jutting ridge, around whose base
     Winds our deep Vale, two heath-clad <u>Rocks ascend</u>
     In fellowship, the loftiest of the pair
     <u>Rising to</u> no ambitious height, yet both,
     O'er lake and stream, mountain and flowery mead,
     Unfolding prospects fair as human eyes
     Ever beheld.   ('Poems on the naming of places', ll.1–7, p.120)

7.   Watching, with upward eyes, the tall tower <u>grow</u>
     <u>And mount</u>, at every step, with living wiles
     Instinct – to rouse the heart and lead the will
     By a bright ladder to the world above.
                                         ('Ecclesiastical sonnets', ll.7–10, p.354)

8.   But lo! the Alps, <u>ascending</u> white in air,
     Toy with the sun and glitter from afar.   ('Descriptive sketches', ll.50–1, p.9)

Movement in an upward direction tends to be aesthetically appreciated. Cogni-tively speaking, it also tends to be associated with a positive value (as in the con-ceptual metaphor GOOD IS UP, Lakoff 1987). However, to attribute motion to a solid would be a relatively rare case in poems as Kames (2005) notes, not to mention that the entities which are described as moving in these extracts are 'Temple', 'Rocks', 'tower' and 'the Alps', which we presume by our general beliefs are grand in size and immobile. These entities, including both natural entities ('Rocks' and 'the Alps') and artificial structures ('Temple' and 'tower'), however, are depicted here to either ascend aloft from the earth on their own or possess the potential to do so (see the underlined words in the extracts).

In Extract 5, the upward movement of the 'Temple' is a pure imaginary act that happens only in '[the] mind's eye'. In Extract 6, a static scene unfolds itself as a dynamic event before the persona, when the 'Rocks' are described as 'ascend[ing]' and 'rising'. One may suggest that these upward movements arise from the transmuting effect of the persona's physical vision combined with his imaginative vision.

In a similar vein, Extract 7 describes the 'tall tower' as 'grow[ing] and mount[ing]'. The perceived movement of the 'tower' arguably arises from the fact that the persona is visually scanning it from the bottom to the top with his 'upward eyes'. In other words, it is the persona's eye sight that is moving upward. Imagine this scenario when one is shifting the eye sight from the bottom to the top: one tends to raise the head and cannot help but open the mouth. This action, I suggest, embodies the state of being amazed and 'the heart' being 'roused' as described in the poem. Likewise, Extract 8 captures a captivating and dynamic scene where the sunshine is thrown upon the Alps. It can be inferred that most likely the sunshine is moving from the summit of the mountain to its base, and its downward movement creates the illusion that the Alps is moving in the opposite direction. This explains why the Alps are portrayed as 'ascending white in air'.

To pinpoint the fictive motion contained in these extracts enables me to examine the spiritual and imaginative dimension of the Wordsworthian representation of nature. For some readers, these fictive upward movements might evoke the scenario of ascending to heaven or in Wordsworth's words 'to the world above' ('Ecclesiastical sonnets', XLII, 10). The most fundamental message behind these fictive upward motions then is that a physical ascent tends to give rise to a spiritual ascent. The description of upward motion, coupled with lofty height and great dynamicity in these extracts, I suggest, also achieves a sense of the sublime. Kant (2007) makes a distinction between two types of the sublime: the mathematical and the dynamic. The mathematical sublime can be achieved through a description of enormous distance, enormous volume, enormous height, enormous depth and so on. In the above extracts, the mathematical and the dynamic are fruitfully combined to conjure up a heightened sense of sublimity. The increase of height helps bring about an imaginative transformation in that object, elevating the commonplace to the sublime, and the persona seems to attain a dignity and aloofness that sets him apart from the worldly to the divine. Most interestingly, the Latin ety-mology of the word *sublime* means the very sense of upward movement. Although each of these extracts presents a *fictive* upward movement, one may suggest that the virtual motion of the scene helps achieve a sense of sublimity and transcen-dence (Barth 2003), with the Wordsworthian imagination (Barth 2003; Eilenberg 1992; J. Jones 1954; Liu 1984; Ruoff 1973). In short, it seems that a witnessing of the ascent leads to the ecstatic contact with a reality beyond the physical.

If these fictive upward movements are all achieved with a Wordsworthian imagination, the following extract presents a fictive motion that arises from a visual act.

9.   The Vicar answered, – 'No disdainful pride
      In them who rest beneath, nor any course
      Of strange or tragic accident, hath helped   40
      To place those hillocks in that lonely guise.
      – Once more look forth, and follow with your sight
      The length of road that from yon mountain's base
      Through bare enclosures <u>stretches</u>, 'till its line
      Is <u>lost</u> within a little tuft of trees;
      Then, <u>reappearing</u> in a moment, <u>quits</u>
      The cultured fields; and up the heathy waste,
      <u>Mounts</u>, as you see, in mazes serpentine,
      <u>Led</u> towards an easy outlet of the vale.
      That little shady spot, that sylvan tuft,   50
      By which the road is hidden, also hides
      A cottage from our view; though I discern
      (Ye can scarcely can) amid its sheltering trees
      The smokeless chimney-top. –
          ('The churchyard among the mountains', ll.38–54, p.669, emphases added)

This extract is part of a poem about the churchyard memorial, where a 'Vicar' explains the life stories of many of the country people who lie buried in the churchyard. I will first draw attention to the middle part of the extract (ll.42–9). This part comprises a rather long sentence, which depicts the gradual unfolding of the 'road' to its static observer. It can be regarded as an extended *coextension path*. What is factive here is the stationary 'road', and what is fictive is the representa-tion of the 'road' as moving and constantly changing its state: the fictive motion is coupled with fictive absence ('lost') and fictive occurrence ('reappear'). One can identify the fictive motion verbs ('stretch', 'mount') and fictive change verbs ('reap-pear', 'quit', 'lead'). The verbs 'stretch', 'mount', and 'lead' indicate a continuation of a state in a relevant period of time. The other three words 'lost', 'reappear' and 'quit' indicate an action which take place in a sudden instant. However, in this context, 'lost' only indicates the beginning of a process of being hidden by the trees; the phrase 'in a moment' indicates that the road is hidden by the trees for a period of time, no matter how short it is. Equally, the verbs 'reappear' and 'quit' respectively mark only the ending of a process of being lost in the trees and stretching along the cultured fields. In all, these verbs and the durative adverbial either directly or indirectly serve to highlight and prolong the temporal dimension of the fictive dynamicity.

The dynamicity is not only manifested by the above verbs and time adverbials, but also by prepositions, such as 'through' (l.44), 'up' (l.47) and 'towards' (l.49). In fact, a sense of dynamicity is felt even before the main verb 'stretch' (l.45) is introduced, given that the preposition ('through') is syntactically inverted before the verb and this preposition invokes a strong sense of dynamicity by encoding the *path* of movement (for an extended discussion of 'through', see Tyler & Evans 2003).

The sentence (ll.42–9) is so vividly represented that it brings the path before the mind's eye of the reader. In addition, it requires the reader to take an active role in mentally scanning the scene. Indeed, it seems that one cannot help but mentally picture the contour of the road. In this way, the visual and mental scanning process experienced by the persona is enacted by the reader. In doing so, the reader is easily 'drawn' into the landscape.

The grammatical structure of the sentence seems clear but until the final moment (l.49) it may pose a potential difficulty. What one may find striking is the passive voice of 'led' in the final line 49, given that most of the rest of the verbs (in their active voice) depict the road as a wilful and self-propelled agent. In order to explain this use, we need therefore to answer a (seemingly) simple question: what are the agent and patient of this verb (what is led by what)? By identifying the subject of the preceding verbs ('lost', 'reappear', 'quit' and 'mount') as the '[road's] line', one may perhaps attribute the subject of 'led' to this noun as well; obviously, the 'line' cannot refer to the whole contour of the road, given that all these verbs ('lost', 'reappear', 'quit', and 'mount') only indicate either a beginning or an ending of a steady-state process. In other words, the action these verbs denote only occurs over a short period of time. Still, the 'line' here is only a short segment of the whole contour, which is most possibly what the eye can capture at a time. It is interesting to note that 'the line' as the unchanging subject refers to a changing referent. For the verb 'lost', it refers to the short length of road that is right before the road is hidden by the trees; for the verb 'reappear', it refers to the length of road that is right after the road is hidden by trees; for the verb 'quit', it refers to the length of road that comes right after the cultured fields; for the verb 'mount', it refers to the short length of road that just starts climbing up the heathy waste. Here the static subject role is assumed by a dynamic referent. The underlying reason is of course the changing sight or attention of the observer. Following this line of reasoning, we may say that it is the short segment of the line that is led by the observer's sight towards the outlet.

The grammatical difficulty this sentence poses, I argue, creates a processing maze for the reader, so to speak. Therefore, it turns out that the reader is invited to be led by the view of the road passively and submissively, although we cannot be sure whether this effect is intended by the poet. It transpires that the persona, who initially seems to exert an active eye, actually has passive sight, and is seized and carried along by what he sees.

Ordinary coextension fictive motion sentences such as 'This fence goes from the plateau to the valley' are so conventional that one may not perceive the dynamicity in the representation. I argue that this Wordsworthian extended extension path sentence, however, takes the coextension path to a new level and arouses a strong sense of dynamicity by the use of the iconicity between the lexical choice, syntax and fictive motion representation, thus inviting the reader into the literary world.

3.3   The hedge-rows run

10.   FIVE years have past; five summers, with the length
      Of five long winters! and again I hear
      These waters, rolling from their mountain-springs
      With a soft inland murmur. – Once again
      Do I behold these steep and lofty cliffs,
      That on a wild secluded scene impress
      Thoughts of more deep seclusion; and connect
      The landscape with the quiet of the sky.
      The day is come when I again repose
      Here, under this dark sycamore, and view   10
      These plots of cottage-ground, these orchard-tufts,
      Which at this season, with their unripe fruits,
      Are clad in one green hue, and lose themselves
      'Mid groves and copses. Once again I see
      These hedge-rows, hardly hedge-rows, little lines
      Of sportive wood run wild: these pastoral farms,
      Green to the very door; and wreaths of smoke
      Sent up, in silence, from among the trees!
      With some uncertain notice, as might seem
      Of vagrant dwellers in the houseless woods,   20
      Or of some Hermit's cave, where by his fire
      The Hermit sits alone.
                  ('Lines composed a few miles above Tintern Abbey', ll.1–22, p.165)

'Tintern Abbey' is generally regarded as an autobiographical poem, wherein Wordsworth recounts his revisit to the bucolic setting of his childhood. It consists of five verse paragraphs and the above lines constitute the first paragraph. The criticism of this poem has been dominated by a historical reading. Many critics have generally agreed on the important role of the natural description in the first paragraph. Mack, for example, states:

> The objects that are absorbed into 'Tintern Abbey' [...] – 'these hedge-rows', 'these pastoral farms', these 'wreaths of smoke', 'the sounding cataract', 'the tall rock, the Mountain, and the deep and gloomy wood' – are held in place, justified, by their relation and their meaning to Wordsworth the experiencer.
>
> (Mack 1982:235)

Mack's observation typifies the common practice of treating the description of nature in the first paragraph in relation to the persona's mood and thoughts. Departing from this line of argument, I will, following Miall (2000), focus on the style of landscape description embodied in this paragraph in particular relation to the picturesque tradition. Miall draws attention to the description of 'hedge-rows' in particular.

> Once again I see
> These hedge-rows, hardly hedge-rows, little lines
> Of sportive wood run wild:

Criticising an attempt to read these lines either as a move towards abstraction (see J. K. Chandler 1982) or as a blurring of fact and fiction (see McFarland 1992), Miall (2000:9) argues that 'Wordsworth rather carefully describes the process of his seeing as it unfolds'. To Miall, the re-qualifying of the 'hedge-rows' as 'hardly hedge-rows' necessitates a second glance and therefore replicates Wordsworth's own process of observation. He further interprets this as Wordsworth's attempt to supersede the picturesque tradition, given that for this tradition, 'what is "agree-able in picture" has already been selected, arranged, and rendered static' (2000:8). In agreement with Miall (here quoting William Gilpin 1802), I shall point out further textual evidence that points to this observation.

The paragraph under discussion opens the poem with a description of the passing of time: 'FIVE years have past'. Later in the text, the temporal progression is further encoded in the sentence 'The day is come' (l.9). These two characterisa-tions of time encode a metaphorical conceptualisation of time in terms of move-ment. In this imagined movement, time is construed as moving with respect to a static persona. Consider our two possible ways of conceptualising this movement: TIME MOVING versus EGO MOVING (compare 'Christmas is approaching us' and 'We are approaching Christmas'; Evans 2004:209; see also Lakoff & Johnson 1980;

Traugott 1978). In other words, the persona witnesses that days come and go; only he remains static. The stasis of the persona in the temporal progression is reinforced by the actual passivity of the persona implied in a range of static (perhaps only physically) characterisations of the persona: 'again I hear' l.(2), 'Once again/ Do I behold [...]' (ll.4–5), 'when I again repose' (l.9), and 'Once again I see' (l.14). One may suggest that although the persona is static, he is participating in the great movement of eternity: the lapse of time.

Whether it is TIME MOVING or EGO MOVING, we are essentially associating time with a horizontal movement. On a closer examination, the repeated use of 'again' in the extract points to another manner of time conceptualisation: what Evans (2004) identifies as the *cyclical* conceptualisation of time. This extract involves both manners of conceptualising time: the elapse of time is perceived as a horizontal movement; the persona's visiting of the place is conceived as a cyclic motion, when broadly conceived against the recurrent cycles of seasons and nature. In the poem, both manners of time conceptualisation are reconciled to generate a sense that there is something unchanged in the changing time.

Having discussed the temporal movement involved in the extract, I will move on to the physical movement, both actual and fictive. In the surrounding scene, one can easily ascertain some actual motions, such as the waters 'rolling' (l.3) and the 'wreaths of smoke' being '[s]ent up' (ll.17–18). Interestingly however, one can also see a wide range of fictive movements in the static scenes:

a. 'these steep and lofty cliffs' [...] <u>connect</u>/The landscape with the quiet of the sky' (l.5, ll.7–8)
b. 'these orchard-tufts' [...] '<u>lose themselves</u>/'Mid groves and copses' (l.5, ll.13–14)
c. 'Once again I see
   These hedge-rows, hardly hedge-rows, little lines
   Of sportive wood <u>run</u> wild: these pastoral farms
   <u>Green to</u> the very door;' (ll.14–7)

Be it the 'steep and loft cliffs', the 'orchard-tufts', the 'hedge-rows' or the 'pastoral farms', neither are capable of moving nor conducting a volitional act. As I will show, the underlined words reveal a fictive representation of these scenes. By way of illustration, I shall focus on the third fictive representation about the 'hedge-rows' and 'pastoral farms'. Kaiser interprets these images in the following way:

> [T]he hedge-rows could be indicative of sheep herding, since they were often used as fences to contain sheep. Just as the unseen shepherds watch over the unseen flock here, so too do they take care of the hedge-rows. These are not rigid hedge-rows; they are 'little lines of sportive wood run wild'. It is as if the cottage-dwellers

> are more like the parents than the planters of these rows of trees. The trees function
> as hedge-rows, yet they maintain their wildness. The cottages are 'green to the very
> door' like the unripe fruits, the cottages have become part of nature, and as such
> they do not disturb this scene.   (Kaiser 2007:49)

Kaiser aptly interprets the 'hedge-rows' as both a cultural symbol and a per-sonified poetic image. The farms' merging into 'the very door' is also appropri-ately understood as the indication that 'cottages have become part of nature'. In other words, one can barely take issue with this interpretation itself. My point is that although Kaiser has convincingly suggested what these images culturally and semantically *mean* to him, he fails to explicate what do these lines *do* to the reader. Here, I echo Olson's (1997) and Hatlen's (1989) appeal to treat a poem as a 'kinetic event' and shift attention from the symbolic value to the cognitive pro-cessing of the images.

I shall begin my analysis with the characterisation of the 'hedge-rows' as 'run[ning] wild'. Due to its formulaic use, 'run wild' does not always activate the sense of actual running. Even in sentences such as 'These hedges run along the garden', the dynamicity lies only in the observer's dynamic visual attention. In this context, however, there can be a literalisation involved in the prefabricated phrase 'run wild', given that the hedge-rows are portrayed as 'sportive'. The very word is closely associated with literally running. In other words, a reactivation of the dynamic sense of the word 'run' is not impossible in this context. This is, of course, not to say that we actually mentally 'see' the 'hedge-rows' as running, but a strong sense of dynamicity may be evoked.

Thanks to Rice (personal communication), my attention was brought to the verbless structure 'Green to the very door'. He suggested that it evoked a strong sense of movement to him. In trying to account for this feeling, Rice compared two sentences 'Beyond the trees is a river' and 'She is running', and he suggested that the former sentence aroused a stronger sense of movement than the latter. Part of the reason, Rice noted, lies in that although the verb 'run' in the latter sentence would unequivocally arouse more kinetic sensation than the preposition 'beyond' in the former sentence, the path information encoded in 'beyond' provokes a greater sense of space than the verb 'run'. It seems that, to Rice, the spatial information is more important than the kinaesthetic resonance in evoking a sense of movement, and the dynamicity of the very verbless struc-ture 'Green to the very door' turns on the spatial information captured in this expression.

In general agreement with Rice's observation regarding the verbless expres-sion in the extract, I would venture to claim that the verbless expression mainly derives its power from the word 'green'. Supposing we extend the verbless expression to a full sentence such as 'These pastoral farms extend (with) their greenness to the very door', so much beauty and dynamicity of the original sentence would be evaporated. Firstly, verbs like 'extend' tend to evoke a movement with a rigid trajectory, and thus carry a sense of limitedness and boundedness, whereas one association (among many) of the word 'green' is Spring, which boasts a vast and unbounded expanse of greenness. In other words, read in the context of a Romantic poem, the word 'green' tends to evoke a sense of vastness and unboundedness.

Secondly, it is argued that the preposition *to* codes the orientation and goal information, and profiles the landmark of an event (Evans & Tyler 2004). In the expression 'Green to the very door', the goal ('the door') is therefore profiled by the preposition 'to' and the intensifier 'very' helps reinforce the prominence of the goal. While 'extend' and many similar verbs also suggest a sense of purposeful and determined act, 'green' is closely associated with season and hence a natural happening. My point is that 'green' can thus mitigate this intentionality by drawing attention to the boundless path of the event. 'Extend', however, draws too much attention to the intention, the landmark and the bounded path. In doing so, it limits nature and more importantly constrains the reader's imagination in picturing this scene.

Thirdly, as introduced in Langacker's framework, a verb profiles a process that evolves through conceived time. It follows that the use of any verb (with any tense) here would introduce the temporal dimension in the conceptualisation of this scene, whereas the verbless expression conveys a sense of timelessness by the very absence of a verb. In short, the word 'green' suggests a sense of unboundedness in both space and time, thereby epitomising the grace and abundance of the farms, or the ubiquity of nature.

Moreover, I suggest that the reader may also undergo a strong bodily resonance, immanently imagining a running experience. It would be possible that this arises from the running *schema* (Rumelhart 1975; also known as *frame, domain,* or *idealised cognitive model*), which is activated by the phrase 'run wild' in the preceding sentence. In other words, the stylistic environment also plays a part in rendering this verbless structure so powerful by triggering a strong kinaesthetic resonance.

In summary, I have explored the coexistence of two alternative manners of time conceptualisation and then moved on to the fictive motion contained in this extract. Both aspects of the text combine to generate a strong sense of dynamicity and signals Wordsworth's effort to transcend the picturesque tradition. In Wordsworthian nature, landscape is not observed in a static manner, but is dynamically experienced and represented.

To close this section about fictive motion in Wordsworth's poems, I have looked at various static images that take on a dynamic character, four of which are specified in the titles of the subsections 'light and shadow travels', 'the mountain rises' and 'the hedge-rows run'. Images of this type represent a natural environment which has an 'active existence', in Goatly's words (2007: 307), that is, nature is not just a static state of being, but takes on energy in Wordsworth's works.

4.   Discussion: dynamicity, fictivity and subjectivity in Wordsworthian nature

I have shown that the mixture of apparently disparate passages analysed above, when read under the category of fictive motion, can be taken as an under-explored but a significant aspect of Wordsworth's treatment of nature. Wordsworth builds the fictive motion into the very fabric of his verse. These examples shed light on Wordsworth's fundamental attitude towards nature and the way he represents nature in his works.

Most of the instances of fictive motion I have analysed point to the fact that Wordsworth represents nature as not immediately present but unfolding along a temporal dimension. In other words, these instances embody Wordsworth's view of nature-as-process instead of nature-as-object. This dynamicity of representation helps to impart life to entities in nature. As my analysis has shown, the inanimate entities in nature are endowed with voluntary motion. This also reveals the relationship between outer motion and inner emotion, or the interchange between the inner feelings and the outer world. Moreover, the dynamicity in representing nature invites readers into the natural world and enhances the interactivity between the reader and the represented world.

Furthermore, Wordsworth's works are endowed with such fictivity that unmoveable entities such as the cliff/mountain, the road and hedge-rows are depicted as dynamic. Related to fictivity is the subjectivity displayed in Wordsworth's representation. With respect to the fictivity and subjectivity, Wordsworth himself gives us a remarkable testimony in his *Essay, Supplementary to the Preface*:

> The appropriate business of poetry, […] her appropriate employment, her privilege and her *duty*, is to treat of things not as they *are*, but as they *appear*; not as they exist in themselves, but as they *seem* to exist to the *senses*, and to the *passions*.
> (Wordsworth 1837: 316, original italics)

In short, Wordsworth has deeply imbued nature with dynamicity, fictivity and, in all, his subjectivity. Taken as a whole, the dynamicity, fictivity and subjectivity embodied in his works reveal important aspects of his allegedly ambivalent attitude towards the picturesque tradition. In the extracts I have analysed, Wordsworth celebrates a dynamic and animate rather than a static and pictorial nature. My study in this chapter thus provides evidence for Wordsworth's attempt to write beyond the picturesque tradition, which is closely associated with a static manner of representing landscape. In all, the dynamicity, fictivity and subjectivity that are embodied in Wordsworth's literary representation of fictive motion offer us a new lens to view his representation of nature and more specifically his attitude towards the picturesque tradition.

CHAPTER 13

The cognitive poetics of *if*

Craig Hamilton

> Language, as we know it, is a superficial manifestation of hidden, highly abstract, cognitive constructions. Essential to such constructions is the operation of structure projection between domains. And therefore, essential to the understanding of cognitive constructions is the characterization of the domains over which projection takes place. Mental spaces are the domains that discourse builds up to provide a cognitive substrate for reasoning and for interfacing with the world.
>
> (Fauconnier 1997:34)

1.   Introduction

Since the 1990s, interest in cognitive poetics has grown. More and more scholars have become interested in how insights from cognitive science in general, and from cognitive linguistics and cognitive psychology in particular, can move the study of language or literature forward. Despite their different backgrounds and concerns, those scholars who have taken the cognitive turn with their research share a desire to better understand how the mind works. A guiding principle in cognitive poetics is that studying the language of literature is one way of studying the imagination. As I aim to show in this chapter, studying conditional constructions in English poetry may help us better understand the poetic mind.

Conditionals are rarely studied in depth in literary criticism although in other disciplines, according to Kaufmann (2006:6), 'Conditionals are among the most extensively studied linguistic constructions.' Harding (2011) is one of the few to have studied conditionals in literature, but there is plenty of research on this construction in linguistics, psychology and philosophy (see e.g. Dancygier & Sweetser 2005; Declerck & Reed 2001; Fauconnier 1985, 1997; Frosch & Byrne 2012; Gomes 2008; Haiman 1978; Horn 2000; Larsson 2009; Oberauer 2006; Schriffrin 1992; Thompson et al. 2005; Traugott 1985; van Canegem-Ardijns & van Bell 2008). However, despite the amount of research on conditionals in these disciplines, Byrne & Johnson-Laird boldly state, '"If" is a puzzle' (2009:282). While this chapter will not solve the puzzle once and for all, it does aim to explain how conditional constructions have been used in English poetry from Chaucer to Atwood.

2.   Conditional usage

The importance of conditionals becomes clear when looking at corpora. For example, in the BYU BNC (Davies 2004), the word 'if' is 41st in frequency of use. Likewise, in the Lancaster BNC (Leech, Rayson, and Wilson 2001), 'if' is 6th in frequency of use as a conjunction (out of 50 listed), and 50th in frequency of use overall. Corpora also show that conditionals with 'if' are ubiquitous in literature. For example, the Oxford BNC (www.natcorp.ox.ac.uk) gives 253,679 tokens for 'if,' while the BYU BNC (corpus.byu.edu/bnc) gives 230,887 (see *Table 2.1*). These numbers show that 'if' is used *very* frequently, which offers evidence to support Dancygier and Sweetser's (2005:276) recent claim: 'Thinking and talking about the "Real World" is constantly, pervasively, and inevitably composed of cognition and talk involving other mental spaces besides "Reality"'. According to Swan (2005:233), we generally use conditionals 'to talk about uncertain events and situations; things which may or may not happen, which may or may not be true, etc.' As we will see later in this chapter, the same holds for poets.

Table 2.1. BYU BNC data (Davies 2004)

Context	Words	Tokens for 'if'	Frequency per million words
Spoken	9,963,663	47,033	4,720.45
Fiction	15,909,312	40,075	2,518.96
Academic	15,331,668	32,745	2,135.78
Newspapers	10,466,422	17,093	1,633.13

Leech, Rayson, and Wilson based *Word Frequencies in Written and Spoken English* (2001) on version 1.0 of the BNC from 1995, which contained 100,046,235 words. They found that 'if' was used more frequently in imaginative writing, including fiction, than in informative writing. Furthermore, the very high loglikelihood given for 'if' suggested there was a *statistically significant* overuse of 'if' in imaginative writing relative to informative writing in the Lancaster BNC (see *Table 2.2*)

Table 2.2. Lancaster BNC data (Leech et al. 2001)

Context	Words	Frequency of 'if' per million words
Imaginative writing	18,439,114	2,488
Informative writing	71,230,923	2,022

In the BYU Corpus of Contemporary American English (COCA), which contains more than 385,000,000 words from sources since 1990 (www.americancorpus.org), there are 899,044 tokens for 'if' distributed across a range of contexts (see *Table 2.3*)

Table 2.3. *COCA at BYU data*

Context	Words	Tokens for 'if'	Frequency per million words
Spoken	78,819,050	248,998	3,158.98
Fiction	74,877,712	205,069	2,738.72
Magazines	80,661,327	191,242	2,370.93
Newspapers	76,331,043	146,322	1,916.94
Academic	76,190,503	107,423	1,409.93

The BYU BNC data in *Table 2.1* and the Lancaster BNC data in *Table 2.2* corroborate the COCA data in *Table 2.3*. All these data reveal two important things. First, 'if' is a really high frequency item compared to other words in the corpora, meaning it is used very often. Second, although *Tables 2.1, 2.2,* and *2.3* show that 'if' is used *less often* in literary texts than in speech, they nevertheless show that 'if' is still used *more often* in literary texts than in other written genres. Because conditionals with 'if' occur often in literature, studying them may tell us more about the poetic mind.

3. Definitions

So many scholars study conditionals that terminological inflation is inevitable. The 'if clause' is sometimes called the *protasis* and the 'then clause' the *apodosis*. I shall use P for the protasis and Q for the apodosis for simplicity's sake here. In the literature, a further distinction is often made between indicative and subjunctive conditionals. Indicative forms include both predictive and non-predictive types. For example, Larsson (2009: 201) calls (1) predictive:

1. If he is in Paris, then he is happy.

Meanwhile, Dancygier & Sweetser (2005: 110) call (2) a speech-act conditional:

2.   If you need help, my name is Ann.

While (1) and (2) are *indicative* types, Horn (2000: 317) would call (2) an 'Austinian conditional' since (2) is clearly non-predictive. There are *subjunctive* types as well. For instance, Larsson (2009: 201) calls (3) counterfactual:

3.   If he were in Paris, then he would be happy.

And yet, Frosch & Byrne (2012: 55) would call (3) a 'subjunctive' conditional. Clearly, overlapping terms may seem like obstacles to studying conditionals, and Gomes (2008: 221–2) has shown that many of these labels can be confusing. But to me, this reveals just how rich the research has been.

To continue, many English grammars (Swan 2005) use terms like *zero, first, second,* and *third* to categorize conditionals. Example (4) is a so-called zero conditional with present tenses in P and Q:

4.   If you *play* ice hockey, you *are* crazy.

In turn, (5) is a first conditional with present tense in P and *will* in Q:

5.   If you *run*, you *will* catch the train.

Example (6) is a second conditional with past tense in P and *would* in Q:

6.   If I *knew* anything about cricket, I *would* understand it.

Finally, (7) is a third conditional with past perfect in P and *would* with present perfect in Q:

7.   If Trevor Francis *had played*, Detroit *would have won*.

However, Carter, Hughes & McCarthy (2000: 70) show that not all forms fit strictly into these four neat patterns, including their examples (8)–(12) below. In this chapter I shall extend the four categories to include variations of the forms noted by Carter, Hughes & McCarthy (2000: 70). I therefore see (8) and (9) as zero conditionals with imperatives in Q:

8.   If you suffer from headaches, take Hedex.
9.   If you want it, why not go and get it?

In turn, I see (10) as a first conditional with future forms in Q, and (11) and (12) as first conditionals with modals in Q:

10.   If she finds out, she's going to kill me.
11.   If David doesn't come, you must ring me.
12.   If you have a toothache, you should see a dentist.

While the zero, first, second, and third taxonomy accounts for many examples, expanding the categories makes sense. The potential verb forms in P may vary little, but the verb forms in Q can (and do) vary at times (I will return to this point in Section 5).

My approach follows that of other cognitive linguists. As Dancygier & Sweetser (2005: 24) state, people are 'brilliant' at making inferences, including those that arise from conditionals. Someone who says, 'If it rains, they'll cancel the game' (2005: 125), makes an inference. The inference is a cause-and-effect prediction: due to rain (P), the game will not be held (Q). In terms of Fauconnier's (1994, 1997) *mental spaces* theory, 'if' is a mental space builder that immediately distinguishes a speaker's reality or base space from another mental space that is hypothetical, conditional, or counterfactual. In the base space for this example, there is no rain yet (~P) so the game remains scheduled (~Q). In the hypothetical space, however, rain (P) means no game (Q). That is the reality the conditional construction calls into question. What we mean by 'reality,' of course, has a particular meaning here. According to Ronald Langacker, 'It is how we conceptualize a situation, not objective reality, that determines the meaning of a linguistic expression describing it' (1991b: 266). To return to our example, rain (P) will cause the game to be cancelled (Q), although ~P and ~Q reflect reality. One function of many examples with 'if' is thus to contrast two situations: ~P, ~Q, which are given, and P, Q, which are imagined. This contrastive function might explain why conditionals seem so important to poets, as we will see below.

4. Poetic examples

In collections such as *The Norton Anthology of Poetry* (3rd edition; 1983), *An Introduction to Poetry* (9th edition; Longman 1998), and *The Norton Introduction to Poetry* (7th edition; 1999), readers may see that conditionals have been part of English poetry for centuries. Because it is impossible in this chapter to discuss every example from these three anthologies, thirteen instances have been chosen to briefly discuss the form over the years. The examples chosen are rather representative, hence my selection of them.

Let us begin by considering (13) from Chaucer's initial description of the Prioress in 'The General Prologue' of *The Canterbury Tales*:

13. Of small houndes hadde she that she feede
     With roasted flessh, or milk and wastelbreed;
     But sore wept she if oon of hem were deed,
     Or if men smoot it with a yerde smerte

     (original c.1380; this text from *Norton* 1983: 9)

The last two lines above may be rendered in modern English as: 'But she would weep sorely if one of them died,/Or if men beat one hard with a rod.' Here we see that the Prioress weeps (Q) either when a dog of hers dies (P1) or when one is hit hard (P2). This is not the only conditional in this part of *The Canterbury Tales*, but there are two points worth making. First, there are two P clauses for one Q clause here. The most common form (*If P, Q*) is symmetrical (one P, one Q), but Chaucer's choice is asymmetrical. Second, the last two lines of (13) have a *Q if P* form since Q, the effect, is stated before the causes (P1, P2). The *Q if P* causal relationship can also be expressed in standard *If P, Q* form (Dancygier & Sweetser 2005:239), but the inverted form is poetic. The construction is also causal in that each P causes Q. It is also hypothetical in that, in the moment of this description, the Prioress is *not* weeping (~Q) as her dogs are *not* suffering (~P). The poet's reality space contains ~P, ~Q, which is given. However, P, Q are in the conditional space, which is postulated.

In (14), from 'The Unquiet Grave,' we see the following lines near the end of the poem:

14.   'You crave one kiss of my clay-cold lips;
       But my breath smells earthy strong;
       If you have one kiss of my clay-cold lips,
       Your time will not be long'
                              (original c.1400; this text from *Norton 1983*:76)

In this 14th century anonymous ballad, a young man visits the grave of his beloved for a year, longing for one last kiss. Yet the deceased warns him that a kiss could kill him. The standard *If P, Q* form is used in (14), which is an example of what Dancygier & Sweetser call 'threat conditionals with *will* forms in the Q clause' (2005:83). While 'have' is in P, 'will' is in Q. Using 'will' in Q rather than 'going to' may seem less threatening, but the relative certainty of the prediction remains clear. Since a tense change in P can force a tense change in Q, using 'had' in P entails using 'would' in Q. Yet such changes would weaken the force of the persona's threat. Here the conditional is hypothetical. In the reality space, the man is alive (~P) and cannot kiss the dead woman (~Q). In the hypothetical space, kissing her (P) would unfortunately be fatal (Q). Contemplating that bleak outcome is meant to dissuade the man from his desire, hence the woman's strong warning.

Although (14) might seem a rather extreme warning, consider (15) from the end of Shakespeare's Sonnet 116. 'Let me not to the marriage of true minds/Admit impediments' opens the sonnet, and it ends with this couplet:

15.   If this be error and upon me proved,
       I never writ, nor no man ever loved.
                              (original 1609; this text from *Norton 1983*:190)

Shakespeare uses an *If PP, QQ* form here in challenging readers to prove him wrong. In the penultimate line, 'this' refers to the argument he made about unconditional love in the preceding 12 lines. Proving (P2) Shakespeare wrong (P1) is equated with arguing *not only* that he never wrote anything (Q1), but *also* that nobody was ever in love before (Q2). The patent absurdity here of Q1 and Q2 reveals a parameter of scale in the conditional construction, which may relate to what Dancygier & Sweetser call 'scalar reasoning' (2005: 253–5). When Q is obviously false, P cannot be true. Shakespeare's extreme Q clauses counter anybody who might disagree with him. That is how he reassures readers at the end that what he has said about love in the sonnet is right. As he does in Sonnet 30, Shakespeare ends Sonnet 116 with a conditional to summarise his argument concisely. On a scale of possibility, the sheer impossibility of both Q clauses means that neither P1 nor P2 are possible, thus validating the reality space, as it were, and negating the hypothetical space.

Example (16) is from Sonnet 9 in John Donne's *Holy Sonnets*, written mainly in the 1620s and published in 1635. The sonnet opens as follows.

16. If poisonous minerals, and if that tree
     Whose fruit threw death on else-immortal us,
     If lecherous goats, if serpents envious
     Cannot be damned, alas, why should I be?

                    (original 1635; this text from *Norton 1983*: 221–2)

The first four lines contain four P clauses for one (interrogative) Q clause. This asymmetry seems to reflect Donne's attempt to gather arguments against the purpose of original sin. The sonnet's many rhetorical questions are also iconic of asymmetry: one asks God many questions; most are never answered. After becoming ashamed of debating with God, Donne ends with a more symmetrical *Q if P* conditional: 'That thou remember them, some claim as debt;/I think it mercy [Q] if thou wilt forget [P].' He thus defines 'mercy' as God's willingness to 'forget' our sins. Donne's use of 'wilt' in P (now an archaic form of 'will') may seem unusual, since 'will' most often appears in Q. But in speech-act conditionals – as in, 'If you will take a seat, I will get the doctor' – it is common, especially to be polite. That is to say that pragmatic factors may have influenced his choice of 'wilt' in P, given the explicit contrast between what it is real (~Q, ~P) and what is conditional (Q, P) in (16).

We move from Donne in the 17th century to Blake in the 18th century in our discussion of Blake's 1789 poem, 'The Chimney Sweeper.' In this poem, a young chimney sweep has a dream about his hard life. The boy dreams of an angel setting dead boys free, and Blake ends the poem with this couplet:

17. Though the morning was cold, Tom was happy and warm;
     So if all do their duty they need not fear harm.

                    (original 1789; this text from *Longman 1998*: 39)

P has a present tense verb ('do') while Q has a modal auxiliary and main verb ('need not fear'). Blake's verb choices reflect a positive (or at least neutral) epistemic stance about P and Q being possible, as opposed to a negative stance that past perfect verbs would represent. He also argues that Q results from P, implying in turn that ~P leads to ~Q. As Tom in the poem understands the consequences (~Q) of not doing his 'duty' (~P), fear seems to compel him to work (P) in order to stay 'happy and warm.' Like other poems by Blake about the plight of poor children in London circa 1800, there is a sad tone here, partly based on the terrible logic of the conditional in the conclusion in (17).

Just as the Romantic Movement continued from the 18th century to the 19th, so too did the use of conditionals. For instance, in (18), which is from Shelley's famous 1820 poem, 'Ode to the West Wind,' Shelley exhorts the wind to:

18.   Be through my lips to unawakened earth
      The trumpet of a prophecy! O Wind,
      If Winter comes, can Spring be far behind?
                    (original 1820; this text from *Norton 1983*: 622)

Just as he did in 'Mont Blanc' in 1817, here Shelley ends 'Ode' with a conditional in interrogative form. This gives readers the impression of uncertainty for at least three reasons. First, Shelley's use of 'if' here rather than 'when' is significant. While 'if' is a marker of neutral or negative epistemic stance toward the content of P, 'when' is a marker of positive stance (Dancygier & Sweetser 2005: 48). Nothing could be more certain than the four seasons each year, yet Shelley seems uncertain. Second, while Shelley's use of the *If P, Q* form is rather conventional, the interrogative weakens his certainty here. Just as 'if' is less certain than 'when,' so too is a question less certain than a declaration. Third, using simple present tense with 'if' in P reveals that, in conditionals, P is 'not itself predicted' (Dancygier & Sweetser 2005: 44); rather, Q is what is normally predicted. Had Shelley used past tenses, the effect would have been very different, as in: 'If Winter came, could Spring be far behind?' Changing 'comes' to 'came' and 'can' to 'could' makes the conditional even less certain, of course. And yet, it is important to note that the grammatical features of this construction help explain where the impression of uncertainty comes from.

Examples (19) and (20) are from the 19th century poet, Elizabeth Barrett Browning. She ends her 1844 sonnet, 'Grief', as follows in (19):

19.   Touch it: the marble eyelids are not wet -
      If it could weep, it could arise and go.
                    (original 1844; this text from *Longman 1998*: 396)

She describes true grief as the silence of a statue, with modal auxiliaries in both P and Q. The epistemic stance here is more negative than positive since 'could' rather than 'can' is used. In the persona's reality space (~P, ~Q), getting up and leaving are impossible since she is unable to overtly express her feelings. The hypothetical situation in P, Q contrasts with the reality of ~P, ~Q. Example (20), the poet's famous Sonnet 43 from 1850 that opens with the question, 'How do I love thee?', ends with these lines:

> 20.   Smiles, tears, of all my life; and, if God choose,
>   I shall but love thee better after death.
>   (original 1850; this text from *Longman* 1998:397)

In Browning's famous poem, she tries to explain her love with many examples. She ends with the conditional in (20), which has a subjunctive in P and modal auxiliary with main verb in Q. The persona is alive (~Q) rather than dead (Q), and the choice of God (P) she refers to will presumably only be made in death, not in life (~P). Again, the contrast of mental spaces is between reality (~P, ~Q), where her love is strong, and the hypothetical space where, God willing (P), her love is even stronger (Q). The subjunctive signals a neutral-to-negative stance in P, which 'shall' reinforces in Q. One of the senses of 'shall' can be paraphrased as 'to be allowed to do X' in the context of giving permission, and God presumably has the authority to guide what the persona feels. That is why P is not marked as more likely with a present tense verb, or with another stative verb such as 'prefers'.

Walt Whitman's *Song of Myself*, containing 1,346 lines and 52 sections in its final 1881 version, is home to one of the most famous ambiguous lines in the history of poetry. The last eight lines of this epic poem are as follows, in (21):

> 21.   I bequeath myself to the dirt to grow from the grass I love,
>   If you want me again look for me under your boot-soles.
>
>   You will hardly know who I am or what I mean,
>   But I shall be good health to you nevertheless,
>   And filter and fiber your blood.
>
>   Failing to fetch me at first keep encouraged,
>   Missing me one place search another,
>   I stop somewhere waiting for you.
>   (original 1881; this text from *Norton* 1983:764)

Whitman's conditional – 'If you want me again look for me under your boot-soles' – has perplexed readers for years. However, its *If P Q* form, with present tense in P and imperative in Q, is rather conventional. As Dancygier & Sweetser state (2005:174), there are four main conditional patterns: [a] *If P, Q*; [b] *If P Q*; [c] *Q, if P*; and [d] *Q if P*. In Whitman's *If P Q* line, the P and Q clauses are more mutually dependent than they might be had Whitman separated them with a comma (e.g. *If P, Q*). Whitman's omission of 'then' is also noteworthy. In conditionals, 'then' is 'a deictic reference for a mental space', and its absence limits the kinds of causal and alternative inferences that are often possible when using 'then' explicitly (Dancygier & Sweetser 2005: 145, 147). Thus, in (21) *If P Q* yields ambiguous interpretations as it forces readers to relate P to Q without 'then.' Moreover, the mutual dependence of P and Q is more predictive than causal. *Looking for* the persona may not cause the reader to *want* the persona once more, nor does the reader's desire to see the persona *cause* the persona to be 'under' his or her feet. Instead, this can be seen as a speech-act conditional as the persona is 'under your boot-soles' (Q) *regardless* of P.

The last four examples are from 20th century poetry. Example (22) is from Wilfred Owen's famous anti-war poem, 'Dulce et Decorum Est,' completed in spring 1918. The poem ends as follows:

> 22. If in some smothering dreams you too could pace
>   Behind the wagon that we flung him in,
>   And watch the white eyes writhing in his face,
>   His hanging face, like a devil's sick of sin;
>   If you could hear, at every jolt, the blood
>   Come gargling from the froth-corrupted lungs,
>   Obscene as cancer, bitter as the cud
>   Of vile, incurable sores on innocent tongues, –
>   My friend, you would not tell with such high zest
>   To children ardent for some desperate glory,
>   The old Lie: *Dulce et decorum est*
>   *Pro patria mori.*   (original 1918; this text from *Norton 1983*: 1037)

Owen has two P clauses for one Q clause here: 'If … you too could pace…' and 'If you could hear…' lead us to 'My friend, you would not tell…' The asymmetrical form nevertheless evokes alternatives. First, 'you' can see and hear the awful death of the soldier (P), so 'you' do not tell children the 'old Lie' (Q). Second, 'you' are far from the Western Front, and because 'you' do not hear the soldier dying, 'you' continue to tell children the 'old Lie.' This is the reality space (~P, ~Q), according to the persona. Yet (22) gives rise to a counterfactual reading because of its *irrealis* (P, Q). According to Fauconnier and Turner, 'the usual methods of analyzing counterfactuals … have paid scant attention to the dynamic powers of the imagination' (2002: 32), including our ability to imagine the terrible situation Owen portrays. As Harding notes, a counterfactual is 'the verbal expression of two distinct cognitive representations – the representation of what actually was, and the representation of what might have been – [and they are] communicated by using specific linguistic forms that mark one set of events as counterfactual' (2011: 26). In (22), the reader's presence at the scene is imagined. The counterfactual signs are not only 'if' but also 'could pace,' 'could hear,' and 'would not tell.' Just as we can use 'when' to express our *certainty* of P, so too can we use 'if' to express our *uncertainty* about the likelihood of P (Dancygier & Sweetser 2005: 46). Owen's modals also represent a particular epistemic stance toward P. Fauconnier (1994: 112) argues that the tense used in P reflects the cognitive status of P. With present verbs, the status of P is more certain. With past tenses, the status of P is either less certain or uncertain; with past perfect tenses, the status of P is generally uncertain. Owen's verbs, in other words, yield the counterfactual reading.

Unlike Owen, D.H. Lawrence uses a more conventional *If P Q* form in (23), which is from his short ironic poem, 'The English Are So Nice!'. The first ten lines are as follows:

23.   The English are so nice
So awfully nice
They are the nicest people in the world.

And what's more, they're very nice about being nice
About your being nice as well!
If you're not nice they soon make you feel it.

Americans and French and Germans and so on
They're all very well
But they're not *really* nice, you know.
They're not nice in *our* sense of the word, are they now?

(original 1932; this text from *Norton 1983*: 955–6)

In this 1932 poem, Lawrence seems to be aware of the fact that 'nice' originally meant 'foolish' or 'ignorant' circa 1300. What is more, here he argues that P (not being 'nice') is the condition to be met for Q (being snubbed by the English). This *If P Q* example is also predictive as readers can infer that, 'If you're not English, then the English will snub you.' Despite Lawrence's confidence in the matter, he uses 'if' rather than 'when' in (23). According to Dancygier & Sweetser, 'if' sometimes 'marks a relation of causal contingency' (2005: 46), unlike 'when.' While 'if' points to what is possible, 'when' points to what is inevitable. Lawrence's verb choices are also important. As Dancygier & Sweetser (2005: 126) note, 'In general, tense use in conditional structures in English does reflect semantics, including mental-space structure.' In the conditional line in stanza two from (23), 'are not', 'make' and 'feel' are all present tense forms. This gives the predication its force. This so-called 'present-for-future' tense in English conditionals is common, and it 'characterizes the background clauses of predictive constructions' (Dancygier & Sweetser 2005: 43). However, the confident epistemic stance is somewhat diminished by the use of 'if', thus creating some tension in the poem and perhaps prompting readers to interpret the poem as ironic or sarcastic.

Example (24) is from 'A Blessing,' a poem written in 1961 by American poet James Wright. The short poem ends with these lines:

24.   Suddenly I realize
      That if I stepped out of my body I would break
      Into blossom.   (original 1961; this text from *Longman 1998*: 509)

While there is nothing very unusual about the *If P Q* form, what Wright does with it is poetic. The moment of epiphany is a hallmark of modern lyric poetry, the moment when whatever the poet finally understands or realises essentially becomes the poem's *raison d'être*. The preterit in P, and modal auxiliary with main verb in Q, mark the persona's neutral-to-negative epistemic stance toward the likelihood of P and Q occurring. The technique of contrast is common in stylistic analysis, and we only need to compare variations on Wright's form to see what the effects would be with different lines. (27) below repeats (24) above for ease of analysis:

25.   Suddenly I realize
      That if I step out of my body I break
      Into blossom.

26.   Suddenly I realize
      That if I step out of my body I will break
      Into blossom.

27.   Suddenly I realize
      That if I stepped out of my body I would break
      Into blossom. (1998: 509)

28.   Suddenly I realized
      That if I had stepped out of my body I would have broken
      Into blossom.

Reading (25), (26), (27) and (28), in that order, we move through zero, first, second and third conditionals. In terms of epistemic stance, (25) is positive, (26) is positive-to-neutral, (27) is neutral-to-negative, and (28) is negative. This puts Wright's actual verb choices in (27) into clearer perspective. The impossibility of P arguably gives the image in Q greater poetic force in (27). Neither (28) nor (25) would create that effect, although (26) might seem an acceptable alternative to (27). The cognitive status of P, or Q for that matter, helps explain how Wright's final lines can have an impact on readers.

Our final example for discussion is (29), which is from Margaret Atwood's short ironic poem, 'This is a Photograph of Me.' This 1966 poem opens with 14 descriptive lines, before ending with these 12 lines:

29.   (The photograph was taken
the day after I was drowned.

I am in the lake, in the center
of the picture, just under the surface.

It is difficult to say where
precisely, or to say
how large or small I am:
the effect of water
on light is a distortion
but if you look long enough,
eventually
you will be able to see me.)

(original 1966; this text from Norton 1983: 1373–4)

These lines are one long parenthetical statement, which sets them apart from the rest. Ironically, the poem literally describes the landscape more than the persona. The persona is in the lake yet Atwood writes in line 13, 'In the background there is a lake.' Thus, the persona cannot be seen in a lake which is merely in the background of a photograph of her. Atwood ends this odd poem of 'distortion' with an *If P, Q* conditional construction. While P has a present tense verb, Q has a future verb phrase with the modal auxiliary 'will'. Atwood uses 'be able to' rather than 'can', keeping with grammatical rules for what follows 'will'. As Dancygier and Sweetser argue, future 'will' can be predicative in its semantics (2005: 91), and in predictive conditionals, P is normally a premise and Q is a consequence of P. That is usually why present tense is used in P and 'will' is used in Q (Fauconnier 1997: 85). Atwood's persona predicts Q based on P, or that, 'if you look long enough,/eventually/you will be able to see me.'

Many factors produce the sense irony in (29). Atwood sounds less certain by using 'if' rather than 'when.' She also sounds somewhat less certain by using 'you will be able to' rather than 'you are going to be able to.' And yet, the present form in (P) is more positive than negative in its epistemic stance, thus lending the prediction (Q) its credibility. In other words, in a form that normally expresses some degree of certainty, there are linguistic signs of uncertainty. In reality (~P), looking hard at a photograph with a lake in the background will *not* enable us to see a person under the lake who drowned the day before the picture was taken (~Q). But Atwood's conditional at the end of the poem suggests that the impossible (~P, ~Q) is possible (P, Q). That helps give the poem its ironic tone.

5. Discussion

It may seem odd to make generalisations about conditionals in seven centuries of poetry in English based on only thirteen items, but the findings thus far reveal four things. First, of Dancygier & Sweetser's (2005:174) four patterns, there are eight instances of *If P, Q* (Examples 14, 15, 16, 18, 19, 20, 22, 29), four instances of *If P Q* (Examples 17, 21, 23, 24), one instance of *Q if P* (Example 13), and no instances of *Q, If P*. Three of the *If P Q* examples come from after 1880, maybe due to an evolution in punctuation standards. But there seems to be little change in preference over time, and the conventional form is most prevalent.

Second, symmetry is more common than asymmetry. Only three Examples (13, 16, 22) have an unequal number of P and Q clauses, while the other ten Examples (14, 15, 17, 18, 19, 20, 21, 23, 24, 29) are symmetrical. Presumably, if the symmetrical form is most common in natural usage, then the same seems true in poetic usage. Extreme counterexamples exist, of course, such as Kipling's 'If.' That famous poem, written in 1896 and published in 1910, contains thirteen P clauses for only two Q clauses (see Stockwell's 2005 analysis). But poets generally seem to prefer using conditionals symmetrically.

Third, some poems end with conditionals, arguably to conclude a poem's argument. This is why they are part of the rhetorical structure of poetry. Related to this are questions in conditional form at the end of poems, which seem like speech-act conditionals with a pragmatic function. Shelley's 'Ode to the West Wind' (18) or 'Mont Blanc' are famous examples of this pattern. Ending with a rhetorical question in this form is an excellent way to hold onto a reader's attention afterwards. According to Thompson et al. (2005:239), 'the function of a conditional is to elicit a process of hypothetical thinking in the listener,' and this is equally true for readers. Mary Oliver, for example, used the following line in her 1990 poem, 'Singapore,' which was set in the Singapore Airport: 'If the world were only pain and logic, who would want it?' (Norton 1999:109). This is line 32 in a poem of 38 lines. Oliver starts line 33 with the phrase, 'Of course, it's not,' yet her verbs already reflect neutral or negative epistemic stance, making the answer redundant. What is more, answering the rhetorical question, in the entire last stanza no less, lessens the poetic force of the conditional.

Fourth, among the types mentioned in Section 2 of this chapter, usage seems balanced between first and second conditionals, especially when we extend the categories for various modals in Q. There seem to be five instances of first conditional use (Examples 14, 17, 18, 20, 29) and six examples of second conditional use (Examples 13, 15, 16, 19, 22, 24). While there are only two instances of zero conditional use (Examples 21 and 23), there are no instances of third conditional use (i.e. with past perfect in P, and modal auxiliary with past perfect in Q). Why might this be? Neutral epistemic stance can be found in both first and second forms. Positive stance is common in zero conditionals and negative stance in third conditionals. The certainty represented by zero conditionals might make poets uncomfortable, which may explain why the form is not used often. Regarding first conditionals, Thompson et al. (2005: 254) say that their 'interpretation … takes place in the context of the goals and position attributed to the writer of the statement.' Such a statement makes perfect sense now in cognitive poetics, but it openly contradicts what literary critics used to call the 'intentional fallacy,' which was the belief that readers could not and should not infer writers' intentions from texts. Meanwhile, the popularity of second conditionals in poems might be due to their ability to reflect either neutral or negative epistemic stance. This is where use of modals becomes crucial. According to Langacker (2008a: 307), 'At a given moment epistemic judgments pertain to either future occurrences or present situations. But in either case a modal indicates that the grounded process is not yet accepted as real. It is future in the sense that its incorporation in the speaker's conception of reality remains to be accomplished.' As for third conditionals, the tendency to give them counterfactual readings might be why poets seem to avoid them. If zero and third conditionals reflect the extremes of epistemic stance, this could explain the preference observed for first and second conditionals. The poetic mind seems to prefer imagining what is possible or likely (P, Q) rather than what is impossible or counterfactual (~P, ~Q).

6. Conclusion

In this chapter, I have tried to show that conditionals are a fundamental part of English poetry's rhetorical structure. Corpora show that they are used more frequently in literary texts than in other kinds of writing. In poems, their function is to contrast real situations (~P, ~Q) with imaginary situations (P, Q), be they hypothetical or conditional or counterfactual. Following Fauconnier, I see 'if' as building imaginary situations that can be characterized as mental spaces, although I have excluded mental space diagrams from this chapter. Following Dancygier & Sweetser, I also argued that verb forms in conditionals can mark epistemic stance, yet without making constant distinctions between the epistemic stance of poets and personae. Verb choices cannot be overlooked in conditionals because, as Dancygier & Sweetser state, 'One more layer of 'past' morphology adds one more layer of 'distance,' either temporal or epistemic' (2005: 60). Thus, the more 'distance' there is, the less certainty there is, which influences epistemic stance. Given the basic contrast between P, Q, and ~P, ~Q, it is important to recall the concept of reality central to cognitive linguistics. As Langacker wrote:

> It is our conception of reality (not the real world per se) that is relevant to linguistic semantics. When reality is at odds with a speaker's view of it, the latter obviously prevails in determining his use of any grammatical markers serving to indicate the status of a situation as real or unreal. Linguistically it is important that speakers believe in the existence of a 'real world' and distinguish it from worlds they regard as purely conceptual, but the validity of this belief is of no direct concern. Reality, of course, is not restricted to the physical. Part of a person's conception of reality is the recognition of his own mental activity, including the fact that he has a conception of reality. Part of this conception as well is the recognition that other people have conceptions of reality that differ in some respects from each other and from one's own. It is further realized that that any of these reality conceptions, including one's own, may be inconsistent and in error on many points. Convoluted though they are, considerations of this sort are crucial for the semantic analysis of certain predicates and grammatical constructions. (Langacker 1987: 114)

While Langacker admits that the things we must consider may well be 'convoluted,' they remain nevertheless important for our research. In this chapter, I have focused on just one kind of grammatical construction (conditionals with 'if') in one specific context (anthologies of poetry for students). I have tried to expand our knowledge of how poets imagine the hypothetical, with the help of concepts in cognitive linguistics. Although seven examples were made up for definitional purposes, the other 27 examples in this chapter are attested. This is because, as Dancygier & Sweetser write (2005: 14), 'The claim that *If P, (then) Q* is true whenever P and Q are both true seems nonsensical to anyone examining real linguistic conditionals.' Almost all examples discussed here are *real*, not invented. However, I have relied on ideas from various cognitive linguists to clarify the form and function of conditionals in poetry, a topic which is often overlooked in poetics. Elsewhere, Oberauer (2006: 277) has warned against any 'ad hoc marriage contrived for the sole purpose of accounting for the present data,' yet I have tried to link literary criticism with the work done by the cognitive linguists I cite.

Finally, in Section 1, I spoke of studying the imagination for a specific reason. Statements like this one, by Jonathan Culler (1997: 31), are all too common in literary studies: 'The literary work is a linguistic event which projects a fictional world that includes speaker, actors, events, and an implied audience (an audience that takes shapes through the work's decisions about what must be explained and what the audience is presumed to know).' There are no human beings in that statement, although the agent doing the actions Culler mentions is not a text but a human mind. Writers and readers map, project, and (ultimately) make meaning;

disembodied texts do nothing alone. As I see it, to study conditionals in literature is one way to more fully understand the imagination, but there are others
of course. As for the future, more data from more sources in various forms (e.g.
inverted forms without 'if') could be studied. More examples could teach us more
about the frequency of the conditional and epistemic stance in poetry. Readers'
responses to them in context could also be studied to evaluate the salience of these
constructions. Likewise, genetic criticism could tell us how much revision poets
put into their conditionals. Concerns like these, while not addressed in this chapter, could no doubt be topics for future research.

CHAPTER 14

Representing the represented

Verbal variations on *Vincent's Bedroom in Arles*

Alina Kwiatkowska

The present chapter focuses on several poems inspired by the well-known painting by Vincent van Gogh, popularly known as *Vincent's Bedroom in Arles*. The painting exists in three versions, subtly different, the first one dated 1888 and the other two in 1889. The investigation of the variant construals of its ekphrastic renditions may tell us something both about artistic freedom and about its limits.

This case of ekphrasis is interesting because the relatively minimalistic work seems less promising as an inspiration for ekphrastic poems than the ones more prototypically chosen for such purposes. It is ostensibly just a picture of an interior, presumably created to explore some painterly techniques. It is evident, however, that the viewers' interest in it stems not from what it shows, but what they believe it conveys or stands for.

The painting shows a rather ordinary bedroom. No human protagonist is explicitly shown. The only element that may be regarded as an expressive marker are the vivid colours (louder in the second version). Though any real-life room is a fairly large and complex entity, a picture obviously reduces its scale, so the scene seems easy to grasp at a glance. The nominal form of the work's title (van Gogh simply entitled it 'The Bedroom' – '*De Slaapkamer*' in the original Dutch) also suggests that the unexceptional static scene can be *summarily scanned* by the beholder. However, this is not exactly how this painting is usually viewed. Its display in an art museum, and its present status of a 'masterpiece', trigger a special mode of super-attentive viewing, with the beholders taking time to examine each of its components separately. This is only one of the many ways in which the temporal element enters this deceptively simple work.

There is more happening in the painting than meets the eye, in quite a literal sense. The descriptive title under which the work is popularly known, *Vincent's Bedroom in Arles* (note the informal use of the first name rather than the more formal surname, and the possessive construction), reflects the beholders' perception of the painter's intimate connection with the represented room. His presence – in the role of the room's inhabitant and the scene's implicit protagonist – is evoked metonymically by the items of furniture and other practical objects: the washbasin, the mirror, some items of clothing. It is certainly part of the beholder's mental picture, as it is deemed essential for the proper interpretation and appreciation of the work.

The tendency to view the content and form of a work of art as an emanation of its maker's personality and biography is prevalent among the members of the art public, despite the protestations of the critics (see especially Roland Barthes' [1977] essay 'The death of the author'). Practically all of the poems of interest here reflect this assumption, with some authors even explicitly pointing out some of its sources:

> Carl Jung said rooms are a symbol
> Of the self
> What part of the self
> Is this room, Vincent?   (Laura Scheffer [2012] 'Bedroom in Arles')

There is indeed some justification for this view. Since the artist was rendering his own bedroom, in the process of painting he cannot have been looking at the scene impassively. It was obviously imbued, for him, with his personal circumstances, his experience and memory of using the objects in the room. In this sense the work, as a record of specific embodied experience, has a history going far beyond the artist's pure perception during the act of creation. However, what level and scope of experience is encodable in an image and transferable to the viewers may be a matter of dispute. Emotional states can be expressed through form, and then recognised, but only at a low degree of precision, as it is not possible to adequately convey their unique causes (Langacker's [2008a: 61–2] concept of different *compositional paths*, though of course originally used in another context, comes to mind here). Nevertheless, as shown by the poems discussed below, the viewers still hope that a close enough study of the work will let them retrieve some of the original experiences responsible for the artist's genius.

Talking about ekphrasis, one has to consider the varying levels at which the vital elements of the creative process are perceptually grasped and conceptually construed. These are the levels of (1) the actual scene; (2) its representation by the painter; (3) the interpretation of the painting by the viewer. Further on, the viewer becomes (4) an author, whose presence may or may not be revealed in his poem, e.g. as implied (imagined) in the scene alongside the characters. Finally, there is the level of (5) the reader's interpretation of the poem. An ekphrastic poem can elaborate on any of those levels. In the present chapter, the main focus is on levels (3) and (4), while the others are relatively neglected.

While more prototypical poems on paintings zoom in on the content of the artworks (though frequently also backgrounded by external knowledge, e.g. of an earlier cultural text, as in the case of *Landscape with the Fall of Icarus* by Pieter Brueghel), the poems inspired by *Vincent's Bedroom* tend to treat the painting as merely affording mental access to the drama of the painter's life – an approach motivated by the fact that the 'literal' content of the work does not seem to have much narrative potential. This is an important consideration, as narration is a defining feature of the genre. Ekphrastic poems always set out to tell a story, whether it is one of what is happening in the painting, in the poet's mind, or in the artist's life. Ekphrasis is not quite the same thing as description, contrary to the popular belief, and to the suggestion contained in its most widely accepted, but too simplistic definition as 'the verbal representation of visual representation' (Heffernan 1993: 3).

The exploration of the difference between description and ekphrasis in this particular case is facilitated by the existence of a unique example of the former. The artist himself described his painting in substantial detail in his letters to his brother Theo and to Paul Gauguin (letters no. 705 and 706 respectively in Jansen et al. 2009). This matter-of-fact description by the observer who was looking at the real scene when producing its visual representation, and was then interested in conveying the details of this representation to the addressees as faithfully as possible, gives us a basis for the comparison with the ekphrastic accounts, whose authors are naturally farther removed from the original creative situation and whose agenda is rather different from that of the artist.

One of the primary concerns in descriptions is the problem of the selection and reduction of the material. Every picture is packed with a staggering amount of data, despite the fact that by the time an author sets down to describing it, the total volume of the information has already been reduced twice: initially by the perception of the painter, as it imposes some order upon the mass of raw sensory impressions by backgrounding the less important ones; then in the act of depiction, when every artist abstracts from the original scene. An accurate linguistic rendering of this data would require many more than the thousand words suggested by the popular saying. If in practice descriptions do not run into many pages of text, it is only because of the natural limitations of production and reception. The describer is guided by the general principle of least effort (for himself and the addressee), and is often constrained by the limited space available. Consequently he tries to extract only the most relevant information from the picture, so that it can be presented in the briefest possible form.

Van Gogh's description of his painting (the first version of 1888) in a letter to his brother seems to achieve a proper balance between informativeness and brevity:

> [The painting shows] simply my bedroom, but the colour has to do the job here, and through its being simplified, by giving a grander style to things, to be suggestive here of rest or of sleep in general. In short, looking at the painting should rest the mind, or rather, the imagination.
> The walls are of a pale violet. The floor – is of red tiles.
> The bedstead and the chairs are fresh butter yellow.
> The sheet and the pillows very bright lemon green.
> The bedspread scarlet red.
> The window green.
> The dressing table orange, the basin blue.
> The doors lilac.
> And that's all – nothing in this bedroom, with its shutters closed.
> The solidity of the furniture should also now express unshakeable repose.
> Portraits on the wall, and a mirror and a hand-towel and some clothes.
> The frame – as there's no white in the painting – will be white.
> (…) you can see how simple the idea is. The shadows and cast shadows are removed; it's coloured in flat, plain tints like Japanese prints.
> (Letter to Theo van Gogh, Arles, 16 October 1888. No. 705 in Jansen et al. 2009)

The artist's description is not of the actual room, but of its pictorial representation (though as the picture is fairly realistic, it also carries information about the set-up of the real scene). His inclusion of the sketches of the composition in this letter and in the letter to Gauguin shows that he regarded its structure as highly important. It is thus interesting to examine the structure of his description. He begins with a global outlook on things (mentioning the 'bedroom' and the 'interior'), proceeds to describe the basic architectural elements of the room ('the walls', 'the floor'), the largest and front-most items of furniture ('the bed' and 'chairs'), the bedding accessories ('sheet', 'pillows', 'bedspread'), the smaller and more back-grounded furniture items ('the dressing-table', 'the basin'), the even smaller and less prototypical items ('portraits', 'mirror', 'towel', 'clothes' – in the order from less to more potentially removable ones). The description is roughly centripetal, with the window – the perspective point in the middle – also mentioned at a mid-point in the text. It is evident that this 'simple description' of the picture, i.e. one whose predominant purpose is a 'literal', no-frills rendering of the picture's content, displays structural similarity between the organisation of the text and of the process of perception (specifically attention-focusing).

This is of course not surprising to a cognitive linguist. This orientation has long taken for granted the perceptual basis of linguistic structure, in particular the relation between the visual segregation of elements into *figure and ground* and the order of mention of those elements in a sentence or a larger text (see e.g. Talmy 2000, 2007 on attention phenomena). Simple descriptions thus diagrammatically represent the levels of attentional salience of the elements of a perceived or pictured scene. There is no room here for any further exploration of this topic; but it is worth noting, in the context of our study, that such tendencies limit the possibility of structural improvisation.

Reading van Gogh's account of his painting, we initially have an impression of a canonical offstage *construal* of the subject (cf. Langacker 1991a, 1995). The author is not putting himself explicitly in view, with the banal exception of the possessive pronoun in 'my bedroom'. However, on closer inspection we note that the sentences preceding and following the strictly descriptive section do contain some elements betraying the presence of the writer and so are evidence of his *objectification* (in the sense of Langacker 1991a: 318–19). His explicit statements about the painting ('looking at the painting should rest the mind'; 'you can see how simple the idea is') reveal his involvement, which is perhaps unavoidable considering his dual role as both the maker and the viewer-describer of the picture. It is the former role that takes over as he attempts to explain his creative intentions to the addressee.

It is also worth noting another point at which those roles are collapsed: the expressive use of the colours. The focus on the colours is in fact the foremost thing one notices when reading the descriptions. They are mentioned copiously in the text because they are perceptually prominent in the painting, made so by the artist who had decided they should 'do the job' there. It is quite surprising to read that the described composition of bright colours (pale violet – red – butter yellow – bright lemon green – scarlet red – green – orange – blue – lilac) is supposed to be 'suggestive of rest or sleep in general' or, as van Gogh put it in a letter to Paul

Gauguin written slightly later, to 'express utter repose' (letter no. 706 in Jansen et al. 2009). These are certainly idiosyncratic associations; most people would rather associate bright colour palette with being wide awake. However, as the colours are (figuratively) warm and optimistic, what the painter meant by 'repose' was perhaps some respite from his depression. The description quoted here is of the 1888 version of the painting, where the colours are still relatively balanced. In the second version (1889), they become even more intense, and their contrasts more jarring, which, as suggested by some authors, may reflect the artist's deteriorating nervous state, his increasing agitation. Incidentally, it is interesting that one poet writing about this version of the painting suggests a reverse direction of influence, claiming that it was the colours that made the artist nervous:

> No wonder he sliced his ear,
> jangled by interruptive smudges like these tan chips
> across the sea-green floor
> (Deborah DeNicola [2004] 'Van Gogh's Room')

Another rather surprising statement in the letter is that there is 'nothing in this bedroom, with its shutters closed'. The literal falsity of this claim signals the need to look for a figurative interpretation. The nihilistic 'nothing' connoting a pessimistic outlook on the situation and the mention of the closed shutters make for a suggestion of confinement, as if in a prison cell. This impression is consolidated by the writer's backgrounding of the doors, mentioned in the last position in the letter to Theo, and not at all in the letter to Gauguin (no. 706 in Jansen et al. 2009). In sum, the description, ostensibly balanced and simple like the painting itself, is framed by the mention of some incongruent elements, which may be putting this equilibrium into doubt. Nevertheless, though the presence of this expressive content objectivises the writer, the whole text still keeps fairly close to the work.

Not so with the poetic reactions to the painting, representing the genre of literary ekphrasis. The definition of ekphrasis as the 'verbal representation of visual representation' seems rather misguided in the light of the expectation (which has become conventional in the actual practice of this genre today) that the poems 'should not be considered as one-to-one renditions into words of what a painting shows' and that the authors should 'respond to what they see, rather than dryly recording what is depicted in a painting' (de Jong 2003: 253). As has been already noted, in the case of *Vincent's Bedroom in Arles*, these responses, though triggered by the work, indeed depart considerably from its visually represented content. Though the authors point to the painting as their source of inspiration in the titles of their poems, paradoxically many of them seem not to be paying much attention to the actual artifact, apparently convinced that it does not need to be described, because, as one author rightly notes, 'Everyone's seen it' (Deborah DeNicola [2004] 'Van Gogh's Room'). They would only cursorily mention the colours and some of the objects in the room before quickly moving on to the details of the artist's life (or rather of his death, which casts back a long shadow over the earlier events). They flaunt their knowledge of the painter's mental problems, the fact that he cut his ear, and that he killed himself in a wheat field. One poet makes references to van Gogh's other paintings, writing of 'stars reeling in the night', and 'irises drawn to imagined breezes', which the painter is supposed to be dreaming about (Ed Bennett [2012] 'Vincent's Bedroom in Arles').

Several authors also bring onstage another artist, Paul Gauguin (with whom van Gogh briefly shared his house in Arles), only to then curiously emphasise his absence from the scene. Though featuring prominently in the poems, he is absent not only from the painted room, similarly to Vincent himself, but also from Arles. He is presented as either not having yet arrived there, or having already left. One of the poems takes the cognitive perspective of van Gogh expecting the arrival of Gauguin at his house:

> To think the great Paul Gauguin will sleep there,
> in that small room adjoining my chamber!
> I hope he'll be surprised
> and pleased with all the plans I've made for us.
> (Joanne Cage [2011] 'Vincent van Gogh's "Bedroom in the Yellow House
At Arles". Blue Door, Stage Left')

The poet must have read up on the details of this relationship to be able to put those words in the mouth of van Gogh's poetic persona, and to know that the 'blue door, stage left' she has mentioned in her (sub)title led to Gauguin's room. The use of the word 'stage' reinforces the metaphorical conceptualisation of the bedroom as a setting for the drama that will be soon playing out there. As the external narrator expects the reader to know (the poem does not provide this information), the artist's hopes for this cohabitation proved futile in all respects; the two painters did not get on well together. Another poet also dwells on Gauguin's 'negative presence' (the term coined in 1943 by Jean Paul Sartre [1984] in *Being and Nothingness*) in the town, highlighting it by offering a brief summary of his post-Arles life elsewhere. Through a shift in location and time (marked explicitly in the fragment, for example, by the references to 'the islands', 'Polynesian', and the future form 'he'll'), she has introduced a deictic sub-world (see Stockwell 2002a: 140) into the main text world:

> Gauguin's already gone, burnt out in the islands
> with the bronze Polynesian ladies draped in fuschia
>
> and lime sarongs. He'll lose a leg to gangrene,
> forget Vincent completely, die leaving his paintings
>
> and his notebook, never knowing where we're going,
> why we're here, from whence we've come
> (Deborah DeNicola [2004] 'Van Gogh's Room')

Texts such as these are predominantly based on the information relating only very indirectly to the painting, some of it not verbalised, but understood as shared by the poet and the reader. All in all, we have to do with a very non-standard set of ekphrastic poems, focusing on the normally backgrounded context of the creative act (the painter's biography), i.e. the facts external to the painting, rather than on its essence (the painting's form and content). This reversal is due to the (already mentioned) pressure on providing a narrative, with van Gogh's biography ideally suited for this purpose. Its dramatic details have entered the mass consciousness, notably through the popular 'biographical novel' by Irving Stone, *Lust for Life*, with many editions since its first publication in 1934, and the 1956 film based on this novel directed by Vincente Minnelli, starring Kirk Douglas as Vincent van Gogh and Anthony Quinn as Paul Gauguin. A more recent film (1990), entitled *Vincent and Theo*, was directed by Robert Altman. The artist has acquired a 'celebrity status'; his difficult life and his tragic death at 37 have been 'aestheticised', and are perceived from the present perspective in a romantic light, as part of the trope of the 'mad artist'. A recent biography claims that the painter did not in fact commit suicide, but might have been murdered (Naifeh & Smith 2011). If this hypothesis were confirmed, it might change the perception of his works.

Given the relationship between the information included in the painting and in the poems, it might perhaps be appropriate to think of the whole situation in terms of reference-point and *target*. Langacker uses those concepts in discussing grammatical phenomena at a much lower level of analysis (originally in the discussion on possessive constructions). However, what he has to say about the reference-point construal also fits our case quite well:

> Initially the reference point has a certain cognitive salience, either intrinsic or conceptually determined. (…). To function as a reference point, a notion must first be activated and thus established as an entity currently capable of serving in that capacity. In this initial phase (…), R[eference point] becomes prominent as the focus of C[onceptualizer]'s conception, thus creating the potential for the activation of any element in [its] dominion. However, when this potential is exploited – when R is actually used as a reference point – it is the target thereby reached that now becomes prominent in the sense of being the focus of C's conception. Even as it fulfills its reference point function, R recedes to the background in favor of T[arget].   (Langacker 1999: 174)

Thus viewing the painting (salient enough to initiate the whole creative process of 'poeming'), gives the viewer-poet mental access to the associated conceptual region (*dominion*) of the painter's life story, personality, and supposed emotions (and secondarily the emotions of the poet himself), which become the new focus of the poet's conception.

The turn towards the narrative introduces elements which were not present in the painting. It is symptomatic that although the painting shows an empty room, the poems all have human protagonists. Van Gogh, or 'Vincent', as the authors familiarly address him, is the most obvious of them, but some others also appear as characters in the poems' space: there is the 'negatively present' Gauguin, the poet's persona conversing with 'Vincent', and in one original case (Toshiko Hirata's [2011] 'Van Gogh's Bedroom as I See It', discussed below) even some personified items of furniture! The introduction of those characters turns them immediately into attentional figures, due to the natural anthropocentric orientation of our perception, and the pictured room is demoted to the role of the ground. The static scene becomes animated, as the characters are presented as talking or acting in a sequential mode. Due to this shift, the painting and the poems are obviously 'about' something different: while the former drew attention to the formal qualities of objects and of their representation, the latter are concerned with the psychological motives and intentions of the human user of those objects and of the creator and recipient of the artwork presumably encoding those intentions.

Though both the visual and the verbal representations are only copies of reality (in the words of Langacker 2008a: 536), simulation is 'always attenuated relative to engaged experience'), the painting, based on perception, and rendered in the same visual modality, is more directly connected to the actual world. It can be regarded as largely 'documentary', with the exception of certain mannerisms of the painter's style, e.g. the enhanced colours. Although in this case the poems also make references to facts, on the whole they are more removed from reality, which is accessed only indirectly via the poets' knowledge acquired by reading and viewing earlier works authored by other people. Those include interpretations and psychological speculations by an army of commentators, both scholarly and amateur, that he has been exposed to as a member of the cultural community. The loosening of the links with reality makes space for the creation of fictional worlds, in which the characters distant in time and space interact, the narrator describes an image never painted, and items of furniture talk and feel emotions.

The experience and knowledge which the painter and the poets bring into their works are widely divergent. While van Gogh painted the bedroom that was familiar to him and ordinary by the standards of the time (which is why, perhaps, he might have wanted to dramatise it a bit with his use of colours), someone viewing the painting today may regard it as exotic, stylised and 'artsy' (not necessarily in the positive sense). The poets cannot access the painter's experience; however, some are still trying to recreate it on the basis of available information, putting themselves mentally in his place. Alternatively, they put both the painter and themselves in the same *mental space*, in a classic act of *blending*. Combining elements from different input spaces, as in the case of the debate between Kant and a contemporary philosopher described by Fauconnier & Turner (1996), the modern poet converses with 'Vincent' as if they were present in the same room. The poet-protagonist is of course equipped with additional knowledge. Simultaneously conversing with the artist and observing the situation from his vantage point in the present, he has a broader temporal perspective on van Gogh's life. He is able to see it as a closed whole, while some of the facts are still unknown to the artist at the time he was creating the work.

While the above remarks refer to the poems in question more generally, I will now consider some of them in more detail. I have actually found some twenty poems inspired by van Gogh's 'Bedroom'. The limitations of space do not let me discuss them all here. Neither will I attempt to make my analyses exhaustive; I will only focus on those aspects of the texts that seem the most interesting. The poets are relatively unknown, some even amateur, but this study makes no pretension of evaluating literary merit. If anything, the 'naïve' renditions are perhaps of greater interest to us, since they are presumably less contrived, closer to 'natural' perception. The discussion of those specific cases will close this chapter.

Sheena Blackhall: 'Vincent's Bedroom in Arles, Painted 1888'

In this poem (1989), the perspective is that of the viewer, the narrator seemingly identical with the author. Her attention is initially drawn by the central element of the painting – the window. It becomes a perceptual figure because of an anomaly: by definition, windows are openings looking out onto some landscape; but this one 'opens onto paint'. While this is of course literally true of all painted windows, pictorial convention would dictate that they should hint at the existence of some outside world. Here, the windowpanes remain opaque. The poet/narrator takes it as 'a clue' that the painter opted for an inward-directed look; his 'brush was a living thing, /An eerie inward peeper'. The viewer's/narrator's attention is then drawn by another anomaly: there is a big, 'solid' bed, a ground for a conventional figure, but here, the expected figure is absent: 'there isn't a sleeper'. Acting on the aforementioned clue, the narrator takes this as signaling the painter's inability to sleep, a consequence of his depression and/or his agitated mental state. The perspective oscillates between those of the narrator/viewer, and of the poem's disturbed protagonist. Both may be perceiving the tilt of the pictures on the wall as 'ominous'. The word is another attractor; it directs attention to the pictures, personifying and embodying instability, signaling the very real threat of a 'fall', a tragic ending.

> They're barely defying gravity;
> Shouldn't they fall,
> Up-ended tightrope walkers?

While the first half of the poem, ending on this high emotional note, is based on the perception of the actual painting, with the narrator's references to the represented objects: the window, the bed, the pictures on the wall – the second half begins rather unexpectedly with a completely different image. In contrast to the previous one, it is an image the artist 'never painted', though he is claimed to have 'carved' it in the mind of the poem's narrator/author. This imaginary painting in her head is much less realistic than the one of the bedroom. In fact, it resembles a surrealist artwork with its oneiric imagery of 'a telephone box / High on black rocks / Of no-talkers, / Alight on a troubled sea' (no wonder van Gogh never painted it, as it is definitely not his style). However, as in the first half of the poem, the image is symbolic of mental states and emotions, though of a different person and in a presumably different situation. Once again, the poet relies on an anomaly to create an attentional figure. As signaled by the presence of the phrases 'a telephone box' and 'no-talkers', the theme of this fragment is communication, or rather the question of its (im)possibility in a troubled world. The semantic opposition between the phrases creates a tension that demands resolution.

Assuming that the symmetrical construction of the poem, despite the different imagery and different focus in its two halves – on the painter and on the narrator, respectively – is indicative of a similarity or connection between the two protagonists, let us now try to pinpoint this link. The poet brings it to the fore with the explicit 'I like that' in the second line, pertaining to what she sees as the artist's admission of his disinterest in the outside world. Her inclusion of herself in the viewing frame signals that the poem may be serving the purpose of self-reflection as much as the reflection on the artist or his work. The connection is further enhanced by the poet's employment of the second-person address form, which brings herself and the painter into the same blended mental space. On the other hand, the integration is not complete: the questions asked by the poet/narrator are rhetorical ones. The artist remains mute throughout. Not so his painting, which speaks to he narrator, and acts as an intermediary between the two minds, encouraging and facilitating communication. It is the telephone box mentioned in the poem, a potentiality of a direct conversation across space and time.

Adam Strickson: 'Vincent and I discuss "Bedroom at Arles" (Version 3)'

As already signaled in the title, Strickson (2004) performs a feat of conceptual integration, creating a fictional world out of the elements of two reality-based mental spaces. He employs a conversation frame, maintained throughout the poem. The conversation ends with the question-statement in the last line: 'You haven't listened to a word I've said, have you?' Despite the title, the 'discussion' is paradoxically one-sided, as the painter has chosen to turn a deaf ear to the speaker's arguments. It is rather a talking to, triggered by the jolt experienced by the narrator on seeing the bedroom painting (thematised in the poem; its explicit mention begins the whole tirade).

> Vincent, this picture
> is an affirmation of pain.
> I can't believe you think
> looking at it
> rests the brain. (…)

The poem's narrator remains at the level of the text, playing the role of one of its characters. His first-person voice is that of an active participant in the fictional encounter, co-present with the painter in the same integrated story space. Some linguistic indicators suggest that he is visiting him at the mental institution the real van Gogh was staying at shortly before his death. As the painter's persona remains silent, the cognitive viewpoint throughout the poem is solely that of this inside observer. Co-temporal with the painter, he possesses no knowledge of the events that are going to unfold some time after this ineffective conversation has ended. Nevertheless, on seeing the bedroom painting, he recognises it as disturbing; he is particularly worried about 'the three inch nails' hammered into the walls (the hangers for the pictures above the painted bed), and the blacked-up window. The sense of an imminent collapse, cued by such elements, makes him intensify his efforts at helping the painter (e.g. by confiscating his gun, hidden in his room 'behind a Japanese print'; he describes such actions retrospectively), and persuading him to change his lifestyle. The narrator's construal of van Gogh's character may be glimpsed from his tirade, and it is clear that he perceives his unresponsive interlocutor as a total failure. Few contemporary readers of the poem, possessing the knowledge unavailable to the protagonists, would agree with this evaluation.

From the vantage point of an external observer, this narrator, who has assumed the role of a level-headed friend and mentor to van Gogh, comes across as well-meaning but somewhat patronising, as he is trying to straighten out the painter's life, guided by his own sense of what makes a man happy ('a bouquet of children'; 'a wife'; 'a baguette and some Belgian chocolate'; a window that is not blocked up with 'mucky bricks'). This is so kitschily mundane as to be almost comical, not to be treated seriously. We begin to realise that despite the 'I' in the title, the poet does not wish to be identified with the narrator (perhaps an unwelcome aspect of his ego?). He has deliberately entrapped him inside the poem's world, to indicate that he is distancing himself from his naïvety, and from the futility and absurdity of his arguments. Though working in a different medium, the poet is an artist himself; this bias makes him sympathise with van Gogh, who, he knows, could not be changed. He has consequently represented the painter as completely ignoring the talk of a happier life; as preoccupied only by the fact that he had 'run out of paint'. The author thus subscribes to the cultural cliché of happiness precluding greatness: confiscating van Gogh's gun would have saved his life, but killed his art. Not all of the readers would share this view; some may disagree with this stereotypical equation of madness and unhappiness with artistic talent, holding the poet in turn to be naïve and incurably Romantic.

David Jibson: 'Vincent'

Note how the poem discussed above involves some circular embedding in that it has the persona of the poet enter the world of the painter that contains the painting which inspired the poem. The painting also appears inside the painter's world in David Jibson's (2012) poem. Here the author explicitly indicates ('I can see you...') his status as an observer of a situation that plays itself out in his imagination:

> I can see you in your bedroom studio in Arles
> at three in the morning,
> candles standing on odds and ends of furniture
> strategically placed around a home-made easel.
>
> On the canvas, a half finished painting
> of the other side of the room (...)

The poet strangely imagines the painter working at night (one wonders whether this idea was perhaps inspired by the exhibition at the Nevada Museum of Art of the painting known as *Study by Candlelight*, which may or may not be a self-portrait of van Gogh, its authenticity yet to be determined). Although not absolutely impossible, such a setting is highly unlikely, and the actual painting contains no signs of originating in this way. This is then a fictional scene motivated by the author's choice to focus on the painter's presumed psychological state (sleeplessness, nervous desperation), using metaphorical imagery:

> Your face flickers even more than the candlelight
> with an unsteady light of desperation
> that is perhaps the flickering light
> of hope going out.

Michael Dylan Welch: 'Bedroom in Arles'

The poem by Michael Dylan Welch (2012) is another one whose first-person narrator (presumably identical with the author) is convinced he knows what could have made van Gogh happy.

This time he is not addressing the painter, but rather putting himself onstage, pushing van Gogh to the side, but inviting a comparison, leaving the judgement to the implied reader. Not surprisingly, this ego-centric poem with an objectively construed narrator begins with the description of the latter's own bedroom, zooming in on the items that have to do with books and reading. The first two lines suggest the poet's elation and contentment with their role in his life:

> My bedside books are dreams to drink,
> paths to lap up, absinthe to imbibe.
> I have reading glasses now,
> and tall stacks of books seem as rickety as me,
> till a new bookcase finds room in the house.

Having proclaimed his happiness with his way of life, he then points out the lack of books in van Gogh's bedroom – and so presumably in his life – taking pity on the artist, and suggesting that this lack was instrumental in his depression: 'Even a bullet to the chest / cannot end / such bookless, dreamless sadness'. However, the purpose of the poem is not only to declare the superiority of the lifestyle choices of this particular author over those of the famous painter; it also, and perhaps primarily, declares the superiority of word over image: books are claimed to be opening new prospects ('words / show me the road where I will go'), while the painter's only 'dreams / may be the colours in paintings / hung carelessly on vivid walls, / yet the window stays closed/ to tomorrow'.

Toshiko Hirata: 'Van Gogh's Bedroom as I See It' (transl. Jeffrey Angles)

The fact that this poem (2011) has been translated from the Japanese would be an obstacle in discussing its finer grammatical details. However, its basic conceptual structure has I believe been well-preserved. The title specifies the perspective explicitly as that of the author-narrator and sets the stage for an original conceptualisation. The author perceives the items of furniture in the painting as a group whose internal hierarchies are determined by their bulk. She anthropomorphises them, suggesting that they are members of a family, ascribing the family roles on the basis of their relative size. Thus the chairs are children (the larger 'an older brother' and the smaller 'a younger sister'). 'The table is mother to the chairs', and the 'giant' bed is their father. This close-knit family is facing a serious crisis:

> The chair and table are standing
> But the bed is lying down
> It is not doing so well these days
> "Get better, daddy"
> "Get better, darling"
> The wife and her two children
> Watch over it with worried expressions.

In fact, the bed is perceived as dying: he 'doesn't have much longer/ The blood that has drained from him/ Has stained the floor an ominous color' (the author is evidently referring to the second version of the painting, the one with the more dramatic colour scheme).

This image is partly based on the author's visual perception of the painting (the relations between the shapes, the colours), but partly also motivated by what she has read about van Gogh's life (and death): 'The artist who painted this/Shot himself in a wheat field … The artist who painted this/Was not blessed with family'. Thus the verb 'see' from the title must be interpreted as referring both to sensory and to mental perception. The juxtaposition of those explicit references to biographical facts and the vivid personification suggests their connection. Is the author suggesting that the painting encodes the artist's perception of the furniture as the caring family he was longing for, and that the bed was his (metaphorical and metonymic) self-portrait? In this case the title of the poem should read, more accurately, 'Van Gogh's Bedroom as I Believe He Saw It'. Or is the poet just amazed by the irony of fate, by life imitating art, when she notes the formal/visual analogies between the painted scene and the real scene of the painter's death ('The color of the bed in the room/So strongly resembles the color of wheat/While the walls of the room/So strongly resemble the color of the sky/Stretching over the field of wheat')? Placing verbal elements side by side, she seems to be leaving it up to the reader to establish the connections and arrive at their own interpretation.

Dónall Dempsey: 'Little Girl Lost in Vincent's Bedroom'

In a manner almost like that of a tabloid headline, designed to make the reader curious and impatient to move on to the story, the title of Dempsey's poem (accessed 2013) contains no fewer than three elements that need further specification. First, it introduces a 'little girl', who we know is neither part of the painted space, nor of the painter's biography (at least as it is popularly known). The phrase 'Vincent's bedroom' is also puzzling: it could be interpreted as the painting's title (but then it is not typographically marked as such), or as referring to the actual room. The word 'lost' adds to the suspense (is it meant to be interpreted literally or figuratively?).

Those questions are not immediately explained in the poem. The opening lines refer to the setting, which is gradually revealed as that of the painted room. The phrase 'outside the half shut / shutters' indirectly points to the narrator's vantage point inside the room; this intuition is confirmed several lines later by the explicit 'here / inside Vincent's bedroom'. However, the subsequent lines 'I am lost/ in each stroke / of the brush that / created it' make it clear that the narrator is only mentally putting himself in the bedroom, while he is in fact standing in front of the painting. This realisation activates in the mind of the reader a script of a museum visit (we know that all three of van Gogh's bedroom paintings can only be viewed in this context). The author is thus zooming out on the scene: from the narrator's initial narrow focus on the painted window, through his conceptualisation of himself inside the room, to his physical position in the museum space. As the perspective broadens, there is a centrifugal shift in the narrator's involvement, initially in the painting's content, then in its surface features, until he is shown as ready to notice its context.

At this point, having built up the suspense, the author finally re-introduces the little girl from the title. She belongs to the museum script: she is a very young visitor, brought there by her Mummy. Too young to know the conventions of behavior in such a space, she is natural, lively, and beautiful – 'an exquisite little girl'. Having toddled behind the protective rope in front of the painting, she becomes a figure against the ground provided by the painted setting. Her strong figural quality is a natural consequence of the mechanisms of attention: she is an animated presence, who enters the narrator's field of vision unexpectedly, and moves in front of the static ground. In fact, though she is just some anonymous kid, and the painting is a world-famous masterpiece, she absolutely overbalances it in the narrator's/author's perception. This is attested to by the poem, which also has her as figure. She is mentioned both in the title and in the identical last line; they frame the text, their importance typographically marked by the use of the uppercase (nb. this also brings to mind the cognitive linguistic convention of using the capitals to indicate conceptual representation – though this was presumably not consciously intended here, it is strangely appropriate).

The presence of the girl is a dominant of this narrative of a memorable personal experience. It is in fact made prominent on several levels: the author switches back and forth between text worlds and sub-worlds, changing the focus as he shows her occupying several different positions: in the museum; within the narrator's visual field; inside Vincent's bedroom (having entered its mental representation in the narrator's mind); 'fleshed into the paint' (blending with the formal aspect of the painting as he perceives it); in his memory of the event; in the poem; and finally in the mind of the reader.

> (…)
> It is as if
> she has entered
> Vincent's bedroom
> and finding him
> (not there)
> leaves
> & leaves

the presence of
herself
fleshed into
the paint.
Art &
Reality
combining to create
what now for me
will always be
LITTLE GIRL LOST
IN VINCENT'S BEDROOM.

The poem is also about the blurring of the borders between the world of the painting and the actual world, between art and reality. In the beginning, the narrator is simultaneously present in Vincent's bedroom (mentally) and in the museum (physically), yet the latter only comes to his (and the reader's) attention with the intrusion of the girl into his visual field. Her appearance is a world-builder which brings the whole museum setting into his awareness, and into the poem. Without her, he might have been forever lost in the painting; she brings him back outside it at the same time as she enters the bedroom in his mind. The two spaces of art and reality oscillate and become conceptually integrated. The exquisite little girl is both a living figure against the painted ground, and a real-life masterpiece among the artificial ones. She appears to be a necessary complement to art in both cases – a signal that perfection may be achieved in the blending of the two domains.

Nancy Scott: 'Bedroom in Arles'

Though the poem (2012) bears the title 'Bedroom in Arles', a perceptive reader quickly discovers that it does not in fact refer to the bedroom immortalised in the painting. The text reports, in the artist's voice, on his first days in Arles (the facts here are based on van Gogh's letters, and the form of the poem itself resembles that of a letter, though without references to the addressee). The painter has rented a room at a hotel. He is in low spirits: he likes neither the city ('the brothels, the filth, / the absinthe'), nor the room, for which they are overcharging him and where he finds 'no refuge'. The last lines record his firm resolve:

> Tomorrow, I will look
> to rent a small studio, where I can finally begin to paint.

The rest, of course, is history: this studio will be the Yellow House, the place where he will paint his 'proper', famous bedroom. The poem's clever concept is that it ends without ever mentioning this masterpiece, yet everybody realises that if van Gogh had not painted it, this poem likewise would not have been written. It is like a prequel to 'Star Trek' shot long after the latter became a cult film. It tells of the events which are only important in the light of what followed them. Devoting her poem to those events, and leaving the masterpiece unmentioned (although certainly present in the background), the author is engaging in another game of figure/ground reversal.

Afterword

From Cognitive Grammar to systems rhetoric

Todd Oakley

Linguistic theory is a notoriously conflicted domain of research. Saussure was perhaps the first to point out that the object of investigation is dependent on how one defines language itself, especially so in comparison to other *explananda*, such as chemical valence or the microphysics of magnetization. The same is even more dramatically the case of minds, in general. Dan Dennett (1981) articulates the problem succinctly in his essay, 'Three kinds of intentional psychology,' when he confesses that his concept of 'intentional systems theory' is 'woefully informal and unsystematic,' but immediately rejoinders that

> the domain it attempts to systematize – our everyday attributions in mentalistic
> or intentional language – is itself something of a mess, at least compared with the
> clearly defined field of recursive functional theory.   (Dennett 1981:41)

Philosophers hate messes. Formal linguists also hate messes. Often times in their attempts to 'clean up' the mess by offering definitions attempting to clearly delineate 'this phenomenon' from 'that phenomenon' they lose touch with the phenomenon itself. They attempt to hammer bigger square pegs into smaller round holes, all the time complaining that the problem is with the holes and not the pegs.

What makes Ronald Langacker's theory of Cognitive Grammar appealing is that it offers round pegs that fit into round holes.

By defining language at the intentional systems level, Langacker preserves features such as meaning and communicative intent that tend to be treated as peripheral facets, or even epiphenomena of a central syntactic engine. It is not too far fetched to regard such syntacto-centric approaches to language as 'square-pegs' of outsized proportion to the phenomenon itself. Cognitive Grammar is one of a handful of approaches that begins with meaning and communication as a basic design parameter and attempts to bring order to the mess, and only resorts to pure syntax or pure phonology as a last resort (when no other explanations suffice).

My motive for rehearsing this line of argument is not to rekindle the firestorm associated with the linguistics wars of the late twentieth-century but merely to offer some stark reasons for why literary studies should find certain approaches to language structure, acquisition, and use more intuitively useful than other approaches, and why the present volume of essays has achieved something significant: a deep engagement with one theoretical approach that presents many paths to sustained literary stylistic analysis. This is no mean feat.

Despite many of its intuitive foundational concepts, Cognitive Grammar is not an easy theory and method to master and apply. I have taught it for over 15 years, and several facets, like *subjectification*, are very difficult for students to grasp without extensive tutelage. I think this is due in part to the phenomenological nature of the key notions underlying it, such as *perspective, attentional prominence*, and *viewing arrangement*. It is also easy for them to forget that all acts of language are presentations 'from somewhere,' thus confounding a clear understanding of subjectivity and objectivity as key facets of linguistic construal.

The present volume shows what a Cognitive Grammar of literary stylistics looks like in practice. Notions such as *ambience, texture*, and *resonance* are recurring themes in these chapters, as they each point to a quality of the artifact that is not easily captured by theories of formal grammar; it is a credit to the breadth and depth of Langacker's approach that many of the constituent concepts in Cognitive Grammar – such as *active zones, construal, profiling, summary* and *sequential scanning*, and *usage event, viewing arrangement*, to name but a few – fit so easily and without modification. Compare this state of affairs with constituent concepts in formalist approaches, such as *move alpha, merge, subjacency constraint, theta role*, or *c-command*. None of these concepts is useful for literary stylistics without a prior reduction of the phenomenon in question, which is not to say such a reduction is illegitimate, but only to say that in some sense the *explanandum* shifts from the 'work as textured artifact' to the 'work as instantiation of abstract structural principles.'

This brings me to my central point of this *Afterword*. Cognitive Grammar in literature is one of a family of scholarly enterprises that seeks to understand more precisely the dimension of texts and their cultural ecosystems, an enterprise I like to call *systems rhetoric*. It is no accident that ambience, texture, and resonance are properties of whole artifacts (or significant parts thereof) and not merely structural properties of phrases and clauses, for these notions capture a perduring experience with the 'work,' an experience never out of the stylistician's attentional field but rarely within the linguist's respective attentional fields. The Cognitive Grammar framework, however, makes it much more unlikely for the cognitive linguist to ignore the ambience of a usage event. Cognitive Grammar is one framework for integrating theory at the lowest level of explanation – grammar and constructions – with theory at a higher level of explanation, namely at the level of the artifact. Langacker's sketches of discourse *usage events* and *scenarios*, along with his treatment of *domains, domain matrices*, and *dominions* provide useful and cognitively plausible tools for stylistic and rhetorical analysis to scale up to the artifactual level. The contributions in this volume demonstrate the ways linguistic form and literary meaning find explanation according to a single integrative approach.

This is all very promising. But if literary stylistics is to be regarded as part of an ever more comprehensive enterprise of systems rhetoric, then another question emerges: how can Cognitive Grammar provide explanations for the behaviour of whole systems of texts?

Of course, one answer is to simply avoid the problem altogether by saying that there are no literary systems, *per se*, but merely collections of singular artifacts. The literary *explanandum* begins and ends with the literary work. The contributions in this volume, however, suggest that such an argument is logically circular and a practical impediment to any attempt to go beyond narrow curatorship.

A systems rhetoric founded upon a literary stylistics that is founded upon Cognitive Grammar is, I think, possible. For the remainder of this *Afterword*, I will offer a very brief (and no doubt insufficient) illustration of systems rhetoric taken from forthcoming work with my colleague Vera Tobin on rhetorical questions in the Supreme Court of the United States of America, and its relevance to both Cognitive Grammar and the ontology of the literary work (Oakley & Tobin, in press).

The 1803 majority opinion in the case of *Marbury v. Madison*, penned by the newly appointed Chief Justice John Marshall, is by all accounts the most influential decision in the history of this institution. Cited in over two hundred other opinions emanating from the Court, it is widely regarded as the decision establishing the doctrine of 'judicial review', or the power of the Court to determine if any law passed by any state or by Congress itself meets constitutional muster. If it does not, the Court then has the power to invalidate it. The decision has been instrumental in determining the outcomes of many influential cases, leading to, for instance, the invalidation of the Missouri Compromise, the desegregation of public schools, and placing of limits on executive privilege, each of which had perduring effects on the polity, both good and ill.

A patient reading of Marshall's masterpiece reveals a peculiar stylistic feature not seen in other opinions: a superabundance of rhetorical questions (twenty-seven in total). Thus, a leading textural property of this document is the sheer number of instances where the Court asks questions of the reader for which he or she already knows the answer (or to which the Court assumes its readers will provide the intended answer, *sotto voce*). Yet, a sustained investigation of *Marbury's* citation history among other Court opinions reveals something interesting: virtually no instances of these rhetorical questions appear in the record, as if subsequent judges went out of their way to avoid citing these types of construction. Oakley & Tobin (in press) argue that the jurisprudential reason for rhetorical question avoidance stems in part from the doctrine of *obiter dicta,* statements regarded as opinions of the judge and not extendable to other cases. Why such constructions produce these effects is a problem for Cognitive Grammar and related theories (such as the construction grammars of Fillmore & Kay [1995] or Goldberg [1996]). Why such constructions may be systematically avoided as *rationes decidendi* statements (or 'holdings') requires an explanation based on a theory of legal system, or a theory of document acts in the jurisprudential domain.

Although Langacker does not address the phenomenon of rhetorical questions directly, his theory of discourse stipulates that expressions only acquire meaning within a specific usage event. For instance, the expression, *Could you (please) pass the salt?*, 'instantiates a complex interactive schema in which the question scenario is embedded in the request scenario' (Langacker 2008a:471), thus the question is less a question than a request. Even so, the interrogative dimension is not, in fact, removed altogether but, rather, attenuated but still present as prelude to performing a corresponding physical action in response.

With rhetorical questions, a question scenario is embedded in a declarative scenario, such that the declarative scenario gains prominence. In contrast to many other pragmatic accounts of rhetorical questions (see Rhode 2006), where the assertive scenario completely subsumes the questioning one, Cognitive Grammar stipulates a more nuanced effect from this 'blended' scenario. Once again, all expressions are expressions 'by some agent' from 'somewhere.' The more complex blending of scenarios in one clause serves to 'reveal the speaker' in a manner anathema to jurisprudence. That is to say, rhetorical questions semantically encode the pragmatic judgment of the speaker, often against a more-or-less explicit contrasting judgment, with the effect of disqualifying that judgment as unreasonable, unethical, or otherwise irrational or abusive. Such speaker judgments tend to fall within the category of *obiter dicta*; and grammatical constructions that 'blend' speech act scenarios tend to be regarded as suspect and incapable of being legally binding. Good jurisprudence means sifting through the welter of constructions comprising the whole text and choosing those holdings (*rationes decidendi*) from mere opinions (*obiter dicta*). As a construction type, rhetorical questions tend to be interpreted as contested opinion rather than settled legal principle. Yet, if one were to excise all the rhetorical questions from *Marbury v. Madison*, one would create a textual artifact that loses much of its ambient combativeness, for it was a decision borne from a politically heated contest between the Federalist (e.g. John Marshall, Adams, and the entire federal judiciary) and Republican Democrats (e.g. Thomas Jefferson and James Madison), each of whom regarded the other's position as unreasonable. Rhetorical questions are especially well equipped for expressing doubt about the rationality of one's opponent. Such partisanship tends not to generalize across cases.

Cognitive Grammar explains the dispositional meaning of constructions that can then be paired with an analysis of specific document ecosystems. Systems rhetoric is the next logical step in developing a theory of document acts, or how to do things with paper.

Literary artifacts, however, seem not to operate in the 'closed' systems of American jurisprudence. The very notion of what is literary is a perennially contested category. Literary systems may, in fact, be nothing more than a collection of discrete artifacts. However, there are also two contested views of the systems of literary production among editorial theorists.

The *Definitive Text* approach espoused most prominently by G. Thomas Tanselle (1989), holds that the job of scholarly editors is to reproduce or recreate *the* work. Whatever the means of production, it is the author's final intention and authority that matters. The *Social Text* approach, espoused most prominently by Jerome McGann (1992), holds that the job of scholarly editors is to produce a *variorum* documenting a social process involving editors, typesetters, proofreaders, censors, anthologists, and others. The social text approach is much more widely accepted as theoretically correct than used by editors and curators. For instance, the International Federation of Library Associations and Institutions own functional requirement for bibliographic records adopts a position closer to the definitive text approach when they write: 'A *work* is an abstract entity... Relating *expressions* of a *work* indirectly by relating each *expression* to the *work* that it realizes is often the most efficient means of grouping related expressions' (IFLA 1998).

Tobin & Oakley (in preparation) argue that positing the 'underlying work ontology' is cognitively intuitive and, indeed, necessary for much intellectual work of editing and curating to be accomplished. Our commonplace ways of construing the work in ordinary language tend to issue from a fundamental artifactual stance. More specifically, we argue that fictive change predicates appear as a means of *subjectification*, whereby the dynamic nature of processes are transferred to the more or less static objects and configurations of objects (see Langacker 2008a: 530–31). For instance, it is often the case that sentences like *My cell phone bill gets bigger every year* elicits a role interpretation, such that the object is a series of identical bills with different properties, and not a value interpretation, such that the same piece of paper expands over time. Compare these periphrastic cases with sentences headed by verbs of change, as in *These school girls shorten their skirts every year*, where the role and value interpretations are ambiguous between a different object with different length properties or the same object undergoing change. Such ambiguous construals of literary works are plentiful among literary critics. Hugh Kenner assessed the final three-line version of Marianne Moore's 'Poetry' (which she revised several times after its initial printing in 1919) as 'the one *scarred* by all those revisions' (Kenner 1967: 1432, emphasis added). In other words, 'Poetry' is a continuous object undergoing change rather than a role designation given to multiple, separate objects. Such ways of talking are commonplace among literary critics and editors, many of whom embrace as theoretically correct McGann's social text approach to editorial scholarship. Cognitive Grammar predicts that such fictive change predicates with verbs of change as the profile determinant are going to persist even among language users committed to an ontology sceptical of any underlying work because it is simply the cognitively most persistent way of indicating change; objectifying processes is a dominant mode of engaging with a changing world.

In this respect, I think Cognitive Grammar (and cognitive linguistics in general) demonstrates a need for editorial theorists and other curators to think more deliberately about the way human beings interact with and conceptualise literary artifacts. Part of that conceptualisation should take into account the habitual ways of thinking and talking about them.

The scope of Cognitive Grammar can be extended beyond our understanding of literary works themselves and the issues of perduring human interest they depict to help us understand better the larger ecosystems in which texts operate, be they practical and aesthetic. Such an extended research programme would lead to a 'theory of document acts' (a turn of phrase first used by the philosopher Barry Smith 2012, 2014). Langacker's framework is critical in connecting the construction to the artifact and the artifact to the system. Such a perspective can also be extended to aid literary critics and editorial theorists to think about the paradoxical nature of the 'work.'

References

Ariel, M. (1990). *Accessing Noun Phrase Antecedents*. London: Routledge.

Atwood, M. (1966). *The Circle Game*. Toronto: Anansi Press.

Atwood, M. (1996). *The Handmaid's Tale* [original 1985]. London: Vintage.

Badran, D. (2012). 'Metaphor as argument: a stylistic genre-based approach', *Language and Literature* 21 (2): 119–35.

Balassi, B. (1986). *Gyarmati Balassi Bálint Énekei* [The songs of Bálint Balassi of Gyarmat] (eds P. Kőszeghy and G. Szabó). Budapest: Szépirodalmi Könyvkiadó.

Bánhidi, Z., Jókay, Z. and Szabó, D. (1965). *Learn Hungarian*. Budapest: Tankönyvkiadó.

Baldick, C. (2004). *The Oxford Concise Dictionary of Literary Terms*. Oxford: Oxford University Press.

Barańczak, S. (2004). *Ocalone w tłumaczeniu: szkice o warsztacie tłumacza poezji z dodatkiem małej antologii przekładów problemów. Wydanie trzecie, poprawione i znacznie rozszerzone* [Saved in Translation: Sketches from a Poetry Translator's Workshop, with a Supplement]. Kraków: Wydawnictwo.

Barsalou, L. (2008). 'Grounded cognition', *Annual Review of Psychology* 59: 617–65.

Barsalou, L. (2009). 'Simulation, situated conceptualization, and prediction', *Philosophical Transactions of the Royal Society* 364: 1281–9.

Barth, J.R. (2003). *Romanticism and Transcendence: Wordsworth, Coleridge, and the Religious Imagination*. Columbia: University of Missouri Press.

Barthes, R. (1974). *S/Z* (trans. R. Miller). New York: Hill and Wang.

Barthes, R. (1977). 'The death of the author', in *Image–Music–Text* (ed. and trans. S. Heath). New York: Hill and Wang, pp. 142–8.

Bechdel, A. (2006). *Fun Home: A Family Tragicomic*. Boston: Houghton Mifflin Harcourt.

Bennett, E. (2012). 'Vincent's bedroom in Arles', *Quill & Parchment* 127 (January 2012). Online at http://www.quillandparchment.com/archives/vol127.html

Bergen, B. and Chang, N. (2005). 'Embodied construction grammar in simulation-based language understanding', in J. Östman and M. Fried (eds) *Construction Grammars: Cognitive Grounding and Theoretical Extensions*, Amsterdam: John Benjamins, pp.147–90.

Blackhall, S. (1989). 'Vincent's Bedroom in Arles, Painted 1888', in *Fite Doo/ Black Crow*. Aberdeen: Keith Murray Publications 1989. Online at http://www.poemhunter.com/poem/vincent-s-bedroom-in-arles-painted-1888/

Boot, I. and Pecher, D. (2010). 'Similarity is closeness: metaphorical mapping in a conceptual task', *Quarterly Journal of Experimental Psychology* 63 (5): 942–54.

Boot, I. and Pecher, D. (2011). 'Representation of categories: metaphorical use of the container schema', *Experimental Psychology* 58 (2): 162–70.

Botting, F. (1996). *Gothic*. London: Routledge.

Bouson, J.B. (1993). *Brutal Choreographies: Oppositional Strategies and Narrative Design in the Novels of Margaret Atwood*. Amherst: University of Massachusetts Press.

Bowdle, B. and Gentner, D. (2005). 'The career of metaphor', *Psychological Review* 112 (1): 193–216.

Bruhn, M.J. (2008). 'Fictive motion from Maine to Milton', Paper presented at the 9th Conference on *Conceptual Structure, Discourse, and Language*. Case Western University, Cleveland, October 2008.

Butler, C.S. and Gonzálvez-García, F. (2005). 'Situating FDG in functional-cognitive space: an initial study', in J.L. Mackenzie and M. de los Ángeles Gómez-González (eds) *Studies in Functional Discourse Grammar*, Bern: Peter Lang, pp.109–58.

Byrne, R. and Johnson-Laird. P. (2009). '"If" and the problems of conditional reasoning', *Trends in Cognitive Sciences* 13 (7): 282–7.

Cage, J. (2011). 'Vincent Van Gogh's "Bedroom in the Yellow House At Arles". Blue Door, Stage Left'. Online at http://jrc-sourwoodmountain.blogspot.com/2011/09/vincent-van-goghs-bedroom-in-yellow.html.

Caesar, A. (1993). *Taking it Like a Man: Suffering, Sexuality and the War Poets: Brooke, Sassoon, Owen, Graves*. Manchester: Manchester University Press.

Caink, A.D. (2013). 'Generative grammar and stylistics', in V. Sotirova (ed.) *Companion to Stylistics*, London: Continuum.

Cameron, L. (2007). 'Patterns of metaphor in reconciliation talk', *Discourse and Society* 18 (2): 197–224.

Campbell, P. (1999). *Siegfried Sassoon: A Study of the War Poetry*. Jefferson: McFarland.

Carter, R., Hughes, R. and McCarthy, M. (2000). *Exploring Grammar in Context*. Cambridge: Cambridge University Press.

Casasanto, D. and Dijkstra, K. (2010). 'Motor action and emotional memory', *Cognition* 115 (1): 179–85.

Cervo, N. (1981). 'Catholic humanism in "The Windhover" and "God's Grandeur"', *The Hopkins Quarterly* 8 (1): 33–40.

Chafe, W. (1994). *Discourse, Consciousness and Time: The Flow and Displacement of Conscious Experience in Speaking and Writing*. Chicago: Chicago University Press.

Chandler, J.K. (1982). 'Romantic allusiveness', *Critical Inquiry* 8 (3): 461–87.

Chaparro, A. (2000). 'Translating the untranslatable: Carroll, Carner and *Alicia en Terra Catalana?' Journal of Iberian and Latin American Studies* 6 (1): 19–28.

Charteris-Black, J. (2004). *Corpus Approaches to Critical Metaphor Analysis*. New York: Palgrave Macmillan.

Clark, A. (2011). *Supersizing the Mind: Embodiment, Action, and Cognitive Extension*. Oxford: Oxford University Press.

Clark, A. (2013). 'Whatever next? Predictive brains, situated agents, and the future of Cognitive Science', *Behavioural and Brain Sciences* 36.

Cosgrove, P. (2004). 'Hopkins's "The Windhover": not ideas about the thing but the thing itself', *Poetics Today* 25 (3): 437–64.

Crisp, P. (1996). 'Imagism's metaphors – a test case', *Language and Literature* 5 (2): 79–92.

Croft, W. (2001). *Radical Construction Grammar: Syntactic Theory in Typological Perspective*. Oxford: Oxford University Press.

Croft, W. and Cruse, D.A. (2004). *Cognitive Linguistics*. Cambridge: Cambridge University Press.

Culler, J. (1997). *Literary Theory: A Very Short Introduction*. Oxford: Oxford University Press.

Culler, J. (2002). *Structuralist Poetics: Structuralism, Linguistics, and the Study of Literature* (2nd edn). London: Routledge.

Cupchik, G., Oatley, K. and Vorderer, P. (1998). 'Emotional effects of reading excerpts from short stories by James Joyce', *Poetics* 25 (6): 363–77.

Dancygier, B. (2012). *The Language of Stories: A Cognitive Approach*. Cambridge: Cambridge University Press.

Dancygier, B. and Sweetser, E. (2005). *Mental Spaces in Grammar.* Cambridge: Cambridge University Press.

Das, S. (2005). *Touch and Intimacy in First World War Literature.* Cambridge: Cambridge University Press.

Das, S. (2007). 'War poetry and the realm of the senses: Owen and Rosenberg', in T. Kendall (ed.) *The Oxford Handbook of British and Irish War Poetry,* Oxford: Oxford University Press.

Davidson, A. (1988). 'Future tense: making history in *The Handmaid's Tale',* in K. van Spanckeren and J. Garden Castro (eds) *Margaret Atwood: Vision and Forms,* Carbondale: Southern Illinois University Press, pp. 113–21.

Davis, S. (1984). *Wordsworth and the Picturesque* (Unpublished doctoral dissertation). University of Florida.

Davies, M. (2004). *British National Corpus.* Provo: Bingham Young University.

Declerck, R. and Reed, S. (2001). *Conditionals: A Comprehensive Empirical Analysis.* Berlin: Mouton de Gruyter.

de Jong, J. (2003). 'Word processing in the Italian Renaissance: action and reaction with pen and paintbrush', *Visual Resources* 19 (4): 259–81.

Dempsey, D. (2013). 'Little Girl Lost in Vincent's Bedroom'. Online at http://www.poemhunter.com/poem/little-girl-lost-in-vincent-s-bedroom/.

DeNicola, D. (2004). 'Van Gogh's Room', *Ekphrasis* 3 (4): 17–18. Online at http://www.poemhunter.com/poem/van-gogh-s-room/

Dennett, D. (1981). 'Three kinds of intentional psychology', in R. Healy (ed.) *Reduction, Time, and Reality,* Cambridge: Cambridge University Press, pp. 37–61.

Diller, H.-J. (2012). 'Historical semantics, corpora and the unity of English studies', in M. Fludernnik and B. Kohlmann (eds) *Anglistentag 2001. Freiburg. Proceedings,* Trier: Wissenschaftlige Verlag, pp. 321–37.

Dollar, M. (2004). 'Ghost imagery in the war poems of Siegfried Sassoon', *War, Literature and the Arts* 16 (1/2): 235–45.

Doloughan, F. (2011). *Contemporary Narrative: Textual Production, Multimodality and Multiliteracies.* London: Continuum.

Downes, A.D. (1993). 'Hopkins's epiphanic imagination', in E. Hollahan (ed.) *Gerard Manley Hopkins and Critical Discourse,* New York: AMS, pp. 117–36.

Downes, W. (2000). 'The language of felt experience: emotional, evaluative and intuitive', *Language and Literature* 9 (2): 99–121.

Dowty, D. (1991). 'Thematic proto-roles and argument selection', *Language* 67: 574–619.

Dvorak, M. (1998). 'What is real/reel? Margaret Atwood's "Rearrangement of shapes on a flat surface" or narrative as collage', *Etudes Anglaises* 51 (4): 448–60.

Dworak, K./[Carroll, L.] (2010). Lewis Carroll *Alicja w Krainie Czarów.* Warszawa: Buchmann.

Eagleton, T., (2007). *How to Read a Poem.* Oxford: Blackwell Publishing.

Easthope, A. (1985). 'The problem of polysemy and identity in the literary text', *British Journal of Aesthetics* 25 (4): 326–39.

Edgecombe, R.S. (1994). 'The bow-bend in Hopkins's "Windhover"', *Notes and Queries* 41 (3): 357–8.

Ehrlich, S. (1990). *Point of View. A Linguistic Analysis of Literary Style.* New York: Routledge.

Eilenberg, S. (1992). *Strange Power of Speech: Wordsworth, Coleridge, and Literary Possession.* Oxford: Oxford University Press.

Emmott, C. (1997). *Narrative Comprehension: A Discourse Perspective.* Oxford: Clarendon Press.

Enkvist, N.E. (1981). 'Experiential iconicism in text strategy', *Text* 1: 77–111.

Evans, V. (2004). *The Structure of Time: Language, Meaning and Temporal Cognition*. Amsterdam: John Benjamins.

Evans, V. (2006). 'Lexical concepts, cognitive models and meaning-construction', *Cognitive Linguistics* 17 (4): 491–534.

Evans, V. (2009). *How Words Mean: Lexical Concepts, Cognitive Models and Meaning Construction*. Oxford: Oxford University Press.

Evans, V. (2010). 'Figurative language understanding in LCCM theory', *Cognitive Linguistics* 24 (4): 601–62.

Evans, V. and Green, M. (2006). *Cognitive Linguistics: An Introduction*. Edinburgh: Edinburgh University Press.

Evans, V. and Tyler, A. (2004). 'Rethinking English "prepositions of movement": the case of *to* and *through*', *Belgium Journal of Linguistics* 18: 247–70.

Fauconnier, G. (1994). *Mental Spaces: Aspects of Meaning Construction in Natural Language* [original *Espaces Mentaux*, 1985]. New York: Cambridge University Press.

Fauconnier, G. (1997). *Mappings in Thought and Language*. Cambridge: Cambridge University Press.

Fauconnier, G. and Sweetser, E. (eds) (1996). *Spaces, Worlds, and Grammar*. Chicago: University of Chicago Press.

Fauconnier, G. and Turner, M. (2002). *The Way We Think. Conceptual Blending and the Mind's Hidden Complexities*. New York: Basic Books.

Fillmore, C.J. and Kay, P. (1995). *Construction Grammar*. Manuscript: University of California, Berkeley.

Fillmore, C.J., Kay, P. and O'Connor, M.K. (1988). 'Regularity and idiomacity in grammatical constructions: the case of *let alone*', *Language* 64: 501–38.

Fludernik, M. (1996). *Towards a 'Natural' Narratology*. London: Routledge.

Forceville, C. (2009). 'Non-verbal and multimodal metaphor in a cognitivist framework: agendas for research', in C. Forceville and E. Urios-Aparisi (eds) *Multimodal Metaphor*, Berlin: Mouton de Gruyter, pp. 19–42.

Fowler, R. (1977). *Linguistics and the Novel*. London: Methuen.

Freedman, A. (2009). 'Drawing on Modernism in Alison Bechdel's *Fun Home*', *Journal of Modern Literature* 32: 125–40.

Freeman, M. (2006). 'The fall of the wall between literary studies and linguistics: cognitive poetics', in G. Kristiansen, M. Achard, R. Dirven, F.J. Ruiz de Mendoza Ibanez (eds) *Cognitive Linguistics: Current Applications and Future Perspectives*, Berlin: Mouton de Gryuter, pp. 403–28.

Frosch, C. and Byrne, R. (2012). 'Causal conditionals and counterfactuals', *Acta Psychologica* 141: 54–66.

Fussell, P. (1975). *The Great War and Modern Memory*. New York: Oxford University Press.

Gallet, R. (1991). '"The Windhover" and God's first intention *ad extra*', in P. Bottalla, G. Marra and F. Marucci (eds) *Gerard Manley Hopkins: Tradition and Innovation*, Ravenna: Longo Editore, pp. 55–68.

Gardner, M. (ed.) (1960). *The Annotated Alice: Alice's Adventures in the Wonderland and Through the Looking Glass*. London: Penguin.

Gardner, M. (2000). 'Introduction', in *Alice's Adventures in Wonderland* and *Through the Looking Glass*, New York: Signet, pp. v–x.

Gardner, W.H. (2008). 'Introduction', *Poems and Prose by Gerard Manley Hopkins*. London: Penguin.

Gardner, W.H. and Mackenzie, N.H. (eds) (1967). *The Poems of Gerard Manley Hopkins* (4th edn). London: Oxford University Press.

Gavins, J. (2005). '(Re)thinking modality: a text-world perspective', *Journal of Literary Semantics* 34 (2): 79–93.

Gavins, J. (2007). *Text World Theory: An Introduction*. Edinburgh: Edinburgh University Press.

Gavins, J. and Stockwell, P. (2012). 'About the heart, where it hurt exactly, and how often', *Language and Literature* 21 (3): 33–50.

Genette, G. (1972). *Figures III*. Paris: Editions du Seuil.

Genette, G. (1980). *Narrative Discourse: An Essay in Method*. Ithaca: Cornell University Press.

Genette, G. (1988). *Narrative Discourse Revisited*. Ithaca: Cornell University Press.

Genette, G. (2002). 'Order, duration and frequency' in B. Richardson (ed.) *Narrative Dynamics: Essays on Time, Plot, Closure and Frame*, Columbus: Ohio State University Press, pp. 25–34.

Gentner, D. (1983). 'Structure mapping: a theoretical framework for analogy', *Cognitive Science* 7: 155–70.

Gentner, D. and Markman, A. (1997). 'Structure mapping in analogy and similarity', *American Psychologist* 52 (3): 45–56.

Gibbons, A. (2012). *Multimodality, Cognition, and Experimental Literature*. New York: Routledge.

Gibbs, R. (1994). *The Poetics of Mind: Figurative Thought, Language and Understanding*. Cambridge: Cambridge University Press.

Gibbs, R. (2002a). 'Feeling moved by metaphor' in S. Csabi and J. Zerkowitz (eds) *Textual Secrets: The Message of the Medium*, Budapest, ELTE, pp.13–28.

Gibbs, R. (2002b). 'A new look at literal meaning in understanding what is said and implicated', *Journal of Pragmatics* 34: 457–86.

Gibbs, R. (2006). 'Metaphor interpretation as embodied simulation', *Mind and Language* 21: 434–58.

Gibbs, R. (2011a). 'Are "deliberate" metaphors really deliberate?: a question of human consciousness and action', *Metaphor and the Social World* 1 (1): 26–52.

Gibbs, R. (2011b). 'Advancing the debate on deliberate metaphor', *Metaphor and the Social World* 1 (1): 67–9.

Gilpin, W. (1802). *An Essay on Prints*. London: Cadell & Davies.

Glucksberg, S. (2003). 'The psycholinguistics of metaphor', *Trends in Cognitive Sciences* 7 (2): 92–6.

Glucksberg, S. and Haught, C. (2006). 'On the relation between metaphor and simile: when comparison fails', *Mind and Language* 21 (3): 360–78.

Glucksberg, S. and Keysar, B. (1990). 'Understanding metaphor comparisons: beyond similarity', *Psychological Review* 97 (1): 3–18.

Goatly, A. (2007). *Washing the Brain: Metaphor and Hidden Ideology*. Amsterdam: John Benjamins.

Goldberg, A.E. (1995). *Constructions: A Construction Grammar Approach to Argument Structure*. Chicago: University of Chicago Press.

Goldberg, A. (1996). *Conceptual Structure, Discourse and Language*. Stanford: CSLI Publications.

Gomes, G. (2008). 'Three types of conditionals and their verb forms in English and Portuguese', *Cognitive Linguistics* 19 (2): 219–40.

Gonzálvez-García, F. and Butler, C.S. (2006). 'Mapping functional-cognitive space', *Annual Review of Cognitive Linguistics* 4: 39–96.

Grady, J. (1997). *Foundations of Meaning: Primary Metaphors and Primary Scenes*. (Unpublished doctoral thesis). University of California, Berkeley.

Grady, J. (2004). 'Primary metaphors as inputs to conceptual integration', *Journal of Pragmatics* 37 (10): 1595–614.

Grayson, S.A. (2010). 'Core texts and context: reading poems of World War 1 in 2005–2006', in P.T. Flynn, J–M. Kauth, J.K. Doyle and J. Scott Lee (eds) *Substance, Judgment and Evaluation: Seeking the Value of a Liberal Arts, Core Text Education. Selected Papers from the Twelfth Annual Conference of the Association for Core Texts and Courses*, Lanham: University Press of America.

Green, K. (ed.) (1995). *New Essays in Deixis*. Amsterdam: Rodopi.

Greimas, A.-J. (1971). 'Narrative grammar: units and levels', *Modern Language Notes* 86: 793–806.

Greimas, A.-J. (1976). *Maupassant: La sémiotique du texte: Exercises pratiques*. Paris: Seuil.

Greimas, A.-J. and Courtés, J. (1993). *Sémiotique: Dictionnaire raisonné de la théorie du langage* [original 1979]. Paris: Hachette.

Haiman, J. (1978). 'Conditionals are topics', *Language* 54: 512–40.

Hakemulder, J. (2004). 'Foregrounding and its effects on readers' perception', *Discourse Processes* 38: 193–208.

Halliday, M.A.K. (1971). 'Linguistic function and literary style: an inquiry into the language of William Golding's *The Inheritors*', in S. Chatman (ed.) *Literary Style: A Symposium*, Oxford: Oxford University Press, pp.330–68.

Halliday, M.A.K. and Matthiessen, C.M.I.M. (2004). *An Introduction to Functional Grammar* (3rd edn). London: Arnold.

Hamilton, C. (2003). 'A Cognitive Grammar of "Hospital Barge" by Wilfred Owen', in J. Gavins and G. Steen (eds) *Cognitive Poetics in Practice*, London: Routledge, pp.55–65.

Harbus, A. (2012). *Cognitive Approaches to Old English Poetry*. Cambridge: D.S Brewer.

Harding, J.R. (2011). '"He had never written a word of that": regret and counterfactuals in Hemingway's "The Snows of Kilimanjaro"', *Hemingway Review* 30 (2): 21–35.

Harrison, C. (2013). *Cognitive Discourse Grammar in Contemporary Literature* (Unpublished doctoral thesis). University of Nottingham.

Harrison, C. and Stockwell, P. (2013). 'Cognitive poetics', in J. Littlemore and J. Taylor (eds) *Companion to Cognitive Linguistics*. London: Continuum.

Hart, C. (2010). *Critical Discourse Analysis and Cognitive Science*. Basingstoke: Palgrave Macmillan.

Hatlen, B. (1989). 'Kinesis and meaning: Charles Olson's "The Kingfishers" and the critics', *Contemporary Literature* 30: 546–72.

Heffernan, J. (1993). *Museum of Words: The Poetics of Ekphrasis from Homer to Ashbery*. Chicago: University of Chicago Press.

Hejwowski, K. (2007). *Kognitywno-komunikacyjna teoria przekładu*. Warszawa: PWN.

Herman, D. (2002). *Story Logic*. Lincoln: University of Nebraska Press.

Herman, D. (2009a). 'Beyond voice and vision: Cognitive Grammar and focalization theory', in P. Hühn, W. Schmid and J. Schönert (eds) *Point of View, Perspective, and Focalization: Modeling Mediation in Narrative*, Berlin: de Gruyter, pp. 119–42.

Herman, D. (2009b). 'Cognitive approaches to narrative analysis', in G. Brône and J. Vandaele (eds) *Cognitive Poetics: Goals, Gains and Gaps*. Berlin: Mouton de Gruyter, pp. 79–118.

Hirata, T. (2011). 'Van Gogh's Bedroom as I See It' (transl. Jeffrey Angles), *Action Yes* 1 (15) (Winter 2011). Online at http://actionyes.org/issue15/hirata/

Hobbs, J.R. (1990). *Literature and Cognition*. Stanford: CSLI Publications.

Hoeken, H. and van Vliet, M. (2000). 'Suspense, curiosity and surprise: how discourse structure influences the affective and cognitive processing of a story', *Poetics* 27 (4): 277–86.

Hoey, M. (2005). *Lexical Priming: A New Theory of Words and Language*. London: Routledge.

Hoey, M. (2013). 'Lexical priming', in C.A. Chapelle (ed.) *The Encyclopedia of Applied Linguistics*, Oxford: Blackwell.

Holloway, M.M. (1993). 'An approach to Hopkins through the game motif', in E. Hollahan (ed.) *Gerard Manley Hopkins and Critical Discourse*, New York: AMS, pp. 197–210.

Hopkins, G.M. (1918). *Poems* (ed. R. Bridges). London: Humphrey Milford.

Horn, L. (2000). 'From *if* to *iff*: conditional perfection as pragmatic strengthening', *Journal of Pragmatics* 32: 289–326.

House, H. and Storey, G. (eds) (1959). *The Journals and Papers of Gerard Manley Hopkins*. London: Oxford University Press.

Howells, C.A. (2005). *Margaret Atwood* (2nd edn). Basingstoke: Palgrave Macmillan.

Hugh-Moore, L. (1969). 'Siegfried Sassoon and Georgian Realism', *Twentieth Century Literature* 14 (4): 199–209.

IFLA (1998). *Functional Requirements for Bibliographic Records – Final Report*. International Federation of Library Associations and Institutions. Available: ⟨http://archive.ifla.org/VII/s13/frbr/frbr1.htm⟩

Ingpen, R. (2009). 'Od ilustratora', in L. Carroll, *Alicja w Krainie Czarów*. Warszawa: Buchmann.

Ishiguro, K. (2005). *Never Let Me Go*. London: Faber and Faber.

Jansen, L., Luijten, H. and Bakker, N. (eds) (2009). *Vincent Van Gogh – The Letters. Vol. 4: Arles 1888–1889*. New York and London: Thames and Hudson, in conjunction with Van Gogh Museum and the Huygens Institute.

Jaworski, S. (2000). *Podręczny słownik terminów literackich*. Kraków: Universitas.

Jeffries, L. (2000). 'Don't throw out the baby with the bathwater: in defence of theoretical eclecticism in stylistics', *PALA Occasional Papers* 12.

Jibson, D. (2012). 'Vincent'. Online at http://ekphrasispoems.tumblr.com/vincent

Johnson-Laird, P. (1983). *Mental Models: Towards a Cognitive Science of Language, Inference and Consciousness*. Cambridge: Cambridge University Press.

Johnson, M. (1987). *The Body in the Mind: The Bodily Basis of Meaning, Imagination, and Reason*. Chicago: University of Chicago Press.

Johnson, S. (1990). 'The life of Cowley', in D. Greene (ed.) *Samuel Johnson*, Oxford: Oxford University Press, pp. 677–97.

Jones, J. (1954). *The Egotistical Sublime: A History of Wordsworth's Imagination*. London: Chatto and Windus.

Kaiser, R. (2007). 'Unity in the valley: transcendence and contiguity in Wordsworth's "Tintern Abbey"', *Limina* 13: 45–53.

Kames, H.H. (2005). *Elements of Criticism* (ed. P. Jones, 6th edn) [original 1762]. Indianapolis: Liberty Fund.

Kant, B./[Carroll, L.] (2010). Lewis Carroll *Alicja w Krainie Czarów*. Poznań: Vesper.

Kant, I. (2007). *Critique of Judgement* (trans. J.C. Meredith) [original 1790]. Oxford: Oxford University Press.

Kaufman, G. (1972). *God, the Problem*. Cambridge: Harvard University Press.

Kaufmann, S. (2006). 'Conditionals', in K. Brown (ed.) *Elsevier Encyclopedia of Language and Linguistics* (2nd edn), Amsterdam: Elsevier, pp.6–10.

Kay, P. and Fillmore, C. (1999). 'Grammatical constructions and linguistic generalisations: the *what's doing X to Y?* construction', *Language* 75 (1): 1–33.

Kenesei, I., Vago, R.M. and Fenyvesi, A. (1998). *Hungarian*. London: Routledge.

Kenner, H. (1967). 'Artemis and Harlequin: review of *The Complete Poems of Marianne Moore*, *The National Review* 19, December 26th, 1967, p.1432–3.

Kirk, D.F. (1962). *Charles Dodgson Semeiotician* (University of Florida Monographs, No. 11). Gainesville: University of Florida.

Klaniczay, T. (ed.) (1985). *Pallas Magyar ivadékai*. Budapest: Szépirodalmi Könyvkiadó.

Koller, V. (2005). 'Critical Discourse Analysis and social cognition: evidence from business media discourse', *Discourse and Society* 16 (2): 199–224.

Koller, V. and Davidson, P. (2008). 'Social exclusion as conceptual and grammatical metaphor: a cross-genre study of British policy making', *Discourse and Society* 19 (3): 307–31.

Kőszeghy, P. (2008). *Balassi Bálint: Magyar Alkibiadész*. Budapest: Balassi Kiadó.

Kozak, J./[Carroll, L.] (1997). Lewis Carroll *Przygody Alicji w Krainie Czarów*. Warszawa: Czytelnik.

Kuiken, D. and Miall, D.S. (1994). 'Foregrounding, defamiliarisation and affect: response to literary stories', *Poetics* 22: 389–407.

Kuiken, D., Miall, D.S. and Sikora, S. (2004). 'Forms of self implication in literary reading', *Poetics Today*, 25 (2): 171–203.

Labov, W. (1972). *Language in the Inner City*. Philadelphia: University of Pennsylvania Press.

Lacayo, R. and Grossman, L. (2006). '10 Best Books', *Time* [Online]. Available: http://www.time.com/time/magazine/article/0,9171,1570801,00.html

Lakoff, G. (1987). *Women, Fire and Dangerous Things: What Categories Reveal About the Mind*. Chicago: University of Chicago Press.

Lakoff, G. (1993). 'The contemporary theory of metaphor', in A. Ortony (ed.) *Metaphor and Thought* (2nd edn), Cambridge: Cambridge University Press, pp. 202–51.

Lakoff, G. and Johnson, M. (1980). *Metaphors We Live By*. Chicago: University of Chicago Press.

Lakoff, G. and Johnson, M. (1999). *Philosophy in the Flesh: The Embodied Mind and its Challenge to Western Thought*. Chicago: University of Chicago Press.

Lakoff, G. and Turner, M. (1989). *More Than Cool Reason: A Field Guide to Poetic Metaphor*. Chicago: University of Chicago Press.

Langacker, R.W. (1987). *Foundations of Cognitive Grammar Vol. 1: Theoretical Prerequisites*. Stanford: Stanford University Press.

Langacker, R.W. (1991a). *Concept, Image, Symbol: The Cognitive Basis of Grammar*. New York: Mouton de Gruyter.

Langacker, R.W. (1991b). *Foundations of Cognitive Grammar, vol. II: Descriptive Application*. Stanford: Stanford University Press.

Langacker, R.W. (1993). 'Grammatical traces of some "invisible" semantic constructs', *Language Sciences* 15: 323–55.

Langacker, R.W. (1994). 'The limits of continuity: discreteness in cognitive semantics', in C. Fuchs and B. Victorri (eds) *Continuity in Linguistic Semantics*, Amsterdam: John Benjamins, pp. 9–20.

Langacker, R.W. (1995). 'Viewing and cognition in grammar', in P.W. Davis (ed.) *Alternative Linguistics: Descriptive and Theoretical Modes*, Amsterdam: John Benjamins, pp. 153–212.

Langacker, R.W. (1999). *Grammar and Conceptualization*. Berlin: Mouton de Gruyter.

Langacker, R.W. (2000). 'A dynamic usage-based model', in M. Barlow and S. Kemmer (eds) *Usage-Based Models of Language*, Stanford: CSLI, pp. 1–64.

Langacker, R.W. (2001). 'Discourse in Cognitive Grammar', *Cognitive Linguistics* 12 (2): 143–88.

Langacker, R.W. (2002). *Concept, Image and Symbol: The Cognitive Basis of Grammar* (2nd edn). Berlin: Mouton de Gruyter.

Langacker, R.W. (2005). 'Construction Grammars: Cognitive, Radical, and less so', in M. Ibáñez, F.J. Ruiz and S. Peña Cervel (eds) *Cognitive Linguistics: Internal Dynamics and Interdisciplinary Interaction*, Berlin: Mouton de Gruyter, pp. 101–59.

Langacker, R.W. (2007a). 'Cognitive Grammar', in D. Geeraerts and H. Cuyckens (eds) *The Oxford Handbook of Cognitive Linguistics*. Oxford: Oxford University Press, pp. 421–62.

Langacker, R.W. (2007b). 'Constructing the meaning of personal pronouns' in G. Radden, K–M. Kopcke, T. Berg and P. Siemund (eds) *Aspects of Meaning Construction*, Amsterdam: John Benjamins, pp. 171–88.

Langacker, R.W. (2008a). *Cognitive Grammar: A Basic Introduction*. New York: Oxford University Press.

Langacker, R.W. (2008b). 'Sequential and summary scanning: a reply', *Cognitive Linguistics* 19 (4): 571–84.

Langacker, R.W. (2009). *Investigations in Cognitive Grammar*. Berlin: Mouton de Gruyter.

Langacker, R.W. (2010). 'Control and the mind/body duality: knowing vs. effecting', in E. Tabakowska, M. Choiński and Ł. Wiraszka (eds) *Cognitive Linguistics in Action. From Theory to Application and Back*, Berlin: Mouton de Gruyter, pp. 163–208.

Larsson, S. (2009). 'Review of *Conditionals in Context* by Christopher Gauker (MIT Press, 2005)', *Language* 85 (1): 201–203.

Lausberg, H. (1998). *Handbook of Literary Rhetoric: A Foundation for Literary Study* (trans. M.T. Bliss, A. Jansen and D.E. Orton, eds D.E. Orton and R.D. Anderson). Leiden: Brill.

Leech, G., Rayson, P. and Wilson. A. (2001). *Word Frequencies in Written and Spoken English*. London: Longman [see also http://ucrel.lancs.ac.uk/bncfreq/]

Leech, G. and Short, M. (2007). *Style in Fiction: a Linguistic Introduction to English Fictional Prose* (2nd edn). Harlow: Pearson Longman.

Lees, F.N. (1950). 'The Windhover', *Scrutiny* 16 (1): 36.

Levenston, E.A. and Sonnenshein, G. (1986). 'The translation of point of view in fictional narrative', in J. House and S. Blum-Kulka (eds) *Interlingual and Intercultural Communication*, Tübingen: Gunter Narr Verlag, pp. 49–59.

Levy, L.B. (1966). 'Hawthorne and the sublime', *American Literature* 37 (4): 391–402.

Liu, A. (1984). 'Wordsworth: the history in "imagination"', *ELH* 41 (3): 505–48.

Longman (1998). *An Introduction to Poetry* (9th edn, ed. M. Panero). New York: Addison-Wesley-Longman.

Louw, B. and Milojkovic, M. (2013). 'Semantic prosody', in P. Stockwell and S. Whiteley (eds) *The Handbook of Stylistics*, Cambridge: Cambridge University Press.

Low, G., Littlemore, J. and Koester, A. (2008). 'Metaphor use in three UK university lectures', *Applied Linguistics* 29 (3): 428–55.

Lucas, J. (1988). 'Places and dwellings: Wordsworth, Clare and the anti-picturesque', in D. Cosgrove and S. Daniels (eds) *The Iconography of Landscape: Essays on the Symbolic Representation, Design and Use of Past Environments*, Cambridge: Cambridge University Press, pp. 83–97.

McCallum, E. (2009). 'Lost in the *Fun Home*: Alison Bechdel's Gothic queers', in M. Duperray (ed.) *Gothic N.E.W.S.: Exploring the Gothic in Relation to New Critical Perspectives and the Geographical Polarities of North, East, West and South*. Paris: M. Houdiard.

McFarland, T. (1992). *William Wordsworth: Intensity and Achievement*. Oxford: Clarendon Press.

McGann, J. (1992). *A Critique of Modern Textual Criticism*. Charlottesville: University of Virginia Press.

McHale, B. (1989). *Postmodernist Fiction*. Cambridge: Cambridge University Press.

McHale, B. (1992). *Constructing Postmodernism*. London: Routledge.

Mack, M. (1982). *Collected in Himself: Essays Critical, Biographical, and Bibliographical on Pope and some of his Contemporaries*. London: Associated University Presses.

McLaughlin, R. (2012). 'Post-postmodernism' in J. Bray, A. Gibbons and B. McHale (eds) *The Routledge Companion to Experimental Literature*, London: Routledge, pp. 212–23.

McLellan, J. (1984). 'Did Queen Victoria write *Alice in Wonderland?*', *The Gazette*, Montreal, February 11, 1984.

McRae, K. and Boisvert, S. (1998). 'Automatic semantic similarity priming', *Journal of Experimental Psychology: Learning, Memory and Cognition* 24: 558–72.

Maldonado, R. (2010). 'Grammatical voice in Cognitive Grammar', in D. Geeraerts, Herbert Cuyckens and Hubert Cuyckens (eds) *The Oxford Handbook of Cognitive Linguistics*, Oxford: Oxford University Press, pp.829–68.

Mariani, P.L. (1970). *A Commentary on the Complete Poems of Gerard Manley Hopkins*. Ithaca: Cornell University Press.

Marianowicz, A./[Carroll, L.] (1955). Lewis Carroll. *Alicja w Krainie Czarów*. Warszawa: nasza Księgarnia.

Mason, W. (2004). 'Don't like it? You don't have to play', *London Review of Books* 26 (22), pp. 17–19.

Matlock, T. (2004a). 'Fictive motion as cognitive simulation', *Memory & Cognition* 32 (8): 1389–400.

Matlock, T. (2004b). 'The conceptual motivation of fictive motion', in G. Radden and K.U. Panther (eds), *Studies in Linguistic Motivation*, Berlin: Mouton de Gruyter, pp. 221–48.

Matlock, T. (2010). 'Abstract motion is no longer abstract', *Language and Cognition* 2 (2): 243–60.

Matsumoto, Y. (1996). 'How abstract is subjective motion? A comparison of coverage path expressions and access path expressions', in A.E. Goldberg (ed.) *Conceptual Structure, Discourse and Language*, Stanford: CSLI Publications, pp. 359–73.

Miall, D.S. (1998). 'The Alps deferred: Wordsworth at the Simplon Pass', *European Romantic Review* 9: 84–102.

Miall, D.S. (2000). 'Locating Wordsworth: "Tintern Abbey" and the community with nature', *Romanticism on the Net* 20. [http://id.erudit.org/iderudit/005949ar]

Moeyes, P. (1997). *Siegfried Sassoon, Scorched Glory: A Critical Study*. Macmillan: Basingstoke.

Müller, K. (2000). 'Re-constructions of reality in Margaret Atwood's literature: a constructionist approach', in R.M. Nischik (ed.) *Margaret Atwood: Works and Impact*, Woodbridge: Boydell & Brewer, pp. 229–57.

Nabholtz, J.R. (1964). 'Wordsworth's guide to the Lakes and the picturesque tradition', *Modern Philology* 61: 288–94.

Naifeh, S. and White Smith, G. (2011). *Van Gogh: The Life*. New York: Random House.

Nesset, T. (2009). 'Review of *Cognitive Grammar: A Basic Introduction* (2008), R. Langacker', *Journal of Linguistics* 45 (2): 477–80.

Nikiforidou, K. (2012). 'The constructional underpinnings of viewpoint blends: the *Past + now* in language and literature', in B. Dancygier and E. Sweetser (eds), *Viewpoint in Language*. Cambridge: Cambridge University Press, pp. 177–97.

Nischik, R.M. (1991). *Mentalstilistik: Ein Beitrag zu Stiltheorie und Narrativik, dargestellt am Erzählwerk Margaret Atwoods*. Tübingen: Narr Verlag.

Norton (1983). *The Norton Anthology of Poetry* (3rd edn, ed. A.W. Allison). New York: Norton.

Norton (1999). *The Norton Introduction to Poetry* (7th edn, ed. J.P. Hunter). New York: Norton.

Noyes, R. (1968). *Wordsworth and the Art of Landscape*. Bloomington: Indiana University Press.

Nuyts, J. (2001). *Epistemic Modality, Language, and Conceptualization: A Cognitive-Pragmatic Perspective*. Amsterdam: John Benjamins.

Nuyts, J. (2005). 'Brothers in arms? On the relations between cognitive and functional linguistics', in F.J. Ruiz de Mendoza and S. Peña (eds) *Cognitive Linguistics: Internal Dynamics and Interdisciplinary Interaction*. Berlin: Mouton de Gruyter, pp.69–100.

Nuyts, J. (2006). 'Modality: overview and linguistic issues', in W. Frawley, E. Eschenroeder, S. Mills and T. Nguyen (eds) *The Expression of Modality*, Berlin: Mouton de Gruyter, pp. 1–26.

Nuyts, J. (2007). 'Cognitive linguistics and functional linguistics', in D. Geeraerts and H. Cuyckens (eds) *The Oxford Handbook of Cognitive Linguistics*. Oxford: Oxford University Press.

Oakley, T. and Tobin, V. (in press) 'Sometimes the whole is less than the sum of its parts: toward a theory of document acts', *Language and Cognition* 6.1.

Oatley, K. (1994). 'A taxonomy of the emotions of literary response and a theory of identification in fictional narrative', *Poetics* 23 (1–2): 53–74.

Oberauer, K. (2006). 'Reasoning with conditionals: a test of formal models of four theories', *Cognitive Psychology* 53: 238–83.

Ogden, J.T. (1973). *The Power of Distance in Wordsworth's Prelude. PMLA* 88 (2): 246–9.

Ohmann, R. (1964). 'Generative grammars and the concept of literary style', *Word* 20: 423–39.

Olney, J. (1993). *The Language(s) of Poetry: Walt Whitman, Emily Dickinson and Gerard Manley Hopkins*. Athens: University of Georgia Press.

Olson, C. (1997). *Collected Prose* (eds D. Allen and B. Friedlander). Berkeley: University of California Press.

Ortony, A. (ed.) (1979). *Metaphor and Thought*. Cambridge: Cambridge University Press.

Palmer, F. (1986). *Mood and Modality*. Cambridge: Cambridge University Press.

Parrinder, P. (ed.) (2012). *H.G. Wells: The Critical Heritage*. London: Routledge.

Perkins, M. (1983). *Modal Expressions in English*. London: Francis Pinter.

Phelan, J. (1996). *Narrative as Rhetoric: Technique, Audiences, Ethics, Ideology*. Ohio: Ohio State University Press.

Phelan, J. (2005). *Living to Tell About It: A Rhetoric and Ethics of Character Narration*. New York: Cornell University Press.

Phillips, B. (2005). 'The negative style of David Foster Wallace', *The Hudson Review* 57 (4): 675–82.

Pinker, S. (2007). *The Stuff of Thought: Language as a Window into Human Nature*. New York: Viking.

Pragglejaz group (2007). 'A practical and flexible method for identifying metaphorically-used words in discourse.' *Metaphor & Symbol* 22: 1–39.

Price, U. (1810). *Essays on the Picturesque, as Compared with the Sublime and the Beautiful* [original 1794]. London: J. Robson.

Propp, V. (1968). *Morphology of the Folktale*. Austin: University of Texas Press.

Quintilian (2001). *The Orator's Education* (trans. and ed. D.A. Russell). Cambridge: Harvard University Press.

Radden, G. and Dirven, R. (2007). *Cognitive English Grammar*. Amsterdam: John Benjamins.

Rehder, R. (1992). 'Inside out: omnipotence and the hidden heart in "The Windhover"', in A. Mortimer (ed.) *The Authentic Cadence: Centennial Essays on Gerard Manley Hopkins*, Fribourg: University Press of Fribourg, pp. 169–99.

Rescher, N. (1968). *Topics in Philosophical Logic*. Dordrecht: Reidel.

Rhode, H. (2006). 'Rhetorical questions as redundant interrogatives', *San Diego Linguistics Papers*2 (1): 134–68.

Rice, C. (2012). 'Fictive motion and perspectival construal in the Lyric', in I. Jaén and J.J. Simon (eds) *Cognitive Literary Studies: Current Themes and New Directions*, Austin: University of Texas Press, pp. 183–98.

Richardson, A. (2010). *The Neural Sublime: Cognitive Theories and Romantic Texts*. Baltimore: Johns Hopkins University Press.

Rivinoja, A. (2004). 'Free Indirect Discourse and third-person pronouns in translation – possible changes in point of view', in T. Puutrinen and R. Jäskelääinen (eds) *Points of View: Papers on Teaching and Research in the English Department*, Savonlinna: Savonlinna School of Translation Studies 4: 75–85.

Rodaway, P. (1994). *Sensuous Geographies: Body, Sense and Space*. London: Routledge.

Rojo, A. and Valenzuela, J. (2003). 'Fictive motion in English and Spanish', *International Journal of English Studies* 3 (2): 123–49.

Rudanko, J. (1982). 'On one NP of "The Windhover": a phonological approach', *Language and Style* 15 (4): 277–82.

Rumelhart, D.E. (1975). 'Notes on a schema for stories', in D.G. Bobrow and A.M. Collins (eds) *Representation and Understanding: Studies on Cognitive Science*, New York: Academic Press, pp. 211–36.

Ruoff, G.W. (1973). 'Religious implications of Wordsworth's imagination', *Studies in Romanticism* 12 (3): 607–92.

Ryan, M–L. (1991). *Possible Worlds, Artificial Intelligence and Narrative Theory*. Bloomington: Indiana University Press.

Salvesen, C. (1965). *The Landscape of Memory: A Study of Wordsworth's Poetry*. Lincoln: University of Nebraska Press.

Sartre, J.-P. (1984). *Being and Nothingness* (trans. H.E. Barnes). New York: Washington Square Press.

Sassoon, S. (1946). *Siegfried's Journey 1916–1920*. London: Faber and Faber.

Sassoon, S. (1983). *Siegfried Sassoon Diaries 1915–1918* (ed. Rupert Hart-Davis). London: Faber and Faber.

Sassoon, S. (1984). *Collected Poems 1908–1956*. London: Faber and Faber.

Sassoon, S. (2000). *Memoirs of an Infantry Officer*. London: Faber and Faber.

Scheffer, L. (2012). 'Bedroom in Arles', *Quill & Parchment* 127 (January 2012). Online at http://www.quillandparchment.com/archives/vol127.html

Schiffrin, D. (1992). 'Conditionals as topics in discourse', *Linguistics* 30: 165–97.

Schneider, C.W. (2010). 'Young daughter, old artificer: constructing the Gothic *Fun Home*', *Studies in Comics* 1: 337–58.

Schubert, T.W. (2005). 'Your highness: vertical positions as perceptual symbols of power', *Journal of Personality and Social Psychology* 89: 1–21.

Scott, C.T. (1974). 'Towards a formal poetics: metrical patterning in "The Windhover"', *Language and Style* 7: 91–107.

Scott, N. (2012). 'Bedroom in Arles', *Quill & Parchment* 127 (January 2012). Online at http://www.quillandparchment.com/archives/vol127.html

Semino, E. (2008). 'A cognitive stylistic approach to mind style in narrative fiction' in R. Carter and P. Stockwell (eds) *The Language and Literature Reader*, London: Routledge, pp. 268–77.

Semino, E. (2009). 'Text worlds' in G. Brône and J. Vandaele (eds) *Cognitive Poetics: Goals, Gains and Gaps*, Berlin: Mouton de Gruyter, pp. 33–71.

Short, M. (1996). *Exploring the Language of Poems, Plays and Prose.* Harlow: Pearson Education.

Sienkiewicz, B. (1992). *Literackie 'teorie widzenia'.* Poznań: Obserwator.

Silkin, J. (ed.) (1979). *The Penguin Book of First World War Poetry.* Harmondsworth: Penguin.

Simpson, P. (1993). *Language, Ideology and Point of View.* London: Routledge.

Słomczyński, M./[Carroll, L.] (1972). Lewis Carroll *Przygody Alicji w Krainie Czarów.* Warszawa: Czytelnik.

Smith, B. (2012). 'How to do things with documents', *Rivisti di Estetica* 50: 179–98.

Smith, B. (2014). 'Document acts', in A. Konzelmann-Ziv and H.B Schmid (eds) *Institutions, Emotions, and Group Agents. Contributions to Social Ontology.* Heidelberg: Springer.

Spector, S.J. (1977). 'Wordsworth's mirror imagery and the picturesque tradition', *ELH* 44 (1): 85–107.

Spiers, M.B. (2010). 'Daddy's little girl: multigenerational queer relationships in Bechdel's *Fun Home*', *Studies in Comics* 1: 315–35.

Spooner, C. (2006). *Contemporary Gothic.* London: Reaktion Books.

Staels, H. (1995). *Margaret Atwood's Novels: A Study of Narrative Discourse.* Tübingen: Francke.

Staes, T. (2010). '"Only artists can transfigure": Kafka's artists and the possibility of redemption in the novellas of David Foster Wallace', *Language and Literature* 65 (6): 459–80.

Steen, F. and Turner, M. (2013). 'Multimodal Construction Grammar', in M. Borkent, B. Dancygier, and J. Hinnell (eds.) *Language and the Creative Mind.* Stanford: CSLI Publications.

Steen, G. (1999). 'From linguistic to conceptual metaphor in five steps', in R. Gibbs and G. Steen (eds) *Metaphor in Cognitive Linguistics: Selected Papers from the Fifth International Cognitive Linguistics Conference, Amsterdam, July 1997,* Amsterdam: John Benjamins, pp. 197–226.

Steen, G. (2004). 'Can discourse properties of metaphor effect metaphor recognition?' *Journal of Pragmatics* 36: 1295–1313.

Steen, G. (2008). 'The paradox of metaphor: why we need a three-dimensional model of metaphor', *Metaphor and Symbol* 23 (4): 213–41.

Steen, G. (2009). 'From linguistic form to conceptual structure in five easy steps: analyzing metaphor in poetry', in F. Brône and J. Vandaele (eds) *Cognitive Poetics, Goals, Gains and Gaps,* Berlin: Mouton de Gruyter, pp. 197–226.

Steen, G. (2011a). 'From three dimensions to five steps: the value of deliberate metaphor', *Metaphorik.de* 21: 83–110.

Steen, G. (2011b). 'The Contemporary Theory of Metaphor – now new and improved!' *The Review of Cognitive Linguistics* 9 (1): 26–64.

Steen, G. (2011c). 'What does "really deliberate" really mean? More thoughts on metaphor and consciousness', *Metaphor and the Social World* 1 (1): 53–6.

Steen, G., Dorst, A., Hermann, B., Kaal, A, and Krenmayr, T. (2011). 'Metaphor in usage', *Cognitive Linguistics* 21 (4): 765–96.

Sternberg, R. and Sternberg, K. (2011). *Cognitive Psychology* (6th edition). New York: Wadsworth.

Stewart, D. (2010). *Semantic Prosody: A Critical Evaluation.* London: Routledge.

Stiller, R./[Carroll, L.] (1990). Lewis Carroll *Przygody Alicji w Krainie Czarów.* Warszawa: Lettrex.

Stockwell, P. (2002a). *Cognitive Poetics: An Introduction.* London: Routledge.

Stockwell, P. (2002b). 'Miltonic texture and the feeling of reading', in J. Culpeper and E. Semino (eds) *Cognitive Stylistics: Language and Cognition in Text Analysis,* Amsterdam: Benjamins, pp.73–94.

Stockwell, P. (2003). 'Surreal figures', in J. Gavins and G. Steen (eds) *Cognitive Poetics In Practice,* London: Routledge, pp. 13–25.

Stockwell, P. (2005). 'Texture and identification', *European Journal of English Studies* 9 (2): 143–53.

Stockwell, P. (2009a). *Texture: A Cognitive Aesthetics of Reading*. Edinburgh: Edinburgh University Press.

Stockwell, P. (2009b). 'The cognitive poetics of literary resonance', *Language and Cognition* 1 (1): 25–44.

Stockwell, P. (2010). 'The eleventh checksheet of the apocalypse', in B. Busse and D. McIntyre (eds) *Language and Style*, London: Palgrave, pp. 419–32.

Stockwell, P. (2013). 'Atmosphere and tone', in P. Stockwell and S. Whiteley (eds) *The Handbook of Stylistics*, Cambridge: Cambridge University Press.

Strickson, A. (2004). 'Vincent and I discuss "Bedroom at Arles" (Version 3)', *Staple* 59 (Spring 2004). Online at http://www.poetrymagazines.org.uk/magazine/record.asp?id=13669

Suvin, D. (1979). *Metamorphoses of Science Fiction: On the Poetics and History of a Literary Genre*. New Haven: Yale University Press.

Swan, M. (2005). *Practical English Usage* (3rd edn). Oxford: Oxford University Press.

Szentmártoni Szabó, G. (2004). 'Balassi Bálint poézisáról', in *Balassi Bálint és kora*, Budapest: Balassi Kiadó, pp. 43–64.

Tabakowska, E. (1993). *Cognitive Linguistics and Poetics of Translation*. Tübingen: Gunter Narr Verlag.

Tabakowska, E. (2007). 'Point of view in translation', in R. Jääskeläinen, T. Puurtinen and H. Stostesbury (eds) *Text, Processes and Corpora: Research Inspired by Sonja Tirkkonen-Condit*, Savonlinna: Savonlinna School of Translation Studies 5: 69–81.

Tabakowska, E./[Carroll, L.] (2012). *Alicja w Krainie czarów*. Kraków: Bona.

Talmy, L. (1988). 'Force dynamics in language and cognition', *Cognitive Science* 12: 49–100.

Talmy, L. (2000). *Toward a Cognitive Semantics, Vol. 1: Concept Structuring Systems*. Cambridge: MIT Press.

Talmy, L. (2007). 'Attention phenomena', in D. Geeraerts and H. Cuyckens (eds) *The Oxford Handbook of Cognitive Linguistics*, Oxford: Oxford University Press, pp. 264–93.

Talmy, L. (2008). 'Aspects of attention in language' in P. Robinson (ed.) *Handbook of Cognitive Linguistics*, London: Routledge, pp. 27–38.

Tanselle, G.T. (1989). *A Rationale of Textual Criticism*. Philadelphia: University of Pennsylvania Press.

Taylor, J.R. (2002). *Cognitive Grammar*. Oxford: Oxford University Press.

Thomas, D. (2000). *Collected Poems 1934-1953* (eds W. Davies and R. Maud). London: Phoenix.

Thomas, W.K. and Ober, W.U. (1989). *A Mind Forever Voyaging: Wordsworth at Work Portraying Newton and Science*. Edmonton: University of Alberta Press.

Thompson, V., Evans, J.St.B.T., and Handley, S. (2005). 'Persuading and dissuading by conditional argument', *Journal of Memory and Language* 53: 238–57.

Tobin, V. and Oakley, T. (in preparation) 'Shrinking poems and truncated authors: identity compressions and the ontology of the "Work". Unpublished manuscript.

Todorov, T. (1975). *The Fantastic: A Structural Approach to a Literary Genre* (trans. R. Howard). Ithaca: Cornell University Press.

Todorov, T., Ducrot, O. and Porter, C. (1983). *Encyclopedic Dictionary of the Sciences of Language* [original 1979]. Baltomore: Johns Hopkins University Press.

Todorov, T. (1977). *The Poetics of Prose*. Oxford: Blackwell.

Traugott, E.C. (1978). 'On the expression of spatio-temporal relations in language', in J.H. Greenberg (ed.) *Universals of Human Language, vol. 3: Word Structure*, Stanford: Stanford University Press, pp. 369–400.

Traugott, E.C. (1985). 'Conditional markers', in J. Haiman (ed.) *Iconicity in Syntax*, Amsterdam: John Benjamins, pp. 289–307.

Traugott, E.C. and Pratt, M.L. (1980). *Linguistics for Students of Literature*. New York: Harcourt Brace Jovanovich.

Tsur, R. (2003). *On the Shore of Nothingness: A Study in Cognitive Poetics*. Exeter: Imprint Academic.

Tsur, R. (2010). 'Linguistic devices and ecstatic poetry: "The Windhover" – tongue-twisters and cognitive processes', *Journal of Literary Theory* 4 (1): 121–39.

Turner, M. (2006). *The Artful Mind: Cognitive Science and the Riddle of Human Creativity*. Oxford: Oxford University Press.

Tyler, A. and Evans, V. (2003) *The Semantics of English Prepositions: Spatial Scenes, Embodied Meaning and Cognition*. Cambridge: Cambridge University Press.

Ungerer, F. and Schmid, H.J. (2006). *An Introduction to Cognitive Linguistics*. Harlow: Pearson/ Longman.

van Canegem-Ardijns, I. and van Belle, W. (2008). 'Conditionals and types of conditional perfection', *Journal of Pragmatics* 40: 349–76.

van Hoek, K. (2003). 'Pronouns and point of view: cognitive principles of co-reference' in M. Tomasello (ed.) *The New Psychology of Language: Cognitive and Functional Approaches to Language Structure Volume 2*, Mahwah: Lawrence Erlbaum, pp. 169–94.

van Peer, W. (ed.) (1986). 'The theory of foregrounding: the state of the art', *Stylistics and Psychology: Investigations of Foregrounding*, London: Croom Helm, pp. 1–25.

van Peer. W., Hakemulder, J. and Zyngier, S. (2007). 'Lines on feeling: foregrounding, aesthetics and meaning', *Language and Literature* 16 (2): 197–293.

Verhagen, A. (2005). *Constructions of Intersubjectivity: Discourse, Syntax, and Cognition*. Oxford: Oxford University Press.

Verhagen, A. (2007). 'Construal and perspectivization' in D. Geeraerts and H. Cuyckens (eds) *The Oxford Handbook of Cognitive Linguistics*, Oxford: Oxford University Press, pp. 48–81.

Verspoor, M. (1996). 'The story of -ing: a subjective perspective' in M. Putz and R. Dirven (eds) *The Construal of Space in Language and Thought*, Berlin: Walter de Gruyter, pp. 417–54.

Wallace, D. (1989). *Girl with Curious Hair*. New York: Norton.

Wallace, D. (1997). *A Supposedly Fun Thing I'll Never Do Again*. Boston: Little, Brown.

Wallace, D.F. (2004). 'The Soul Is Not a Smithy' in *Oblivion*, London: Little, Brown, pp. 67–113.

Wallhead, (2003). 'Metaphors for the self in A.S. Byatt's *The Biographer's Tale*', *Language and Literature* 12 (4): 291–308.

Watson, J.R. (1970). *Picturesque Landscape and English Romantic Poetry*. London: Hutchinson.

Weber, J.J. (ed.) (1996). *The Stylistics Reader*. London: Arnold.

Wells, H.G. (1898) *The War of the Worlds*. London: William Heinemann.

Welch, M.D. (2012). 'Bedroom in Arles', *Quill & Parchment* 127 (January 2012). Online at http:// www.quillandparchment.com/archives/vol127.html

Werth, P. (1999). *Text Worlds: Representing Conceptual Space in Discourse*. London: Longman.

Whiteford, P. (2001). 'A note on Hopkins' plough in "The Windhover"', *Victorian Poetry* 39 (4): 617–20.

Whiteley, S. (2010). *Text World Theory and the Emotional Experience of Literary Discourse* (Unpublished doctoral thesis). University of Sheffield.

Wilson, S.R. (1993). *Margaret Atwood's Fairy-Tale Sexual Politics*. Jackson: University Press of Mississippi.

Wisker, G. (2010). *Reader's Guides: Atwood's* The Handmaid's Tale. London: Continuum.

Wójcik-Leese, E. (2000). 'Salient ordering of free verse and its translation', *Language and Literature* 9 (2): 170–81.

Wölfflin, H. (1950). *Principles of Art History: The Problem of the Development of Style in Later Art*. New York: Dover Publications.

Wordsworth, W. (1837) *The Poetic Works of William Wordsworth*. London: Edward Moxon.

Wordsworth, W. (2004). *Guide to the Lakes* (ed. E.D. Selincourt). Berkeley: Publishers Group West.

Zaicz, G. (ed.) (2006). *Etimológiai szótár: Magyar szavakés toldalékok eredete* [Etymological dictionary: The origin of Hungarian word-extensions]. Budapest: Tinta Könyvkiadó.

Zanolie, K., van Dantzig, S., Boot, I., Wijnen, J., Schubert, T.W., Giessner, S.R., and Pecher, D. (2012). 'Mighty metaphors: behavioral and ERP evidence that power shifts attention on a vertical dimension', *Brain and Cognition* 78: 50–8.

Zunshine, L. (2006). *Why We Read Fiction: Theory of Mind and the Novel*. Columbus: Ohio State University Press.

Zunshine, L. (ed.) (2010). *Introduction to Cognitive Cultural Studies*. Baltimore: Johns Hopkins University Press.

Index